NORTH AMERICAN INDIAN WARS

NORTH AMERICAN INDIAN WARS

RICHARD H. DILLON

Facts on File, Inc

460 Park Avenue South
New York, NY 10016
A Bison Book

4

First published in the USA by

Facts on File, Inc.
460 Park Avenue South
New York, NY 10016

Produced by
Bison Books
17 Sherwood Place
Greenwich, CT 06830

Copyright © 1983 by Richard H. Dillon

Dillon, Richard H.
    North American Indian Wars.

    Includes index.
    1. Indians of North America—Wars.   I. Title.
E81.D54   973   82-7384
ISBN 0-87196-641-7   AACR2

Designer and Picture Editor: Bill Yenne
Editor: Tom Aylesworth

10 9 8 7 6 5 4 3 2 1
Printed in Hong Kong

Half-title page: **'The only good Indian is a dead Indian'** was the brutal belief of frontiersmen from 1607 to 1890. This representation of a 1790 incident, when the captive sister of scout Eli Washburn escaped and killed her ex-captor in a skirmish, could stand for any era of the Indian Wars.

Title page: Long before whites arrived, Indians of one tribe fought warriors of another. Charles M Russell captured the tradition of counting coups – striking an enemy to prove one's bravery – on a canvas that he titled both **Counting Coups** and **The War Scars of Medicine Whip**.

Below: In 1891, during the Ghost Dance craze but after the bloody Battle – or Massacre – of Wounded Knee on the Pine Ridge Reservation, John C H Grabill photographed Sioux chiefs and warriors in **the council that finally ended the Indian Wars.**

CONTENTS

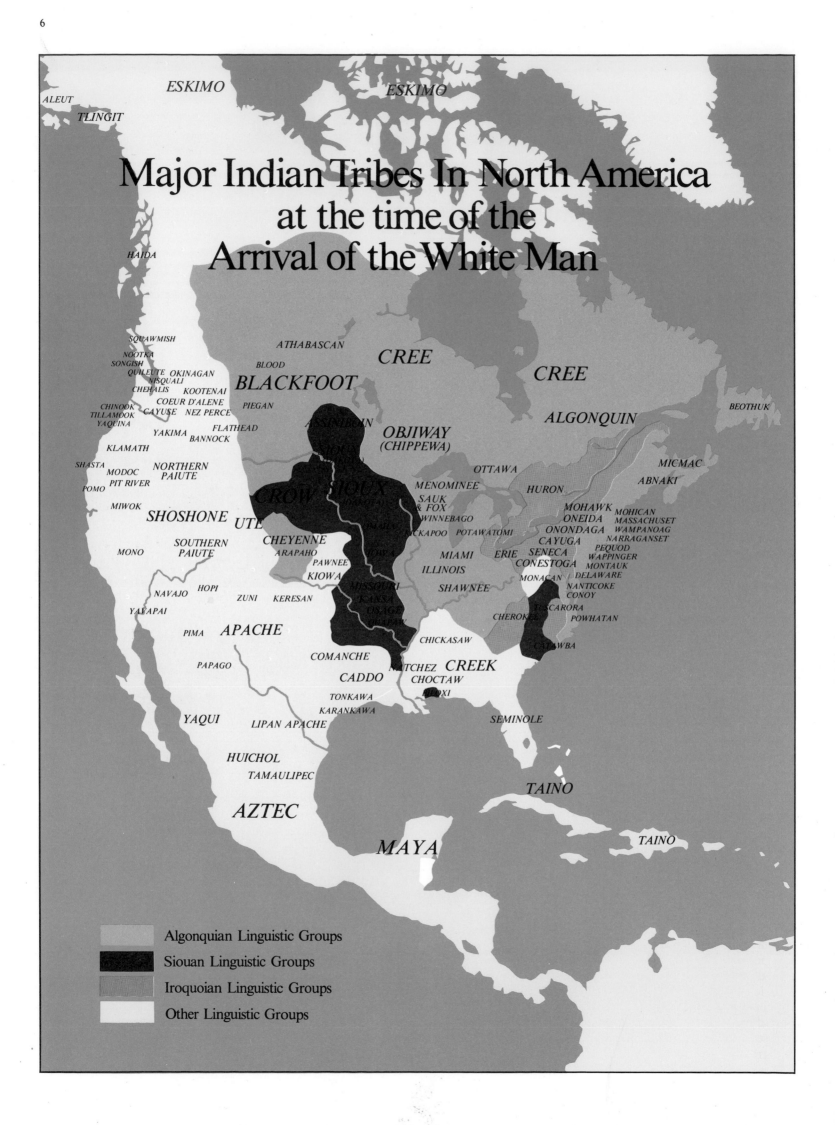

Major Indian Tribes In North America at the time of the Arrival of the White Man

ESKIMO

ESKIMO

ALEUT

TLINGIT

HAIDA

SQUAWMISH
NOOTKA
SONGISH
QUILEUTE OKINAGAN
NISQUALI
CHEHALIS KOOTENAI
CHINOOK COEUR D'ALENE
TILLAMOOK CAYUSE NEZ PERCE
YAQUINA
FLATHEAD
YAKIMA BANNOCK
KLAMATH
SHASTA NORTHERN
MODOC PAIUTE
POMO PIT RIVER
MIWOK
SHOSHONE UTE
SOUTHERN
MONO PAIUTE
NAVAJO HOPI
YAVAPAI
ZUNI KERESAN
PIMA APACHE
PAPAGO
YAQUI
LIPAN APACHE
HUICHOL
TAMAULIPEC

AZTEC

MAYA

ATHABASCAN
BLOOD
BLACKFOOT
PIEGAN

CREE

CREE

ALGONQUIN

BEOTHUK

ASSINIBOIN
OBJIWAY
(CHIPPEWA)
CROW SIOUX
(DAKOTA)
UMAHA
CHEYENNE
ARAPAHO IOWA
PAWNEE
KIOWA MISSOURI
KANSA
OSAGE
QUAPAW
COMANCHE
CADDO NATCHEZ
TONKAWA
KARANKAWA BILOXI

OTTAWA
MENOMINEE
SAUK
& FOX
WINNEBAGO
KICKAPOO POTAWATOMI
MIAMI
ILLINOIS
SHAWNEE
CHICKASAW
CREEK
CHOCTAW

HURON

MICMAC
ABNAKI

MOHAWK MOHICAN
ONEIDA MASSACHUSET
ONONDAGA WAMPANOAG
CAYUGA NARRAGANSET
ERIE SENECA PEQUOD
CONESTOGA WAPPINGER
MONACAN MONTAUK
DELAWARE
NANTICOKE
CONOY
TUSCARORA
CHEROKEE POWHATAN
CATAWBA

SEMINOLE

TAINO

TAINO

Algonquian Linguistic Groups

Siouan Linguistic Groups

Iroquoian Linguistic Groups

Other Linguistic Groups

CONQUISTADORES
1492-1607

In an effort to advance their commercial interests and expand their spheres of influence, Europeans disovered another world. This place that they called the New World was vaster than their wildest imagination and populated by a race of people never before encountered. When the two cultures clashed, conflict was inevitable. The first European antagonists were Spanish Conquistadores and the conflicts were the North American Indian wars, which were to last nearly four centuries.

The violence and brutality, the cunning and duplicity, which characterized European society, were transplanted to American soil by the first Spanish conquerors and by their Portuguese, English and French rivals. The climate proved to be perfect for the growth of these traits; they flourished as if in a hothouse. By sixteenth-century standards the Conquistadores often enjoyed a long life span—when they were not killed by Indians, or murdered by their own men. Cortes died at 62; Pizarro may have been 60 when he was assassinated.

C hristopher Columbus was something of an exception to the rule of cruel *conquistadores*. He wrote of the Arawaks whom he met after his 12 October 1492 landing on San Salvador, now Watling's Island, in the Bahamas: 'They are artless and generous with what they have, to such a degree as no one would believe. . . . Of anything they have, if it be asked for they never say no, but do rather invite the person to accept it, and show as much lovingness as though they would give their hearts. . . . They love their neighbors as themselves, and their speech is the sweetest and gentlest in the world, and they always speak with a smile.' Columbus was as impressed with the skills of the natives as with their amiability: 'They are men of very subtle wit, who navigate all those seas, and who give a marvelously good account of everything.'

As if to prove his humaneness, Columbus kidnapped only six or seven (early accounts differ) Indians for guides to Cuba and Hispaniola, or Haiti, Santo Domingo. He would later take them to Spain to show them off in their native dress. He planned to convert and make servants of many Indians, but by love, he said, not force. It should not be difficult, for, he said: 'They remained so much our friends that it was a marvel.'

Friendship waned, however, and in response to Spanish rapacity and robbery, the Indians destroyed the fort of La Navidad. Columbus had to mount a punitive expedition and send prisoners to the slave markets of Sevilla even after Indian resistance was broken on Haiti in 1495. As Admiral of the Ocean Sea and Governor of Hispaniola, Columbus

Above: America's first Conquistador, **Christopher Columbus**.

began a harsh system of tribute in gold dust. It proved impossible to collect the gold, because the natives died in large numbers from famine, from overwork in the fields and gold mines, from European diseases and massacres. The dream of empire became a nightmare and by 1500, both Columbus and his brother, accused of cruelty and oppression—of Spaniards, not Indians—were shipped back to Spain in chains.

The honor of leading the first expedition into what would become one of the 50 states fell to Juan Ponce de Leon. He seems almost a Quixotic figure, a caricature of a conquistador, because of his futile chase of a fabled, miraculous Fountain of Youth. It was described to him by some Carib Indians who hoped that he would be on his

Above: The caravels of Columbus, the **Santa María, Pinta** and **Niña**, were freighted with the dreams and notions that brought about the first great conflict between the European and American cultures.

way, to anywhere. Actually, Ponce de León was a nobleman who became a tough, no-nonsense soldier fighting in the war with the Moors in Granada. He came to America in 1493 on Columbus's second voyage and continued his military career by supressing an Indian uprising on Hispaniola. He was named Provisional Governor of Puerto Rico after exploring its coast and trading with its Indians.

When Governor General Diego Columbus replaced him as Governor, Ponce de León embarked on his expedition in search of perpetual youth. He named the new land *La Florida* not only because it was so lush with flowers and foliage, but also because he landed on Easter Sunday, *La Pascua Florida*, in 1513.

Ponce de León returned in 1521 to conquer and colonize the peninsula. He landed at Charlotte Harbor, or perhaps Sanibel Island, despite the warnings of the natives. Friendly on his first visit, they had turned against all Spaniards because of the brutality of the slave raiders of Haiti's gold mines like Lucas Vásquez de Ayllón and Francisco Gordillo on the Georgia and South Carolina coasts. Ponce de León landed, anyway, was wounded by an arrow, and later died in Cuba.

The greatest of the *conquistadores* stayed south of what became the USA. Hernán Cortés began his conquest of Mexico in 1519. He mixed diplomacy and violence to capture the Aztec capital of Tenochtitlán and seize the emperor, Moctezuma, as a hostage.

With double irony, when Cortés was absent, Moctezuma's own people stoned the Emperor to death, then rose against the Europeans. Cortés returned only in time to lead his men in a fighting retreat from the city on *La Noche Triste*, the Sad Night of 1 July 1520. But a year later, he recaptured the lake city in a brilliant amphibious campaign.

As Captain General of New Spain, Cortés extended his rule over all of Mexico and Central America. He even sent

explorers to California, rumored to be rich in pearls. But his power was later stripped away and he died in Spain in obscurity.

North America's rough *conquistadores* would prove to be almost gentle compared to the ruthless Pizarros of Peru. An illegitimate swineherd from Spain's backward province of Galicia, Francisco Pizarro literally fought his way up through the ranks to the very top of the military profession. He became Captain General of Peru by conquering the Incas through warfare and treachery. He callously put to death the Inca leader, Atahualpa, after collecting a ransom of gold for his life. Not many years later, Pizarro was assassinated by followers of a victim of his murderous brother, Hernando Pizarro. Hernando was imprisoned for 20 years for his crimes, but his half brother, the rascal, Gonzalo, led a revolt which toppled the King's viceroy before he was himself defeated and beheaded.

Such were the early 'civilizers' of America's Indians.

It was Hernando de Soto who finally followed Ponce de León to Florida. Although he was a lieutenant of the bloody Pizarros in Peru, unlike these men, he was a gentleman, educated in Spain's prestigious University of Salamanca. He was also a fine horseman, perhaps the greatest equestrian of the *conquistadores*.

The King appointed De Soto, now wealthy from Peruvian loot and slaves, *Adelantado*, or Royal Deputy, of Florida. When Charles V gave him the right to explore and conquer that peninsula, almost 20 years had passed since the arrow wound cut short Ponce de León's career. De Soto was eager to explore the region because he had convinced himself that Florida held the treasures of another Peru.

De Soto failed to secure Cabeza de Vaca, as his second-in-command, but that earliest American explorer taught him North American geography. Like Ponce, De Soto landed his force of 620 men—'devout marauders' historian Francis Parkman called them—on the Gulf Coast around Charlotte Harbor or Tampa Bay. He spent months ransacking Florida for riches, which were as non-existent as the magic spring.

The conqueror also sought elusive Indian converts to Christianity and Parkman wrote that the Dons did not neglect the spiritual welfare of those whom they came to plunder—'besides fetters to bind, and bloodhounds to hunt them, they brought priests and monks for the saving of their souls.'

About all that De Soto found of value was a collection of pearls in the possession of a chieftainess, Cutifachiqui, and an interpreter, Juan Ortíz, from Pánfilo de Narváez's shipwreck. He had been saved from certain death by the pleading of a chief's daughter, *a la* Pocahontas and John Smith.

Hernando de Soto made a truly remarkable expedition in 1540–42 through the Indian nations of the American Southeast and even the near Southwest. Making an enormous loop up through Georgia, where he seized a Creek princess as a hostage, and the Carolinas and Tennessee, he moved westward through Alabama and Mississippi. At Mabella, now Mobile, hostile Indians lured him and his men into a trap in a fortified town. But De Soto got them out, in a close call. After discovering the Mississippi River, the conquistador continued his search for gold all the way through Arkansas to northern Texas and Oklahoma.

In Arkansas, De Soto stained his reputation as a gentleman by attacking a village while its Nilco Indians were

Above: On his return to Spain, **Columbus** showed off Indian captives during his triumphal entry into the great city of Barcelona, capital of the province of Catalonia.

asleep. He killed 100 warriors and probably women and children too, before a bow could be strung. He deliberately let the wounded drag themselves away so that they would spread word of the terrible swift sword of Spanish vengeance.

Disappointed and broken in health by fever, De Soto returned to the Mississippi to die. His men buried him at the bottom of the river at night on 21 May 1542, in hopes that the Indians whom he had mistreated would not even know that he was dead, much less be able to dig up his remains for desecration. Before his death, the brave but cruel commander (described by historians as 'much given to the sport of slaying Indians') named his successor. Luís Moscoso managed to lead 311 survivors of the expedition back to civilization in Mexico in 1543.

Francisco Vásquez de Coronado, Governor of the province of Nueva Galicia in Mexico, or New Spain, was chosen by Viceroy Antonio de Mendoza to lead an expedition which more than rivaled De Soto's. Coronado was supposed to follow up on the reports of riches by Cabeza de Vaca (1536), which had been supposedly verified by Fray Marcos de Niza in a 1539 march to, or 'near', the fabulous Seven Cities of Cíbola in what would later become New Mexico.

Coronado set out in 1540 with 300 lancers and 1000 infantrymen, mostly Indian allies. He attacked Hawikuh, the Zuñi village where the Moor, Estevanico, scouting for Fray Marcos, was murdered in 1539. Despite his iron helmet, Coronado was stoned so badly by the defenders on 1 July 1540 that he was knocked senseless and had to be

carried from the field. But his men were victorious. An investigation of this and other pueblos convinced Coronado that there was no gold in Cíbola. When the Hopis of Tusayán, probably in hopes of getting rid of him, told him of gold near a great river to the west, he sent a detachment under Garcia López de Cárdenas to find it. Cárdenas stumbled on the Grand Canyon, but on no gold. Coronado also sent another lieutenant, Melchor Diaz, to meet with Fernando de Alarcón who was exploring the

Gulf of California by sea. Alarcón discovered the Colorado River mouth and followed the stream up to the Gila. Like De Soto, he narrowly missed making contact with Coronado.

After wintering in Tiguex near what was to become Santa Fe, and putting down rebellions in two pueblos, Coronado, in the spring of 1541, pushed on across the high plains to the Texas Panhandle and to the Great Bend of the Arkansas River in Kansas. He expected to find there the Kingdom of Quivira, which the Pueblos had told him about, again probably to get rid of him. In all, Coronado investigated 71 pueblos from Zuñi in the west to Taos in the north and Pecos in the east, but found the fabled 'cities of gold' to be either the adobes of the Pueblos or the rude huts of Wichitas and other plains Indians.

Angered at what he took to be his guile, Coronado hanged his Indian guide, then returned to Tiguex for another winter. There he was accidentally injured in the head in a jousting match. Disillusioned and in poor health from the wound, Coronado returned to Mexico in 1542.

But Coronado's expedition was no failure. It provided Spain with no new gold, to be sure, but with something much more important—a knowledge of, and a claim to, the entire sweep of the American Southwest from California to Kansas. With De Soto's help, this was extended on to the Gulf and Atlantic. Spain's domain in North America, 65 years before England founded Jamestown, now reached from the fortress of San Augustín in Florida to the California coastline above San Francisco, explored by Juan Cabrillo and Bartolomé Ferrelo in 1542.

Unfortunately for the Indians of the Americas, none of the *conquistadores* and *adelantados* paid much attention to 'The Friend of the Indian', Bartolomé de las Casas, except perhaps to curse him as an annoying and meddlesome crank. The Dominican friar who saw the New World's natives as 'quiet lambs, endowed with such blessed qualities', was indefatigable in trying to save the Indians from mistreatment by his fellow-Iberians. Finally, Las Casas was successful. His *New Laws* were enacted in 1542 to protect the natives. During his long crusade, he became not only the historian of the Indians, but their first anthropologist, too. His magnum opus was his *General History of the Indies*.

Las Casas was a propagandist. He may have exaggerated the cruelty of the *conquistadores*, sacrificing the exact truth for 'artistic manipulation' of facts in order to save his beloved Indians. Certainly, he added to the credence of the *Leyenda Negra*, or Black Legend, of the English. This, for political reasons, painted the Iberians as the world's masters of deceit, villainy, cruelty and torture. He described many *conquistadores* as depraved, bloodthirsty monsters in human guise who loved nothing better than stabbing pregnant Indian women in the belly or smashing infants' heads against rocks.

The French

As early as March of 1542, the first 'Frenchman' reached the Atlantic coast of the future USA. He was Giovanni da Verrazano, an Italian in the service of Francis I. He explored from North Carolina to Newfoundland, becoming

Left: Painter Frederick Kemmelmeyer imagined **Columbus's** first steps into the New World on little San Salvador or Watling's Island in the Bahamas of the West Indies.

Above: The **Spaniards** won a well-deserved reputation for cruel treatment of Indians, which the English exploited with their *Leyenda Negra* or **Black Legend** – anti-Spanish propaganda.

Opposite page: **Aztec Emperor Montezuma,** or Moctezuma, was killed (actually stoned to death) by his own people, not by the Spaniards who seized him in order to commandeer his riches.

the first navigator to enter New York Bay and the Hudson River. His men stole a child on the Virginia or Maryland shore, then attempted to kidnap, or rape, a woman till her screams frightened them away. When Verrazano entered Newport Bay, in present-day Rhode Island, impressively dressed Indian 'kings' greeted him—but hid their women. The word was already out about the rapacious Christians.

These Rhode Islanders were the last hospitable Indians that Verrazano saw. In the rest of New England the locals were so suspicious that they would only barter from cliff tops, lowering furs on a line and then hoisting up such trade goods as knives, hooks and bits of iron. When the French tried to land, they were quickly discouraged by a threatening display of bows and arrows.

Historian Francis Parkman probably accurately described the cause of Indian hostility: 'Perhaps some plundering straggler from the fishing banks, some man-stealer like the Portuguese Cortereal, or some kidnapper of children and ravisher of squaws like themselves had warned the denizens of the woods to beware the worshippers of Christ.'

Little is known about Verrazano after he left Rhode Island waters. There were tales that he was killed and eaten by cannibals during another voyage. More likely he was the pirate hanged in 1527 under the alias of Juan Florín.

The Portuguese and the English

As for the Portuguese brothers, Gaspar and Miguel Corte Real, they explored Labrador and, probably, New England in 1500–01 while searching for a route to the Far East. They also seized Indian captives, some of whom drowned horribly, chained in the hold of a sinking ship. The survivors reached Lisbon to be shown off as the kind of docile workers (*Labrador* means laborer)—actually slaves—to be found in North America.

The next Frenchmen to appear on the scene were Jean Ribaut and René de Laudonnière, who explored the Florida coast in the 1560s, made treaties with the Indians, and founded colonies. These settlements were crushed by Spaniards from San Augustín, but not before paintings of the French beachheads by Jacques LeMoyne excited France and the rest of Europe about colonization of the American Southeast.

The English were the earliest rivals of the Spaniards in the New World, with John Cabot making his first landfall barely five years after that of Columbus. He claimed Cape Breton for King Henry VII, then in the next year (1498), apparently sailed the entire littoral down to Spanish waters, though almost all records of the passage were lost when Cabot vanished. His son, Sebastian, searched for a North-west Passage to Asia through the barrier of North America

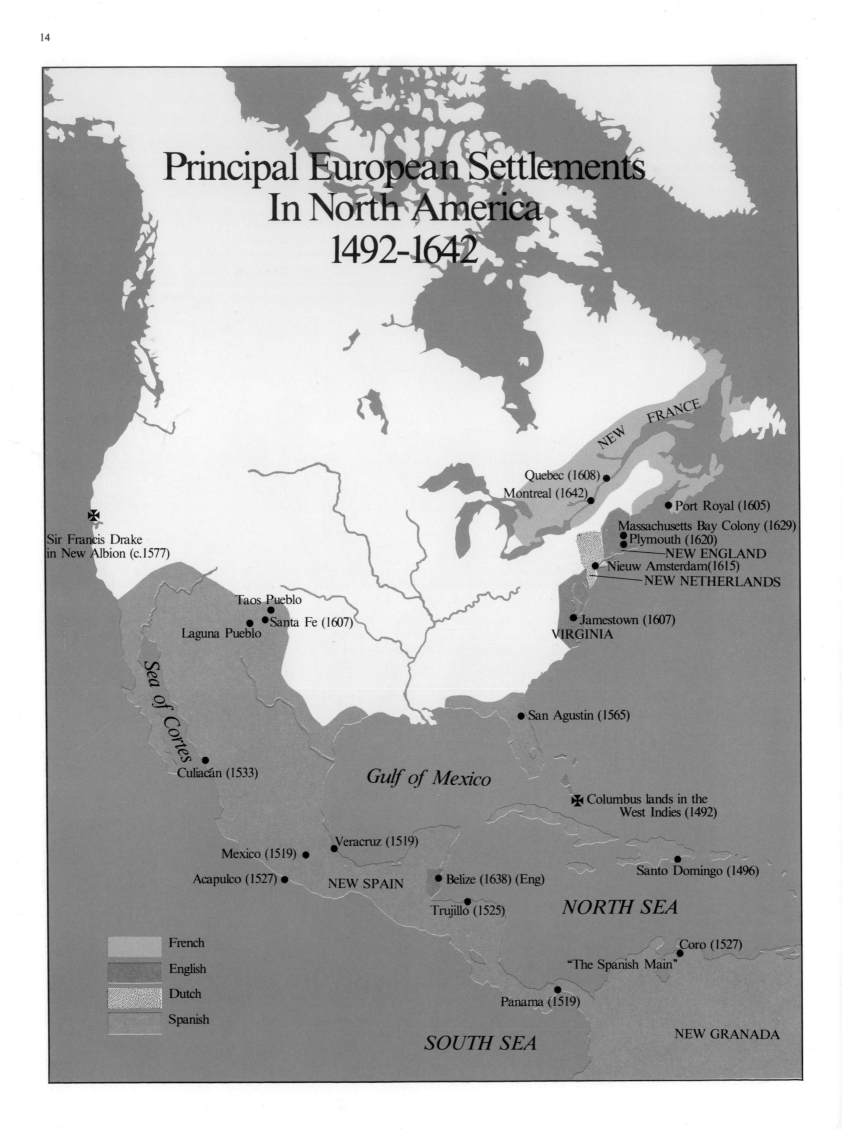

Principal European Settlements In North America 1492-1642

Sir Francis Drake
in New Albion (c.1577)

Quebec (1608)
Montreal (1642)
Port Royal (1605)
Massachusetts Bay Colony (1629)
Plymouth (1620)
NEW ENGLAND
Nieuw Amsterdam (1615)
NEW NETHERLANDS

NEW FRANCE

Taos Pueblo
Santa Fe (1607)
Laguna Pueblo

Jamestown (1607)
VIRGINIA

Sea of Cortes

San Agustin (1565)

Culiacán (1533)

Gulf of Mexico

Columbus lands in the
West Indies (1492)

Veracruz (1519)
Mexico (1519)
Acapulco (1527)
NEW SPAIN
Belize (1638) (Eng)
Trujillo (1525)

Santo Domingo (1496)

NORTH SEA

Coro (1527)
"The Spanish Main"

French
English
Dutch
Spanish

Panama (1519)

SOUTH SEA

NEW GRANADA

and may have reached Hudson Bay, via Hudson Strait, before a mutiny forced him back.

Surprisingly, England's next imperial move in America was on the Pacific, not the Atlantic, coast. In 1579, Francis Drake, soon to be knighted for his circumnavigation of the world, hid out on the California coast north of San Francisco Bay after making raids on Spanish ships and ports. He beached his *Golden Hind* on the shore to clean her bottom of barnacles so that he could make a fast run home to England. While there, he claimed Northern California for Queen Elizabeth, calling it Nova Albion because the cliffs reminded him of Dover. He traded amicably with the Indians and they even crowned him their king.

There was a flurry of interest in Drake's New England, and cartographers such as Hondius and Blaeu were careful to add it to their maps. Books appeared from Richard Hakluyt and Drake's own nephew, and the great Flemish artist, Thomas De Bry, added Indian scenes from New Albion/New England to his popular engravings of history and travels. But, probably fearful of further irritation to Spain, Elizabeth I did not follow up on Drake's exploit. She let Madrid keep California. Britain preferred to look to Virginia.

Meanwhile, Spain was consolidating its position in the Southwest. A half-century after Coronado's magnificent achievement, Don Juan de Oñate colonized New Mexico (1598) with 400 men, women and children, 80 wagons, and 70,000 head of stock. Only the Sky City of Ácoma seriously resisted. But the doughty Spanish soldiers clambered up the cliffs of the high mesa and captured the seemingly impregnible town.

Oñate proved to be a harsh conqueror, treating the brave defenders with unwarranted severity. Most of the warriors were killed in the assault, but he sentenced each survivor to 25 years of slavery—plus the loss of a foot. He sent 500 women and children into 20 years of servitude. He relented only on children under 12 years of age. These he placed in

Above: **Hernando de Soto** (1500?-1542) discovered the Mississippi in 1542. Finding no gold to the west, he returned to it but died and was buried at night to keep his death a secret from the Indians.

the custody of his priests. Luckless visitors to Ácoma were maimed, as a warning; he sent two Hopis home minus their right hands.

Even Madrid could not tolerate the actions of the Oñate. It took 15 years, but he was finally stripped of his honors and fined by a Spanish court.

The Acomans and other Pueblo people had long, long, memories. In 1680, Pope, a San Juan medicine man hiding in Taos, led the Indians in a revolt which drove Oñate's successors out of all New Mexico for 12 years. Popé later became a dictator during a period of wars among the pueblos.

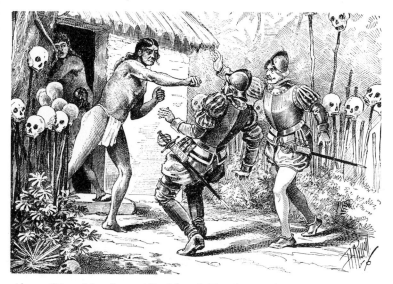

Above: Diego Mendez and Rodrigo de Escobar, acting as spies, entered the Indian camp of Quibian, whereupon Mendez was assaulted by the Chief's son.

COLONIALS
1607-1755

While the English and French efforts to acquire territory in eastern North America were marked by continual though isolated clashes, three incidents occurred that can generally be classified as full-scale wars. The first of these was the Pequot War of 1637, in which the much feared Pequot Indians of the Connecticut River Valley were goaded into open warfare with the settlers. King Philip's War (1675–78) was the most costly the continent had yet seen, with Philip attempting to drive the white man into the sea. Philip was killed in 1676 and two years later the war finally wound down, with the white man still in place. The first two-thirds of the eighteenth century were characterized by ongoing warfare between the French allied with Algonquin-speaking Indians against their respective traditional adversaries, the English in uneasy alliance with Iroquoian-speaking Indians. The conflict became known as the French and Indian War, which set the stage for the Indian conflict with the colonists in the upcoming War of Independence.

I n 1590 John White painted the Algonquin Indians and their farming towns in Virginia. These pictures, reminiscent of those by Jacques Le Moyne, were charming portraits and landscapes, much subtler—and far less bloody —than the engravings of Theodore De Bry and his son, which showed North America as a land of savages butchering Europeans or each other. John White's Indians grew maize, or Indian corn, in rows and hills fertilized with fish. In their slash-and-burn clearings they also tended pumpkins, sunflowers and tobacco. In lieu of scarecrows, they posted sentinels on platforms, whose cries scared pillaging birds away from the ripe corn.

Virginia

The first permanent Anglo-American settlement was Jamestown, Virginia—it nearly didn't succeed. Within just 12 hours of landing on 26 April 1607, the English were fighting a small skirmish with the native Virginians. But fortunately the engagement did not blaze up into a war. Although there were riffraff among the Virginia colonists, they were less greedy for gold than their Hispanic rivals and more content to stay put and till the fields in hoped-for friendship with their Indian neighbors. It was an uneasy peace; but it was peace. Without it, the tiny English enclave had no chance of surviving.

Perhaps the Indians were curious, or merely patient. In any case, as they watched, the colony dwindled from disease and malnutrition. Of the 900 original settlers of 1607, barely 150 were still alive in 1610.

Above: Jamestown, Virginia, was fortunate in having a leader of the great military experience and soldierly courage of **Captain John Smith**.

Opposite page: Massachussetts towns like **Brookfield** and **Deerfield** often came under siege by hostile Indians who employed fire as one of their major weapons of warfare.

The initial 15 years of relative peace on the James River, which in the long run would guarantee the continued existence of an Anglo-America, was in great part the result of the presence of two towering personalities.

The 'king' of the local Indians was called Powhatan, though his real name was Wa-hun-sen-a-cah or Wahunsonacock, sometimes miscalled 'the mighty Weowance'. (An Indian frequently kept his true name a secret and went by an alias or nickname in order to prevent enemies from seizing a part of his soul by means of this too-intimate knowledge of his name or personality.) Powhatan, who lived at the falls of the James River, now Richmond, inherited a collection of five Algonquin ('Falls of the River') tribes from his father, who had fled Spanish incursions to the south. By the time of Jamestown's founding, King Powhatan had expanded the so-called Powhatan Con-

Above: The story of **Pocahontas**'s rescue of Captain John Smith from execution is believable because of the Indian girl's character.

federation to include 32 tribes and 200 villages, perhaps 10,000 people of seaboard Virginia up to the fall line of the coastal rivers.

Captain John Smith described the Chief when Powhatan was about 50 years old. He was well-proportioned and still able-bodied, indeed strong. But he always wore a sour look. There was a real mix of nobility and savagery in the Chief. Grim and suspicious, he was cruel to prisoners and tolerant of the murders of farmers in their very furrows by his young braves. It took more than a grave and majestic presence for Powhatan to win the respect of the settlers. Perhaps the 19th century historian, Wyndham Peterson, described him correctly as a despot who was cruel, but not pitiless, stern yet affectionate at times, and brave, though also wary and subtle. He taught the English to cultivate corn and tobacco, but sometimes refused them corn in starving times in order to keep them dependent on him.

John Rolfe sent samples of tobacco to London as early as 1613. Four years later, export really began—and the Indians were doomed. Tobacco led to frequent clashes over land, as expansion of plantings demanded new fields, sometimes clearings wrested from their Indian owners. More important, it provided the cash crop needed to make English settlement permanent in the South.

Powhatan left no recorded spoken impression of his opponent. But he must have known Captain John Smith to be a formidable adversary. The Englishman was an ex-professional soldier who had fought against the Turks in Hungary and Transylvania. He had been captured and enslaved by them, so hardships were scarcely anything new to him.

Early on, Smith fell into Powhatan's hands while exploring and mapping the colony. He was about to be put to death by having his head bashed in by a war club when Powhatan's 12-year-old daughter, Pocahontas, intervened to save his life. The incident is possibly apocryphal and has been dismissed as 'an exploded story' by many, but it may very well have happened, so strong is tradition. Apparently, Powhatan's daughter inherited all of her father's best traits without his harsh qualities. Her name was Matoaka, but she did not want it used by strangers. Smith wrote: 'The savages did think that, did we know her real name, we should have the power of casting an evil eye upon her.' So she was called by a delightful—and appropriate—nickname, Pocahontas, meaning Playful or Frisky.

As a child, Pocahontas liked to play with colonists' children, turning cartwheels in the dusty streets of Jamestown. As she grew older, she not only donned buckskins but matured into a remarkably adept 'ambassadress' for her father. Since she frequented Jamestown as much as her own village, she was a pledge of peace. But she also worked successfully to restore captives to one side or another and visited the town on other errands of mercy. After she brought provisions to the hungry Jamestonians, she was virtually adopted by the grateful and hard-pressed settlers. Captain Smith said of her: 'She, under God, was the instrument to preserve this colony from death, famine, and utter confusion.' Later warning Smith of an impending raid, subsequently cancelled by her father, she probably saved Jamestown for a second time, the first being her rescue of the Captain from execution. Smith reminisced: 'Blessed Pocahontas, the great King's daughter of Virginia, oft saved my life.'

Captain Smith knew best how to handle the mercurial Indians and, better than anyone else, he realized the vulnerability of his tiny community. So he was determined to maintain good relations with the Indians. In this, he was backed up by the Virginia Company. Its London directors thought, correctly, that peace in Virginia would be cheaper than war. Smith stood his ground when Powhatan withheld corn, and he was infinitely resourceful in the face of the hunger of his people. To attempt to seal their friendship, Smith crowned Powhatan king in 1609. The old soldier complained that the chief was more interested in his gifts than in the copper crown, with all its significant symbolism, which Smith placed on his graying head.

Unfortunately, Captain John Smith was injured in an accident and went to England in 1609. Red-versus-white relations deteriorated immediately. According to William Strachey, a historian of the Commonwealth, the Indians, possibly stimulated by Spanish embassies from Florida, rose in war and 'did spoile and murther all they encountered'. He reported on a 'weroancqua', or queen, of the Powhatan Confederacy who treacherously murdered 14 men in the winter of 1610. Retaliation was automatic and swift; in revenge, the English burned her village and killed her and some of her warriors in a pursuit through the woods.

In an attack on 30 colonists, only Henry Spelman was spared because Pocahontas, in a re-enactment of the Captain Smith episode, intervened to save his life. He lived for years among the Potomac Indians and was later a skilful interpreter for the colonists.

Pocahontas withdrew and did not willingly visit Jamestown after Smith left. She married a warrior named Kocoum, who simply vanished from history, and she lived in a remote Potomac village. Captain Sir Samuel Argall bullied a chief into reluctantly revealing her retreat and Argall seized her for the Governor. He bore her off into what was euphemized as 'honored captivity' in March or April of 1613. She was placed in the care of Sir Thomas Dale and a Reverend Whitaker.

At first, Pocahontas was, naturally, 'exceedingly pensive and discontented' in her captivity, honored or not. But the patient courtesy of the two men won their ward over. She became a Christian and took the name Rebecca. Governor Dale used her as a hostage to keep Powhatan at bay and to ease haggling negotiations over English prisoners. In seizing Pocahontas, Dale was only imitating his predecessor as Governor, Sir Thomas Gates, who tricked, trapped and killed Indians as part of his 'diplomacy' with the red nations.

Curiously, the kidnapping of Pocahontas guaranteed Jamestown's survival, but not in the way Dale expected. The girl had grown up to be a beautiful woman, and the First Secretary and Recorder-General of Virginia, John Rolfe, fell in love with her. There were those who claimed that Rolfe married her 'for the good of the plantation', but it seems to have been a real love match. Rolfe's contemporaries agreed in describing him as 'a gentleman of approved behavior and honest carriage'. The lovers won permission to marry, both from the Governor and King Powhatan. They were married in April 1614 and peace between colonists and Indians was ensured as long as Powhatan should live.

The Rolfes were invited to England as guests of the Virginia Company, and they took Pocahontas's brother along. Lady Rebecca charmed everyone. She was treated like a princess in London and received by the King and Queen. Starting back to Virginia in 1617, she became ill, probably with smallpox, and died at Gravesend on the Thames below London.

Pocahontas became a legend in her own short life span of 21 years. Ben Jonson put her into one of his plays. A small street or courtyard was named for her in London's Ludgate Hill—*Belle Sauvage* Yard, that is to say, the Courtyard of the Beautiful Savage. The Rolfes' lodgings, the Belle Sauvage Inn, were there.

Alas, history has been hard on Pocahontas's memorials. Buried in the chancel of the church at Gravesend, her exact gravesite is unknown and thus not marked, though a fine statue has been erected to her in the churchyard. Even Belle Sauvage Yard is gone, now, obliterated by Luftwaffe bombs in World War II and never rebuilt.

Peaceful coexistence, tested first by Smith's withdrawal from Jamestown and tried further by Pocahontas's departure, ended with Powhatan's death in 1618. If the Chief had been 'sour', his brother and successor, Opechancanough, was bitter with hatred. No one knows the reason for his rancor, unless it was the incident in which Captain Smith had to poke a horse pistol into his ribs, briefly taking him hostage, in order to get himself out of a tight situation.

Opechancanough bided his time, then chose Good Friday, 22 March 1622, to turn on the Englishmen. He had a good excuse, the illegal execution of an Indian, Nemattanow, for the suspected 'murther' of a gentleman named Morgan, who disappeared on a trading trip to the interior. Murderer or an innocent, the Indian made the mistake of wearing the missing man's hat. Morgan's servants shot him.

In a bloody surprise attack, the Indians killed 347 men, women and children, including their devoted teacher and

Above: **Pocahontas or Matoaka,** daughter of Chief Wahunsonacock, usually called Powhatan (the name of his tribe), was captured by Virginians in 1613. She became a Christian convert, taking the name Rebecca, and married John Rolfe in 1614. Pocahontas died at Gravesend on a visit to England (1617), leaving one child, Thomas Rolfe.

would-be Christianizer, George Thorpe. The toll, about one-third of the colony's strength, was far higher than it should have been. Only a fortnight before striking, the Chief had boasted of his upcoming revenge on the English— and to no one else but Governor Francis Wyatt. Only six of 80 plantations were spared, but Jamestown managed a desperate survival because of the warning of a Christian Indian boy, Chanco. He was ordered to kill his master, Mr Pace, but would not do so and, instead, alerted him to the plot.

Inside Jamestown's flimsy walls, the kin of victims dreamed of revenge for the massacre. Pretending to be timid and fearful, the whites seemingly sued for peace. They invited the Indians to a council to draw up a treaty, assuring them—perhaps swearing on their Bibles—that their lives were sacred around the council fires.

The hate-filled Opechancanough was not to be trusted, either, but if he intended treachery, he was forestalled. The white peace-makers pounced on their red brethren, killing many of them. Unluckily for the plotters, one of those who got away was the Chief. When London chided Wyatt for also attempting to poison Opechancanough, Sir Francis retorted: 'We hold nothing unjust that may tend to their ruin'.

Beleaguered little Jamestown decided that its only hope lay in the extermination of the Indians ringing the settlement. Rather than trust them again in peace said Governor Wyatt, 'It is infinitely better to have no heathen among us.' After Opechancanough's betrayal, patrols were sent to destroy Indian villages and crops, to force the redmen to

Above: In crude woodcuts, early American artists depicted Indian attacks on Colonials, a common – but very frightening – frontier event.

withdraw further inland. More natives were killed in Virginia in 1622 than in the prior 15 years.

Hardly a young man when he fled, Opechancanough had to wait for his revenge till long after an uneasy truce began, around 1634, mainly from exhaustion on both sides. He was reputedly 100 years old or more, and had to be carried in a litter when he struck again more than 20 years after his first campaign. He had planned well, mounting a concerted attack by all of the allied tribes within 500 miles of Jamestown.

Opechancanough's first blow was devastating. On 18 April 1644, some 400–500 whites were killed, mostly on the York and Pamunkey Rivers where the old chief was in personal command. But while he had been mustering his strength over two decades, the Virginia population had climbed to 8000 souls. The immediate defeat stung the colony, but was far from crushing it. In fact, the English, under a determined leader, Governor Sir William Berkeley, quickly seized the initiative from the Indians and drove them back into the forest with the fire of their harquebuses, or muskets.

The Chief was defeated, captured and borne to Jamestown. He lay on his litter, still as the death which he anticipated. His eyes were closed and some said that the ancient one no longer had the strength to open his eyelids.

Suddenly, a guard, probably a militiaman who had lost a relative to Indian war clubs, turned his weapon and fired, point blank, at Opechancanough. The ball did not kill the old Indian but, instead, seemed to arouse him. Somehow, he pulled himself to his feet and ordered his startled guards to send for Berkeley. When the Governor arrived, it was to receive a scolding: 'If it had been my fortune to take Sir William Berkeley prisoner, I would not have meanly exposed him as a show to my people.' Dignity replaced the Chief's burning hatred at the end, and he lay quietly down and expired.

All Indian hope of extinguishing Jamestown died with Opechancanough. But guerrilla warfare continued. The General Assembly passed an act for 'perpetuall warre' with the Indians. This was replaced, however, with a peace treaty in 1646 with the new chief, Necotowance. He agreed to pay tribute to the Governor to acknowledge his submission to the Crown.

The British, in turn, established legal boundaries for Indian as well as white lands. However, especially after Berkeley, loyal to Charles I, was forced from office, the British reasserted their unrelenting pressure on Indian lands, expanding their fields of crops up the rivers from Tidewater past the fall line into the Piedmont. At first they seldom seized fields actually occupied by Indians. But as the population grew, such expropriation became common. Naturally, the Indians resisted and the 'injuries and insolences' they committed, such as trespass on private property or stealing and killing strayed livestock, caused retribution. The causes of conflict were rarely race hatred.

Usually it was the result of minor misunderstandings and simple, but irreconcilable, differences, such as in the understanding of property rights. These quickly ballooned into violence.

Real villainy, masked as Indian diplomacy, again reared its head in March of 1656. The Assembly sent Colonel Edward Hill and 100 men, plus Chief Tottopottomoi and 100 Pamunkey warrior-allies, against some Indians who had re-occupied the area of the falls of the James River claimed by the Britishers. Hill was ordered not to use force to expel the intruders. For no good reason, he killed the five chiefs who came to parley with him. Tottopottomoi was then killed in the fight which followed Hill's treachery. The House of Burgesses and Council alike were aghast at the Colonel's base act. They found him criminally guilty and suspended him from office. The Assembly then repealed a law allowing the shooting of Indians for simple trespass. But these actions did not end the warfare.

When Berkeley was restored as Governor in 1671, he found the Indians to be entirely subjected. Less than 1000 warriors remained in the neighborhood of the settlements of 40,000 Englishmen. The Governor frankly welcomed the local Indians' presence—they formed a buffer between the whites and the 'foreign' (wild) Indians of the woodlands.

In 1675 war flared up again in Virginia and Maryland involving militia and Nanticoke Indians who had seized hogs from a planter for an unpaid debt. A vendetta of retaliatory killings followed. Next the peaceful Susquehannocks were surrounded by Maryland and Virginia militiamen and five chiefs 'protected' by the white diplomatic flag were murdered. The Marylanders blamed the Virginians and vice versa. Both colonies, to their credit, held investigations of the atrocities, but the guilty Maryland officer was let off with the usual slap on the wrist, a fine. Now the Susquehannocks, out of sheer instinct for survival, turned hostile.

Berkeley was considered too cautious in Indian affairs by hotheads who supported his young Indian-hating cousin, Nathaniel Bacon. The latter began to prey on the tribes, mostly on those which were peaceful and friendly. Next, Bacon took on the 'Establishment' itself in what became known as Bacon's Rebellion. He usurped power from his cousin, then chased the loyal Pamunkeys into Great Dragon Swamp and killed and captured many of them. Indians and Englishmen alike were relieved when the despicable Bacon died of 'the bloody flux' on 26 October 1676. His revolt was buried with him.

Massachusetts Bay

Far to the north, the settlers of Plymouth Plantation and the Massachusetts Bay Colony were spared the long years of warfare which plagued Virginia. Although the *Mayflower* had some roughnecks aboard, including America's first murderer, the Pilgrims were better-behaved than most Virginians. Plymouth also had a secret weapon. Disease. The *Mayflower* landed its passengers in 1620 in the middle of an epidemic picked up by the Indians from stray Europeans on the New England coast.

The Reverend Cotton Mather was pleased to see Indian settlements laid waste by sickness. He took this to be an act of God, for 'the woods were almost cleared of those pernicious creatures, to make room for a better growth.'

The Pilgrims found that the ruler of much of New

Above: Indian conflicts meant all-out warfare; women and their children were not safe at all from the scalping knives of hostile redmen.

England was the chief of the Wampanoags. His real name was Ousamequin, or Yellow Feather, but was addressed by his title, Massasoit or Great Chief. He lived in Pokanoket, now Mount Hope, Rhode Island. One settler described him in 1621 as being 'a very lusty man, in his best years, an able body, grave of countenance, and spare in speech.'

The equivalent of John Smith in Plymouth was Captain Myles Standish who, according to an 18th century history writer, Thomas Prince, terrorized all of the tribes around him.

Massasoit may have even met Captain John Smith while the latter was exploring and mapping the New England coast. Certainly, the Chief was a reasonable man; already he had permitted sea captains to collect English castaways he had held prisoner. Even more than Powhatan, Massasoit sensed that peace and accommodation were preferable to war in dealing with the strangers. He became their friend and ally.

On 22 March 1621 Massasoit brought his brother, Quadequina, and two leading chiefs, Samoset and Squanto, to a pow-wow in Plymouth. (Samoset was the chief who startled some settlers by walking out of the woods and greeting them, 'Welcome, Englishmen'. He had picked up a few words in their tongue from fishermen on the coast.) Massasoit may have been reticent, but the long harangues droned on, much of them unintelligible to the English, until the latter, as hosts, sealed the treaty with proper ceremony. They gave the chiefs a gill of whiskey. This caused Massasoit, unaccountably, to break out in a sweat. He was probably allergic to alcohol.

In Massasoit's treaty, land, for the first time, was given away by the Indians, not seized by the whites. The Chief handed it to them because it had been emptied of people by the epidemic. 'Englishmen, take this land, for none is

Below: **Captain Myles Standish**, Plymouth Colony's equivalent of Captain John Smith, saved the settlement several times from the Indians. In 1873 an Armstrong & Company lithograph depicted him as he clambered up from a beach at Plymouth on Cape Cod with an Indian guide.

Above: **Roger Williams,** founder of Rhode Island, was a skilled diplomat. He opposed the seizing of land and, instead, purchased it from Chief Canonicus (above) of the Narragansetts. Because of his genuine friendship, the tribe remained peaceful despite provocation by whites.

Right: The **Pequods or Pequots** of Connecticut, 3000 war-like Indians led by Sassacus, dominated neighboring tribes like the Niantics, but were badly defeated in their 1637 war with New Englanders. Most of the survivors of the conflict were massacred by the Mohawks when they fled into their country to avoid the whites.

Above: **Samoset**, a Wampanoag tribe chief, surprised the Pilgrims by welcoming them to New England in passable English.

left to occupy it. The Great Spirit has swept its people from the face of the earth.' Surprisingly, the treaty worked, though Standish had to punish the Massachussetts Indians —and mount a chief's head on the wall of Plymouth's fort— while Governor William Bradford had to outbluff the Indians when they threatened war.

The Pequot War

The Pequot tribe of the Connecticut River Valley was not a party to the treaty. In 1636 the Pequots became restive. They saw themselves squeezed between the English of Massachusetts and Rhode Island, and the Dutch of New Amsterdam and the Hudson River. In 1636 the first Connecticut colony was founded in Hartford. Trouble was bound to occur.

When the Pequot War began in 1636, it broke out in a strange quarter—at sea. John Gallup of Boston, sailing with some friends, found a neighbor's boat under sail, but in the control of Indians. He fired on the vessel, then boldly rammed her and captured a few piratical Pequots too slow to jump overboard.

Reaction was quick, and deadly. Governor Vane of Massachusetts sent a 90-man force to intimidate the Pequots. The whites by mistake killed every Narragansett Indian they could find on Block Island, then burned their lodges. The force did not lose a man in this swift campaign of vengeance.

Naturally the Pequots struck back, almost blindly, though Roger Williams, founder of Rhode Island, per-suaded the stronger Narragansett tribe from joining them in an alliance. The Pequots ambushed families in lonely cabins and killed farm boys behind plows. When there was no immediate reprisal for these murders, they were em-boldened to put 1000 men on the warpath.

Connecticut appealed to Massachusetts for help. Captain John Mason, an old professional soldier, came to the aid of the so-called Nutmeggers. He was cut from the same cloth as Captain John Smith. Mason was another old profes-sional soldier. He had soldiered in the Low Countries before leading immigrants from Dorchester, Massachusetts to found Windsor, Connecticut. At the moment of the crisis, he was in the pay of the Dutch; his job, appropriately, was to harass the Pequots.

In May of 1637 Mason led 80 whites and a hundred Mohicans under the *sachem*, or chief, Uncas, to a rendez-vous with reinforcements at Saybrook Fort. He then proved his powers of persuasion to be superior to those of Pequot's emissaries by convincing a large number of Narragansetts to join him against their old foes.

The expedition ran down Narragansett Bay in small boats. Although a Sunday (no fighting on the Sabbath) and bad weather delayed them, their attack on the Pequot stronghold was a surprise. Mason studied the stockade of 12-foot posts around an acre of ground holding the tribe's wigwams. This aboriginal fortress stood on a hill above present-day Groton, Connecticut.

Mason knew that his Indian allies were unreliable. Chief Uncas was an opportunist who was as likely as not to switch to a winning side in mid-battle. He also knew that Uncas had lived with the Pequots and worse, that their chief, Sassacus, was Uncas's father-in-law.

But the captain was neither discouraged or surprised

Above: **Massasoit**, supreme chief of the Wampanoag tribe, was friendly to the whites, like Samoset, although his son, King Philip, became the deadliest enemy of the New England colonists. In 1621, Massasoit extended the peace pipe to Governor John Carver of Plymouth. He never broke his word though he was sorely tried by the whites.

by the unreliability of his allies. Nor was he intimidated by the impressive stockade or the reversal of usual roles—whites attacking fortified Indians, instead of vice versa. He was pleased just to find the Pequots still ignorant of his stealthy advance. When a patrol reported that there were two gates in the palings, opposite one another, Mason split his force. He rushed both entrances and crashed through them at dawn. He caught the Pequots entirely unaware, but they did not immediately surrender. The warriors fought bravely—like Romans said Benjamin Trumbull—and Mason had a difficult time until he picked up a firebrand, twirled it around his head to fan the flames, and threw it into a wigwam. He shouted over the din of battle, 'God is over us! He laughs his enemies to scorn, making them as a fiery oven!' Mason's second-in-command, Captain John Underhill, followed his example, pitching a torch into another tent. Smoke and flames now confused the defenders, and they broke and ran for the gates. There the soldiers shot them down, and the few who escaped were slaughtered by the Mohicans and Narragansetts who found their courage in time for the kill.

Governor Bradford's report read like an eyewitness account of the bloody battle at Groton. He mixed horror with gratitude at the sight of Indians 'frying in the fire, streams of blood quenching the same, and horrible was the stink and scent thereof; but the victory was a sweet sacrifice, and they [the victors] gave prayer thereof to God.'

Whatever the accurate figure of casualties, 600 or 1000, Mason had scored a smashing victory, losing only two men, plus 20 wounded. Small wonder that Cotton Mather would later write, 'No less than 600 Pequot souls were brought down to hell that day!'

But the Pequot nation was not destroyed. In fact, Mason's victory almost turned into a debacle. On its way back to the boats, the force blundered into a war party, 300 strong. Surprise was with the Indians this time. But Mason extricated his men from a near-trap, got them past the enemy and reached the harbor safely, while fighting a rear-guard action against pursuers.

Shortly, the old soldier was on the march again, hunting down Pequots from Saybrook to New London. Those not killed were enslaved in Massachusetts or Connecticut or sent in chains to Bermuda. A few escaped and found havens in other tribes, but Chief Sassacus made the mistake of choosing the Mohawk tribe as a refuge. The haughty Mohawks cut off his head and sent it to Boston to show that they were not involved in Pequot uprisings.

King Philip's War

The Pequot War was followed by a worse conflict, the

first and only major Indian war in the 17th century. King Philip's War, which began in 1671, decided the fate of New England's Indians.

The Narragansetts, 4000 in all, constituted one-fifth of the Indians in southern New England. White settlements were spreading and threatening to coalesce into a broad unit composed of the 5000 Pilgrims at Plymouth, the 17,000 Puritans of the Massachusetts Bay Colony and Connecticut (10,000), plus the 3000 dissidents of Rhode Island.

The exact cause of the war is unknown. The excuse for the war, as usual, was ridiculous. A suspected murder and the execution of Indian suspects. Probably the violence 'just grew'. It grew out of mounting resentment and resistance by the Indians to white pressure. Though the latter still tended to buy Indian land, not seize it, there were frauds. And the buyers did not understand the Indians' retention of fishing and hunting rights, much like subsoil mineral rights are reserved today in land sales. The English saw the ex-'owners' as trespassers, violators of a legal contract.

There was also Indian annoyance at the growing divisiveness in their villages. Missionaries were converting redmen; settlers were hiring others as laborers; and traders were making the Indians dependent upon them. Most important, the Indians felt hemmed in now, between the English and the Dutch and the implacable Iroquois to the west.

After Massasoit's death, his sons Metacomet and Wamsutta shared power. They seemed to be thoughtful and peaceful Wampanoag *sachems*, and the English named them Philip and Alexander, as symbolic gestures of friendship. Still, troubling rumors of a change of heart in the tribe persisted. So in 1662, Alexander was called to Duxbury.

Alexander handled the questioning by authorities successfully and visited a friend, Josiah Winslow, in Marshfield. Suddenly, the chief came down with a violent fever. He died a few days later, on his way home, and his widow accused the whites of poisoning him. Alexander's brother, now sole chief, made no move for revenge, however. On the contrary, he reaffirmed his father's treaty of peace and friendship.

But peace deteriorated into an armed truce. Rumors of war, probably inspired more by Narragansetts than Wampanoags, echoed through 1667, 1669 and early 1671. Since Philip was the most prominent chief in all New England, he was called to Taunton in 1671. This time, the authorities were more insensitive and peremptory in their demands than ever. They ordered the proud chief to surrender all guns held by his tribe, and they seized his weapons and those carried by his escort.

King Philip was angered by such bullying, but he was not yet ready to resist. He signed the treaty and turned in a few token arms. But most of his braves refused to give up their guns. Philip was recalled, this time to Plymouth, virtually put on trial, and forced to sign a treaty of abject surrender.

This scrap of paper was the last humiliation that Philip could tolerate. He began a plan to push the whites back into the sea. To build a confederation, he sent messengers to tribes asking them to send emissaries to secret war councils. For four years he waited for the proper moment to strike.

On 29 January 1675 an Indian named John Sassamon was found dead under the ice of Assawampsett Pond, 15 miles from Plymouth. He was buried there by Indians, but someone leaked word to the authorities that he had not died of natural causes. The body was exhumed and an investigation suggested that the man had been murdered and thrown into the water.

Sassamon was not just any Indian. He was a convert, raised as a Christian, who not only spoke English well but had studied at Harvard. This civilized or 'white' Indian had astounded both the Indian and white communities when he had reverted to what the settlers called savagery, becoming an aide to Philip, then recanting again and returning to the church, where he became a preacher. Then a new rumor surfaced; just before his death, he had warned the colonists of King Philip's plot. Apparently he had been a spy in the Wampanoags' ranks! The settlers, foolishly lulled by long years of peace—and Sassamon's reputation for cunning as well as plausibility—did not believe him. Philip certainly heard of his spying. And Sassamon was murdered.

An Indian witness came forward and named three Wampanoags as the culprits. None of them admitted his guilt, yet all were tried, convicted and hanged. But Wampapaquan's rope either broke or its hangman's knot slipped. He fell to the ground. Taking this rescue as a good omen, and fully expecting to be spared for turning state's evidence, as it were, he confessed to his part in the crime, blaming the actual killing on his two partners, now deceased. The warrior's reward was to be strung up again.

Philip was angered by the executions and by the betrayal of his machinations. But he was still unready to fight. However, his younger warriors soon forced his hand.

The 'grapevine' warned the village of Swansea of an attack. It was a likely target since it blocked the way from Mount Hope Neck, Philip's home, to Plymouth. As the alarm spread from semi-deserted Swansea to other villages, Governor John Winslow sent a negotiator to Philip. The Chief's insolence *must* have tipped his hand. 'Your Governor is but a subject of King Charles of England. I shall not treat with a subject. I shall treat of peace only with the King, my brother. When he comes, I am ready.'

The young Wampanoags did not wait for Charles II's arrival. On the very day set aside by the Governor's proclamation for fasting and prayers for peace, 24 June 1675, some braves—probably without King Philip's knowledge—struck Swansea. They killed nine persons, mutilating some of them, and wounded two more as they exacted 'blood revenge' for the wounding of one of their number the day before by a citizen when they sacked part of the town. Before the raiders withdrew, they set fire to some of Swansea's buildings, as its inhabitants fled.

The Indians next attacked Taunton, Dartmouth and Middleborough, as messengers hurried to Boston and Plymouth for help. In Boston, drummers beat a roll on the Common for just three hours in order to enlist 110 volunteers. Captain Samuel Mosely marched out and reached the charred ruins on the 26th. He took a chance and sent a detachment toward Mount Hope. The patrol was intercepted, but the skirmish was broken off by Philip after he lost two warriors. Mosley lost one of his dozen men in the patrol.

In the morning, Mosley found himself trapped in blackened Swansea. When the Wampanoags dared him to come out and fight, he immediately obliged. His charge demoralized them and they fled. He then marched to Philip's deserted village, only to find the heads of eight white men on poles. He buried the grisly trophies, burned the village and returned to his base at Swansea.

Meanwhile, a Lieutenant Oakes, marching a small unit to Swansea from Rehoboth, ran into a war party and killed several before they slipped off into the trees. He sent their scalps to Boston to advertise his little victory.

Now, 35-year-old Benjamin Church took to the field. He was a Rhode Islander and always a good friend of the Indians. He really knew them, especially the 'queen' or squaw-sachem, Awashonks, of the Sakonnets. It was the queen who warned him of Philips 'conspiracy,' and it was he who cautioned her not to ally her tribe with Philip. (For a time, she went along with Church, but later, disastrously, joined Philip.) Church urged full use of Indian allies as scouts, trackers, interpreters and soldier-warriors, especially since the Colonials were unsure fighters in marsh or woods. They preferred open country, describing swamp combat as fighting wild beasts in their dens.

Church urged that troops be sent to join him at Pocasset Neck, but his superiors insisted on marching men to Mount Hope. They found the peninsula deserted, just as he predicted. Church had only 36 men in his company, but he took a chance and split his force. With 19 militiamen, he went to Tiverton on Narragansett Bay, covering his movement with three small boats. His surprise advance was given away to enemy scouts when his foolish and green soldiers struck flint and steel to light their pipes. Church cursed this 'epidemical plague of lust for tobacco'. He was also dismayed by his militia's fear of rattlesnakes. He said they were as much afraid of them as of 'the black serpents [Indians] they were in quest of.'

Church found the Indians he was after, all too many of them. An abandoned vegetable garden was literally covered with warriors. Church's coolness prevented panic and his men fought well but had to be rescued by a canoe sent ashore from a sloop. Church was the last to leave shore, in a hail of bullets. Luckily for him and his men, Philip's marksmen were terrible shots. Not one of the whites was even wounded in the engagement.

Captain Matthew Fuller with Church's other 17 men ran into a similar predicament and had to be rescued by boats, also.

The tide of war seemed to turn quickly after Philip's raiding of the five Massachusetts towns. On 19 July 1675 he was trapped in the cedars of Pocasset Swamp near the Taunton River. But he simply sent out some decoys to lure the colonists deeper into the swamp, then ambushed them into a hasty retreat in which they lost seven or eight dead.

The colonists decided to starve King Philip into submission. But, to Church's disbelief, instead of throwing a ring of skirmishers around the swamp, they built a stockade for themselves! Church protested, 'You are building a fort for nothing, to cover the people from nobody.'

Philip spent a cozy fortnight in the swamp while he collected enough canoes, then slipped away to the Connecticut River. His escape would have gone smoothly except that he ran into a force of white-allied Mohicans, or Mohegans. He lost a few warriors to them before getting away to his new allies, the Nipmucks of the Connecticut and its tributaries. Already, they had attacked Mendon on 14 July 1675.

In early August, a force of 20 mounted militiamen under Captains Edward Hutchinson and Thomas Wheeler, guided by three of Reverend John Eliot's 'Praying Indians', ie, Christians, took the field. They still hoped to win over the Nipmucks or, at least, to keep them neutral. There were no Nipmucks at the agreed-upon rendezvous for a parley. The whites pushed on to look for them, over the protests of their Indian interpreters, who smelt treachery. On 2 August a joint war party of Nipmucks and Wampanoags ambushed the force. Eight men were killed outright, three others mortally wounded. Co-commander Hutchinson was also wounded and died a few days later. Wheeler's horse was shot out from under him but Wheeler was rescued, wounded, by his son. The survivors fought a rearguard action back to Brookfield, guided by two of their Praying Indians. The third was captured by the Nipmucks.

The battered force joined 80 very alarmed citizens crowded into Brookfield's garrison house. The Indians burned every other structure. One settler was killed by a musket ball as he ran for the fortified house, another was captured. He was beheaded and his head kicked about in sport by the Indians before being placed on a pole in front of the ruins of his own home, as if to keep an eye on it.

The Indians' attempts to fire the fort were turned back by the defenders' musket fire. The besiegers shot arrows ablaze with flaming tow, but the whites cut holes in the roof and dowsed the fires with water. Twice, men tried to slip away from the log cabin to the woods but were driven back inside.

A midnight full moon disclosed the Indians piling brush and wood against one corner of the building to set it alight. Several citizens ran out and scattered the brands. This operation had to be repeated later and, this time one of the fire-fighters took advantage of the smoke and confusion to get away and run through the woods to Lancaster for help.

The second day of Brookfield's siege came and passed and was replaced by a frightening night lit by the arcs of flaming arrows. The third day was critical. Some Indian strategists loaded a farm wagon with hay, flax, hemp, wood, anything that would burn, and rolled it up against the fortified cabin. There was no way the men could get out to push it away in time. Some got down on their knees and prayed for a miracle. A sudden downpour put out the fire and so dampened the combustibles in the wagon bed that the Indians could not rekindle it.

The miracle was accompanied by a stroke of good luck. The runner did not have to go all the way to Lancaster. He met 70-year-old Major Simon Willard and 50 men—and they were all mounted. Willard galloped to Brookfield's rescue, driving the besiegers away and leaving 80 dead warriors on the field.

The two Praying Indians were so badly abused by the ungrateful whites that they defected to King Philip. One was killed in action, the other captured and sent as a slave to Bermuda. Ultimately, he was rescued by Reverend John Eliot. The third Christian Indian escaped from the Nipmucks and returned to the whites.

Among the stranger legends to come out of King Philip's War was that of the siege of Hadley, Massachusetts. The citizens, locked in the meeting house against rampaging Wampanoags, were led in a counterattack by a mysterious stranger. According to the legend, the man who seemed to appear out of nowhere was none other than the Regicide killer of Charles I, William Goffe, who had fled to Connecticut after the Restoration.

Afterward, Hadley, Northfield, Deerfield, Medfield, Wrentham and other settlements felt the effects of tomahawk and torch. When a party rushed to the relief of Northfield's blockhouse, it ran into an ambuscade which

Above: A classic siege of King Philip's War was the 1675 attack on **Brookfield, Massachusetts,** when fire arrows were used to great effect.

took the lives of 20 volunteers. Deerfield suffered the most, perhaps. Residents on their way to church were attacked in a second raid. Eighty men came from Ipswich to harvest Deerfield's abandoned grain crop. Homeward bound, the drivers of the 18 wagons halted for a rest and a drink in a grove of trees on a stream. There, 700 Indians who had been trailing them killed all but about seven men. Swansea's Captain Mosley heard the distant firing in Deerfield. He hurried to the rescue and, outnumbered as he was, fell on the Indians as they scalped the dead at Bloody Brook. He harassed them till reinforcements came at dusk to drive them off. The loss of at least 68 men with the trapped supply train was described by a New England chronicler as the loss of 'the flower of the County.'

The news was gloomy for New Englanders after the 18 September 1675 affair at Bloody Brook. On the 28th, Northampton was attacked; on 5 October, part of Springfield was burned. An attack on Hatfield was repulsed. In December, Philip went to the powerful Mohawks to seek an alliance. But now the tide began to change. New York's Governor Sir Edmund Andros persuaded the Iroquoian

Above: Several times Indians raided the town of Haverhill, Massachusetts. *Above right:* **Deerfield,** in the Connecticut River Valley, probably suffered more from Indian massacres than any other Massachusetts town.

Mohawks not to join Philip. In fact, the Mohawks threw him out of New York.

But now the Narragansetts, with 3000–5000 men under Chief Canonchet, threw in their lot with Philip. Against them Massachusetts sent 520 men, Connecticut 300, and Plymouth 150. Governor Josiah Winslow of Plymouth took personal command of a force which floundered through the snowy woods on 19 December to attack a supposedly impregnable bastion in the **Great Swamp**. It was something of a repetition of Mason's attack on the Pequot fort.

Winslow split his force and attacked from two sides, but the Massachusetts men were driven back from the log bridge, the only crossing of a moat in front of the stockade, by heavy fire. However, Ben Church was not to be denied. With 30 Plymouth and Connecticut men, he attacked the fort from the rear, forced a break in the stockade and led his men into the compound. Church was wounded three times, but he won the day. In vain, he protested Winslow's burning of the fort's wigwams; the troops needed shelter from the cold.

Winslow pursued the fort's fleeing survivors for 70 miles until the freezing cold forced him to quit. It was a great victory. In one blow, the Narragansetts were smashed. The whites lost 70 or 80 men killed, including 14 company commanders, and about 150 wounded. But 300 warriors were dead, among them 20 chiefs, and probably another 300 old men, women and children.

The Narragansetts had strength for one more attack, however, on 10 February 1676. It fell on Lancaster, Massachusetts. They killed 50 persons and carried off 24 captives. One of them, Mary Rowlandson, survived to write a best-selling book. Her *Narrative* started a whole genre of literature, the Indian Captivity, in 1682. It was in its 15th edition by 1800.

King Philip was still at large. Town after town was attacked and burned. He was so confident of success that

he brazenly ordered his people to plant their corn in Deerfield's abandoned fields. A Captain Turner was sent from Boston to clear the Indians from Deerfield. His dawn assault of 10 May 1676 was so unexpected that some Indians took to their canoes without paddles and were swept over the falls in the Connecticut River. Perhaps Turner exaggerated his success, claiming 300 Indians killed and the loss of only one trooper. In any case, just like Mason 39 years before him, he blundered into a second war party. The troops panicked when someone shouted that King Philip was personally leading the attack. A third of the force was lost, including Turner, before the remainder escaped.

The see-saw campaign continued, with assaults on towns being balanced by 170 Narragansetts being killed or captured in early July in northern Rhode Island and another 80 surrendering at Providence. The colonies finally took stern measures, banning all trade with the Indians and even beginning the impressment or conscription of soldiers.

Benjamin Church was still recovering from the wounds he had received near Kingston, Rhode Island when the Sakonnets turned on Philip and offered to join Church. He made a frontal attack on Philip's headquarters on 20 July. Church almost captured the King and did seize his treasury of wampum, along with his wife and son. They were sold to West Indian slavery for 1 pound sterling each. The colonists also killed from 130 to 173 warriors, depending on the count of different chroniclers.

On 27 July the Nipmucks split. Sagamore John and 180 warriors marched the tribe's main war chief, Matoonas, into Boston as a prisoner. He was bound to a tree and Sagamore John was allowed to shoot him to death.

Now, Philip had only a few loyal followers with him. Everyone else seemed to be a deserter, an informer, a turncoat. Or dead. He cut his hair short as a disguise. His uncle was shot down at his very side. When a warrior urged him to give up, Philip exploded, and clubbed him to death. This act led to the end of King Philip's War. The victim's brother, called Alderman, went immediately to Benjamin Church, 11 August 1676, and offered to guide the Captain

Above: Friendly Indians like the boy **Chanco**, at Jamestown, sometimes warned colonists of attacks.

Right: **King Philip** was killed (1676) by one of his own men, Alderman, who joined the whites and shot him in a swamp.

to Philip's hiding place. The next day, Church's men surrounded the swamp in which the enemy was camped. He sent Captain Roger Goulding and a few picked men to seize Philip. The chief heard them coming and ran for a secret trail. But Church had posted two guards on it, Caleb Cook and the Indian, Alderman. Cook aimed at Philip but his gun misfired. Alderman then fired a double charge into the chief's chest. He fell, face down, in a pool of muddy water.

The militiamen broke out in hearty cheers when Church identified the body as Philip's. He ordered an Indian executioner among his allies to behead and quarter the corpse. Once a friend of the Indians, even of Philip, Church now called him a 'doleful, great, naked, dirty beast'. The butchered remains were denied burial and left to rot or to be torn by wild animals. Church sent Philip's head to Plymouth where it was mounted on a gibbet and remained there as a warning to restive chiefs for 20 years. To Alderman he gave Philip's scarred right hand, injured by an exploding pistol. The Indian took it to Boston as a relic. He exhibited it, preserved in a pail of rum, to gentlemen who would pay him a fee to see it.

The war sputtered on to an end in New Hampshire, where the efficient Church was sent to wind it up. Violence would flare up again after 1688, but it was not part of King Philip's Conspiracy, as the Colonials termed the war. It was an international conflict.

King Philip's War cost the lives of 600 Englishmen and perhaps 3000 Indians. Some 1200 homes were burned and 80,000 head of cattle killed. Surviving Indians were sold as slaves for 30 shillings each. Small wonder that New Englanders had elephantine memories about the conflict. In 1842, 166 years after Philip and his *sachems* burned 52 of New England's 90 settlements, destroying a dozen of them, there was no forgiveness. A convention assembled in Newport to adopt a new state constitution withheld the vote from 'any member of the Narragansett tribe of Indians' because of the bloody alliance with King Philip.

King William's War

Far to the north, Samuel de Champlain had established a permanent French settlement at Quebec in 1608 and a trading post at Montreal by 1611. He allied himself with the Hurons and won the everlasting hatred of the much more powerful Iroquois Confederation by doing so. But, initially, he and his successors were able to push back English influence in upstate New York and Maine.

Explorers like Jean Nicolet and the Sieur de La Salle emulated Champlain. La Salle sent Father Hennepin to the Mississippi River, then descended the great waterway himself in 1682. He went all the way to its mouth on the Gulf of Mexico and took possession of its immense valley for France—naturally, without checking with its Indian inhabitants. An expedition to found a colony at the Mississippi's mouth foundered in shipwreck and Spanish attacks. Wandering in Texas, La Salle was shot by his own men on 19 March 1687.

An alliance of the French and the Abenakis tribe in Maine kept that territory in a state of siege. Sir Edmund Andros attempted to pacify it, without success, during the so-called King William's War. Schenectady was not only sacked, like some New England villages, but the French, after promising 100 captives safety, stood by while their Abenaki allies massacred them.

In 1691, Benjamin Church, now old and fat, forced a few of Maine's *sachems* to sue for peace but, the very next year, Indians and Canadians killed 48 of the village of York's citizens and took 70 prisoners. In 1697, it was the turn of Haverhill, Massachusetts. One of its victims became an early heroine of the Indian wars. Hannah Dustin was resting

a week after the birth of her eighth child when the Abenakis struck Haverhill. She and her baby and the nurse were carried off. When the infant's cries annoyed the Indians, they smashed its head against a tree. That was a blunder for the Abenakis. Hannah waited patiently until her guards relaxed their vigilance. One night, she awoke the nurse and the two women took up hatchets and killed the two warriors, two women and six children of the party that had been holding her captive. Only an old woman and a boy escaped her vengeance. Since the state of Massachusetts offered a bounty on Indians, Hannah was careful to scalp her victims. After she got safely back to Haverhill, she received the sum of 25 pounds sterling for the scalps.

Top left: Between wars, whites romanticized Indians as noble hunters.

Top right: What whites feared most were inter-tribal alliances.

Above: Sometimes, the weaker sex fought back during Indian wars, like Hannah Dustin of Haverhill or the axe-wielding **Mrs Bozarth** (above).

Queen Anne's War

In 1703 the smoldering Indian wars flared up again as part of Queen Anne's War, and on 28 February 1704 it was poor Deerfield's turn to suffer again. Established on the Connecticut River *circa* 1670, that town was the site of massacres in 1675 and 1677. By 1704, 270 people lived in its 41 houses. Once more, it was put to the torch by the hated allies, the 'Indianized-French' and 'Frenchified-Indians' of Cotton Mather's anger. They killed 49 inhabitants and started more than 100 off into captivity. A score or more, however, were murdered on the trail. One who survived was the Reverend John Williams. He was finally ransomed, but his wife was killed when she became too tired to keep up with her fleeing captors. His daughter was adopted by the Indians and never returned to white society, except for occasional visits. Williams wrote another best-seller, along the lines of Mary Rowlandson's narrative. His *Redeemed Captive Returning to Zion* (1707) went through eight editions by 1800. It, and Mrs Rowlandson's book, proved to be very effective anti-Indian propaganda.

The news of the Deerfield horror brought old Benjamin Church into the fray again, though he was now so decrepit that he had to have a soldier always at his side to help him over fallen logs. With 550 men he campaigned in the north, calming things down a bit by a show of force, plus bombast. But not until France's Acadian bastion of Port Royal fell (1711) could Maine folk breathe a little easier.

The Treaty of Utrecht ended Anglo-French rivalry in the north for the moment, but Indian warfare merely shifted southward. The Iroquoian Tuscaroras ('Hemp Gatherers'), irritated by the excesses of frontier traders, went on the warpath in North Carolina in 1711. They were beaten by two South Carolinians, Colonels John Barnwell and James Moore, in 1712–13. Those not sold into slavery at 10 pounds sterling a head to pay for the colonists' campaign expenses, fled northward to join the Iroquois Confederacy in 1715, changing it from the Five Nations to the Six Nations—the Mohawks, Onandagas, Oneidas, Senecas, Cayugas and now the Tuscaroras.

In 1715 the Yamassees of South Carolina repeated the Tuscarora story. They were smashed, the survivors fleeing into Spanish Florida. The powerful Cherokees ('Cave People') now proved a stabilizing influence on the frontier of the South. They remained on good terms with the whites and checked the hostility of the Creeks against the settlers.

Above: On the banks of the Trinity River in Texas the great French explorer, **La Salle,** was treacherously shot by one of his men in 1687. His explorations had taken him down the Mississippi to the Gulf of Mexico, which he claimed for France.

Right: In 1703 the Indians descended on Deerfield, Massachusetts, as they had in 1675 and 1677, murdering or capturing over half of its inhabitants. The violence shown here contrasts sharply with the image of the "noble" redmen shown on the top of the opposite page.

Briefly, between 1721–25, Maine again was a bleeding wound for New England, as French-allied Abenakis resumed their raiding. But they were forced to submit to England by a treaty of 1725.

At last, there was peace in the 13 Colonies, even on the Indian frontier. It would not last.

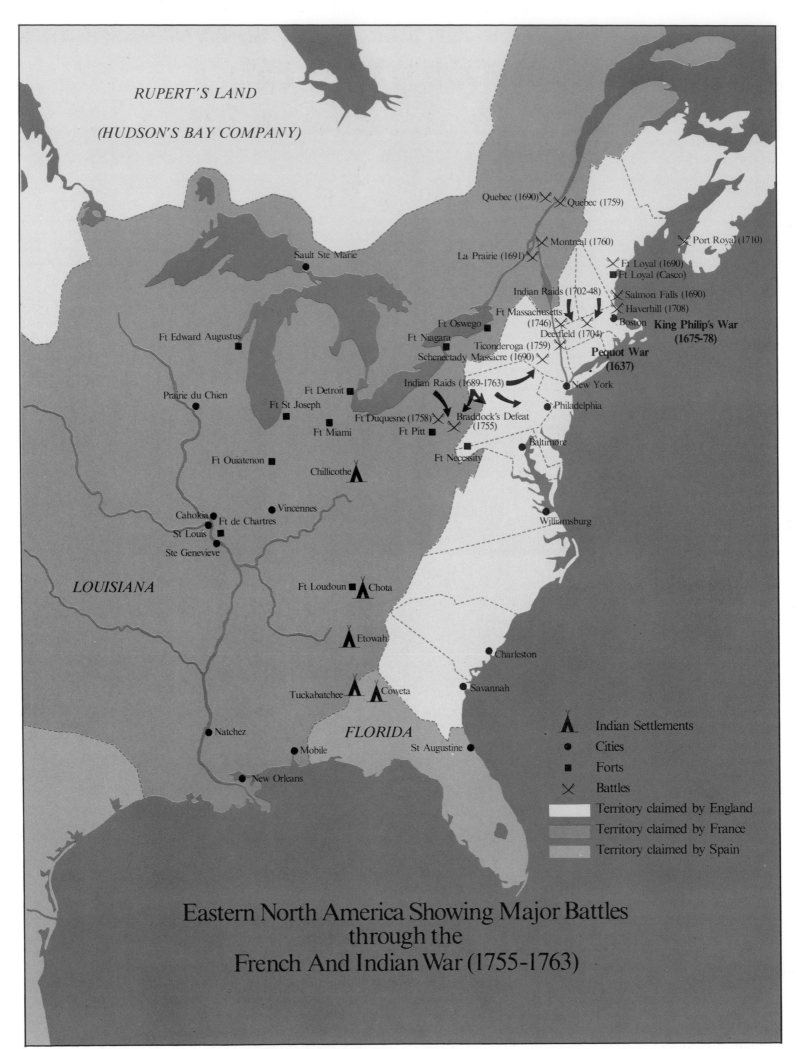

RUPERT'S LAND

(HUDSON'S BAY COMPANY)

Sault Ste Marie

Quebec (1690) ✕ Quebec (1759)

✕ Montreal (1760)   ✕ Port Royal (1710)

La Prairie (1691) ✕

✕ Ft Loyal (1690)
■ Ft Loyal (Casco)

Indian Raids (1702-48)   ✕ Salmon Falls (1690)
✕ Haverhill (1708)

Ft Massachusetts ✕ ● Boston   **King Philip's War**
(1746)   **(1675-78)**

Ft Oswego ✕   Deerfield (1704)

Ft Niagara ✕   Ticonderoga (1759) ✕   **Pequot War**
Schenectady Massacre (1690) ✕   **(1637)**

Ft Edward Augustus ■   Indian Raids (1689-1763)   ● New York

Prairie du Chien ●   Ft Detroit ■   ● Philadelphia

Ft St Joseph ■   Ft Duquesne (1758) ✕ ✕ Braddock's Defeat
(1755)
Ft Miami ■   Ft Pitt ■   ● Baltimore

Ft Ouiatenon ■   Ft Necessity ■

Chillicothe ⛺

Cahokia ●   ● Vincennes
Ft de Chartres ■
St Louis ●   ● Williamsburg
Ste Genevieve ●

LOUISIANA

Ft Loudoun ■ ⛺ Chota

⛺ Etowah

● Charleston

Tuckabatchee ⛺ ⛺ Coweta   ● Savannah

● Natchez   *FLORIDA*

● Mobile   St Augustine ●

● New Orleans

⛺ Indian Settlements
● Cities
■ Forts
✕ Battles
     Territory claimed by England
     Territory claimed by France
     Territory claimed by Spain

Eastern North America Showing Major Battles
through the
French And Indian War (1755-1763)

PATRIOTS

1755-1815

All textbooks agree on the length of the American Revolution, 1775–1783. Yet the dates are misleading in terms of the 13 Colonies' relations with neighboring Indian nations. The War for Independence—from England—was halted in 1783. But the Colonists' war for freedom from attacks by both French-allied and English-allied Indians actually began with the French and Indian War in 1753 and did not end until 1815, with the close of the War of 1812.

One man clearly had seen that the struggle between France and England for domination of the North American continent would ultimately be decided on the frontier, and that the Indians would play a decisive role. William Johnson, later Sir William, was a Mohawk Valley trader who was so honest in his transactions with the Indians at all times that he was appointed His Majesty's Superintendent of Indian Affairs for the Northern Colonies. Since he was married to a Mohawk woman, the Irishman had been made a blood-brother of that tribe. Even more important, his friendship and fair dealing won the allegiance of the powerful Iroquois tribe, who had made him a chief.

Nevertheless, the balance of power on the Indian borders after the Peace of Aix la Chapelle (1748) tipped in France's favor. It was a paradox, because the British and Colonials in 1745 had seized France's New World 'Gibraltar', Louisbourg on Cape Breton Island. (To the dismay of the so-called provincials, Britain gave it back!) But the much more numerous Anglo-Saxons clung to the Atlantic seaboard, yielding control of the Great Lakes–Ohio–Mississippi interior to a relative handful of French and their numerous Indian allies.

The French and Indian War

The inevitable collision between Anglo-Colonists and French-led Indians came in the wilderness of western Pennsylvania. Virginia's governor, Robert Dinwiddie, backed by orders from the King himself, sent Major George Washington, all of 21 years old, on his first important mission. It was also a delicate mission and a difficult one. But, young as he was, Washington was already 'a person of distinction' in gubernatorial eyes. He was to ask the commander of French forces on the Ohio 'his reasons for invading the British dominions while a solid peace subsisted', and to call upon the French to retire from the territory.

Washington's 'force' consisted of an escort of just four men, plus an interpreter and the 48-year-old scout, Christo-pher Gist. He rode up the Indian trail leading to the Forks of the Ohio on 15 November 1753. Once there, he studied the natural fort-site at its apex. He was the first Englishman to see the location of future Pittsburgh. From the junction, a Delaware chief guided Washington to Logstown, where he won the tentative support of some Shawnees and Delawares against the French. At Venango, where French Creek entered the Allegheny River, French officers boasted to him of their plan to take possession of the Ohio River Valley, indeed the whole interior from New Orleans to Quebec via the Wabash, Maumee and Ohio Rivers. They boasted of the power of their line of forts—Le Boeuf, Presque Isle, Niagara, Toronto and Frontenac. True, they admitted, they were badly outnumbered by the English and their Colonial kin, but they considered the Anglo-Saxons too dilatory to prevent the French enterprise.

The creeks were swollen by December rains and too deep to ford, but Washington and his escort bridged them by felling trees and pushed on to Fort Le Boeuf, near today's Waterford, Pennsylvania. The Commandant, Legardeur de Saint-Pierre, refused to discuss the French possession of the land claimed by Britain. But he did warn the young Virginian that he would make prisoners of any Englishmen that he caught in France's Ohio Valley.

George Washington went no farther than Fort LeBoeuf, ten miles from Presque Isle (Erie) on French Creek. But he had seen enough. The fort's walls were almost complete; cannon were in place; 50 birchbark canoes and 170 pine *bateaux* were on the shore, ready to descend the Mississippi to link the Ohio with France's 'lower province' of New Orleans.

The return journey was colder and more fatiguing, made on foot because the horses, left at Venango, were still too weak to be ridden. Slogging along Indian trails buried in freezing snow, Washington composed his report to Dinwiddie in his mind. In his impatience—or distraction—he almost forfeited his life. Wrapping himself in Indian blankets and taking only a gun, hatchet, compass and pack, he took Gist on a shortcut through the woods. An Indian, hiding in ambush not 15 paces from him, fired but missed. Washington made him prisoner. Gist recalled later, 'I would have killed him, but Washington forbade it.' The Major freed his captive that night, then pressed on with Gist to kindle a decoy campfire and hurry ahead all night and the next day before finally resting.

With his hatchet, Washington and Gist hacked out a raft of timber to cross the swollen Allegheny River. But ice floes dumped them in the frigid water and drove them ashore on an island where they suffered terribly from the cold until the river froze solid and they could walk to shore. From there they reached the safety of Gist's Settlement and Washington hurried on to report to the Governor on 16 January 1754.

Dinwiddie, alarmed by Washington's report, sent a small party of woodsmen to occupy the Ohio's forks, the junction of the Allegheny and Monongahela Rivers. He then dispatched reinforcements under Washington. But the French had moved more quickly, ousting the small force and establishing Fort Duquesne. Washington had insufficient supplies even for his weak force, and he was not supported by Indian auxiliaries. Still, he picked up a dozen Mingo Indians to support his 40 soldiers before turning on a party of 33 French and Indians, led by Jumonville de Villiers, which was shadowing him. In the fight he killed 10, including the leader, and captured all the others. Thus, the French and Indian War really began on that day, 28 May 1754, though the term is supposedly synonymous for American actions of the Seven Years War.

Lieutenant Colonel Washington withdrew 10 miles to Great Meadows and erected a stockade which he named, with irony, Fort Necessity. Reinforcements arrived, but in such small numbers that he had to face 900 French and Indians, under the Sieur Coulon de Villiers, brother of the man he had defeated, with barely 400 men. The rainstorm of that 3 July put his swivel cannon out of action and Washington decided to accept the Frenchman's offer of surrender with full honors. He led his men, half of them sick or wounded, out of the Ohio Country and back to Virginia.

Britain finally moved to oust France from the West in 1755, sending over General Edward Braddock. Born in 1695, Braddock entered his father's regiment, the crack Coldstream Guards, as an ensign at the age of 15 and spent the next 43 years in that most exclusive unit in the British Army. His experience in many battles won him the reputation of being a stern disciplinarian as well as the master tactician of the service. Promoted to major general in 1754, Braddock was the obvious choice for Commander in Chief of His Majesty's forces in North America.

The short and stout General Braddock was brave and obstinate. He had, alas, as many weaknesses as strengths. Not only was he arrogant and ill tempered—choleric—he was strictly a 'by the book' tactician, unable to adapt tactics to new situations. He also had almost as much contempt for his own provincials from the 13 Colonies as he did for the Canadians and their 'naked' Indians he planned to thrash. He was clearly a potential victim of his own ego and his own overconfidence.

Braddock arrived at Williamsburg in February of 1755 and spent the spring training and drilling his men before formally assuming command, at Wills Creek, on 10 May. His preparations for the conquest of the Ohio Valley were hampered by inadequate funds, transport, provisions and laborers. The support of southern tribes, such as the Chickasaws, was promised him but no auxiliaries showed up, which was perfectly all right with Braddock. He would count on his professionals to throw the French out. His disdain for partisans, or guerrillas, as well as Indians showed in his supercilious dismissal of offers of aid from the frontiersman, Black Jack, and Chief Scarroyeddy. When Benjamin Franklin warned him that the Indians

Above: A strong, square log fort on the Western border, with a troop of mounted men, was an idealized situation of artistic license.

were not to be disregarded as antagonists, the General tut-tutted him: 'These savages may, indeed, be a formidable enemy to your raw American militia, but upon the King's regular and disciplined troops, sir, it is impossible that they should make an impression.'

The General's personal target was Fort Duquesne, now planted where Dinwiddie and Washington had wanted the key English fort. Other commanders would make uncoordinated attacks on Acadia in Canada, Crown Point on Lake Champlain and Fort Niagara on Lake Ontario. Duquesne was garrisoned by only 500–600 regulars and Canadian militia, plus 800 Indians including both Christians and Chippewas (Ojibwas), the latter probably led by the rising young chief, Pontiac. Braddock expected to have little difficulty in overwhelming Fort Duquesne since he had 1400 smart regulars or redcoats, supported by 450 'blues', or provincials, from Virginia, Maryland and the two Carolinas. He considered himself lucky not to have to depend on the colonial soldiers. They looked like a slothful and languid lot of fellows, hardly fit for military service.

General Braddock began his campaign by hacking a road westward from Fort Cumberland with his 300 axmen. It would be the first such route over the Allegheny Mountains and it was the beginning of the National Road, important in American emigration to the near West. The march began on 10 June 1775 and in eight days Braddock disgustedly found himself but 30 miles out of Cumberland. The column was slowed up by its cumbersome wagons and by the growing number of sick soldiers who were straggling at the rear. For all of his disdain for the 'Frenchies' and their red allies, Braddock was no fool. During the entire march he kept flankers out on each side of the long column, which now stretched for four miles along a 'road' no larger than a bridle path. To flush out ambushers, he kept scouts roving ahead of his advance guard. But at Little Meadows in present-day Pennsylvania the General tired of his snail's pace and decided to split his force. He left 1000 men, including the ill, with Colonel Thomas Dunbar and the heavy, slow, wagons. He then hurried forward with his best 1200 soldiers, plus workmen to improve the Indian trails. Still, the passage through the woods was so difficult that it was 7 July before he reached Turtle Creek, about eight miles south of Fort Duquesne.

Careful to avoid an ambuscade, Braddock crossed the Monongahela River at the upper ford and proceeded down the far bank to re-cross to the right bank again at the second, or lower, ford. He then resumed his march along the rough track, hardly a road, which led to rising ground near the fort.

As Braddock twisted in his saddle to view his column, he must have felt great satisfaction. He had confidence in such officers as Lieutenant Colonel Thomas Gage and Lieutenants Horatio Gates and Charles Lee, both of whom would gain fame in the Revolution. Sir John St Clair's artillery, ammunition train and workmen preceded his smart force of redcoats and somewhat shambling militiamen, well guarded by flanking parties. There was no chance for ambush; no way that the force could come to grief. In fact, he knew that more than one of his officers expected to hear Duquesne blown up, or see it put to the torch by its own dispirited defenders.

Lieutenant Colonel George Washington was so ill that he had to travel in a pallet in one of Dunbar's wagons. He had temporarily resigned his commission in order to serve as an unpaid aide-de-camp to Braddock. He now traded the wagon bed for a saddle horse and rode up to join the General and his other aides, William Morris and Robert Orme. As he watched the advance, in precise formation, of the professional soldiers that 9 July 1775, tramping along to the fifers' tune, 'The Grenadiers' March', Washington thought that it was the most splendid sight that he had ever seen.

It was with difficulty that Captain Hyacinth de Beaujeu, second in command to the Sieur de Contrecoeur, on 8 July persuaded 650 hesitant Indians to join his sortie from the fort with 250 French and Canadian-French. (Probably half of the Indians deserted before a shot was fired.) Beaujeu's orders were to intercept Braddock before he could close with the fort.

English scouts brought back the news that the French were in sight, and Gage's light horsemen pulled up. Harry Gordon, Braddock's engineer, saw young Beaujeu clearly. Wearing a bright red gorget at his throat, he was running along the trail ahead. He even waved, derisively, at the British. But the third volley from Gage's advance party dropped him dead in his tracks.

Braddock was puzzled by the ineffectiveness, otherwise, of Gage's fire. The enemy column, now led by a Captain Dumas, split in two and vanished from sight into the dense woods on both sides of the ravine which the trace followed.

From hiding places behind stumps and the boles of trees, the French and Indians began to pour a terrible fire into the scarlet-coated ranks. The English stoutly maintained their traditional solid red line, a column 2000 yards long, though it was being cut to shreds by the raking fire. Seeing no enemy to aim at, the regulars fired almost blindly in the direction of muzzle flashes and puffs of gunsmoke. But these appeared to come from all points of the compass and the random firing of the redcoats began to hit some of the provincials who had already left the road for better cover. One English officer in the thick of the fight found himself unable to move, wedged in position by falling bodies. And he not once caught sight of a single Indian. The cannon were brought into action, but did little damage to an enemy scattered in the thick forest.

Only the Virginians, led by Captain Thomas Waggener, immediately left the track to fight, Indian fashion, from the woods. They gave as much as they took in musket fire. When Washington offered to take a hillock on the right with his Virginians, again in Indian style, Braddock spurned him and, instead, ordered Lieutenant Colonel Ralph Burton to seize the height with a frontal assault. Once Burton was hit, the charge collapsed.

When a few redcoats yielded to the urgings of their colonial comrades and dared to imitate their backwoods-style fighting, Braddock and his officers drove the 'cowards' back into formation with the flats of their swords, shouting 'Stand and fight!' They ignored the complaints of the rankers—'We would fight if we could see anybody to fight with!'

There was no doubting Braddock's bravery. He tried to rally the advance guard, still (oddly) in column rather than in line-of-battle, but they bolted in a disorderly withdrawal after only 10 minutes of fighting. These bloodied fellows ran into the infantrymen of the main force, who were coming to their aid. Confusion began to turn to panic when a rumor swept the column that the Indians had infiltrated the baggage train to cut off a retreat. Cavalry, infantry and artillerymen all turned and ran, the latter abandoning their cannon. They spread terror among the workmen, who joined the mad dash for the rear.

Four horses were shot out from under Braddock as he tried to restore order. He was wounded in one arm and in the chest. Washington, who had two horses killed under him and his clothing torn by four balls, was not even scratched. Washington more or less took command as Braddock fell from his saddle the last time, coughing bloody froth from his punctured lungs. He tried to salvage an orderly retreat but the withdrawal, by now, was a demoralized, headlong rout. As the withering fire continued unabated from the trees, Washington could not even rally the men after they put the Monongahela between them and most of the enemy.

Braddock's shattered command did not stop retreating for 50 miles, until the men staggered into Dunbar's camp at Great Meadows. Meanwhile, Washington evacuated Braddock from the battlefield by litter, then transferred him to a wagon. Back at Dunbar's camp, four days after he was hit, Braddock died. He was still muttering to his Virginian aide, 'Who would have thought it possible? We shall better know how to deal with them another time'. Sadly, he also died cursing his redcoats and praising the once-despised provincial 'blues.'

Near Great Meadows and Fort Necessity, the site of his earlier defeat, Washington had the General buried with the honors of war and personally read the burial service. But he interred him in an unmarked grave in the middle of the

road named for him. He then had wagons driven back and forth over the grave to obliterate all traces of the burial. He did not want his commander's corpse dug up and mutilated and otherwise desecrated by the Indians. (Braddock's skeleton, with some of his military buttons, was found by a road crew working on Braddock's Road in 1804. It was reinterred under a nearby tree and a plank, reading 'Braddock's Grave' was for years the General's only memorial. In 1913 it was replaced by a proper monument near Farmington, Pennsylvania.)

For three hours, Braddock's men had been easy targets for the hidden snipers. Sixty-three of his 89 officers were either killed or wounded. Of his 1373 men committed, only 459 escaped being killed or wounded. Gage and Gates were wounded, as was Henry Gladwin, who lived to become the heroic defender of Detroit against Pontiac. His conduct was so brave during the disaster that Gage made him a captain in his new 80th Regiment. Later, Gladwin went with a detachment to relieve Fort Niagara, and he commanded the regiment in Gage's absence.

Christopher Gist and his two sons were scouts for Braddock. They got away without injury, as did Daniel Boone, then a 21-year-old civilian teamster and blacksmith. He unharnessed his team and escaped to his father's farm on one of his own horses. The cost to the French and Indians was negligible, barely 60 casualties.

Braddock's defeat was a disaster. It set in motion a domino-like series of setbacks. Dunbar burned his own wagons, destroyed cannon and mortars, ammunition and food, and stampeded back to Cumberland. The grand campaign was abandoned for mere holding actions. A force of 1000 militia and 200 Mohawks sent by Braddock to reinforce William Johnson, who was leading the campaign against Crown Point, ran into an ambuscade and its Mohawk leader, Chief Hendrick, was killed, along with many of his braves and white followers.

Johnson himself, leading 2200 New Englanders against Crown Point, the French stronghold on Lake Champlain's south end, never even got there. But he was, at least, able to hold off the French and Indians who pursued Hendrick's fleeing survivors right up to his hastily thrown-up log barricades. In fact, Johnson and General Phineas Lyman, who took over when the Irishman was wounded, defeated the 700 French regulars of Baron Dieskau, and 600 Indians. Dieskau was wounded, too, captured and stripped. Dragged before Johnson, the Indian agent treated him kindly, though the Mohawks howled for his torture and death in revenge for the loss of Chief Hendrick. When the warriors burst into Johnson's tent to demand that he surrender the prisoner, Dieskau asked his captor what they wanted. 'What did they want? To burn you, by God, to eat you, and to smoke you in their pipes!' But he told the Baron not to fear; the Indians would have to kill him first before they should take a prisoner from him.

Johnson's surprising victory was the only bright spot for England, and it soon faded. He strengthened his post, dubbed Fort William Henry, but with his men mutinous and deserting in the bitter cold of November, he let Lyman preside over a council. The decision was to withdraw. It is

Opposite page: The artist titled his work the *Death of Braddock.* **General Edward Braddock** did not die in his battle of 1755 but a few days later while in the care of George Washington. His defeat was a complete disaster, although he fought very bravely and had four horses shot out from under him before he was downed.

said that his own troopers now jeered him, but Johnson did not mind. The king made him a baronet and Parliament voted him a prize of 5000 pounds sterling.

Fort William Henry was abandoned; the French retained Crown Point, Fort Niagara and Ticonderoga, and menaced Oswego, still being held by Massachusetts Governor Shirley's men. But matters would have been much worse for England after Braddock's debacle were it not for William Johnson and his Indian affairs deputy. George Croghan, Irish-born like his superior, traveled thousands of miles over a period of 16 years to hold powwows, and not only retained the loyalty of most English-allied Indians but persuaded others to defect from France to England. He also helped in the occupation of France's Western forts after 1760.

For the moment, however, the hard work of Johnson and Croghan was offset by the brilliance of France's new commander in the West, the Marquis de Montcalm. Captain John Bradstreet, one of Braddock's subalterns, had built up Oswego, had launched a fleet of 'battoe' (*bateaux*) to control Lake Ontario, and had beat off attacks as he resupplied the post in the spring of 1756. But Montcalm destroyed Oswego in August. Washington noted that this caused a desertion of English-allied Indians back to France's cause. Now Montcalm put France on the offensive all along the frontier. He distributed so many wampum belts of war that he fielded a force of 8000 men.

On his march against a re-garrisoned **Fort William Henry**, Montcalm wiped out several English parties and was aghast when his Indians not only scalped the dead but also cannibalized them. He felt that he could not stop them. He was afraid that if he tried, they might abandon him, or worse, turn on him.

Fort William Henry bravely withstood Montcalm's siege until it was faced with cannon at point-blank range and the Marquis offered the defenders an honorable surrender. He promised to protect them from his Indians. However, no sooner had the provincials left the gate than his Indians pounced on them, stripping off their clothes, then murdering them. Montcalm tried to stop the butchery. He bared his own chest, dramatically, and shouted, 'Kill me, but spare the English!' In their blood lust, the Indians ignored him. One warrior emerged from a room of the fort waving proudly the bloody severed head of a defender. Others fell on the New Hampshire regiment and dragged 80 men away from the French. They killed 50 prisoners and took 200 more as captives to Canada. There, the lucky ones were ransomed by the French. When some semblance of order was restored by his officers, Montcalm burned Fort William Henry and returned to Montreal via Ticonderoga and Crown Point.

In a minor French setback of 1758, a future American Revolutionary general, Captain Israel Putnam, was captured and only narrowly escaped death by torture at the stake. He was a 40-year-old, nearly illiterate fellow from Massachusetts who had won local fame as a youthful hunter, especially after he captured a wolf in its den. After volunteering in Connecticut's army, he joined Major Robert Rogers's force of 500 Rangers, spying on enemy movements around Ticonderoga.

In an unbelieveable act of foolishness for a man of his reputation, Rogers betrayed his position to the enemy by holding a shooting competition with a British officer. Molang, the French partisan, heard the firing and set up an ambush. At the first shots, Captain Putnam halted his men and returned the fire. Another officer brought a company up to his aid but Rogers, bungling a second time in one day, hung back to guard against an attack from the rear—which never came. Putnam's men fought from behind the shelter of trees, but were overrun. The Captain's fusee, or musket, missed fire as he pressed it to the chest of an Indian. The latter took him prisoner and bound him to a tree. For an hour he was exposed to fire from both sides. Many balls lodged in the trunk and more than one passed through the sleeves or skirt of his coat.

When the provincials momentarily fell back, an Indian amused himself by throwing an ax—as if in a circus side-show—to see how close he could come to Putnam without killing him. Then a French officer drew a bead on him, but his musket missed fire. The American begged for treatment as a prisoner of war, but the Frenchman's answer was to drive the butt of his gun into Putnam's face.

Putnam's comrades were left in possession of the field, the French and Indians losing 90 men, but when the latter retreated they took their prisoner along. They stripped Putnam of coat, vest, stockings and shoes, bound his hands tightly together and piled on his back the packs of several of their wounded men. When they finally halted their retreat, Putnam's hands were swollen so badly and his feet so bloodied by rocks that he asked the Indians to either loosen the cords or kill him. A French officer removed his bonds and took away some of his burdens. Then the Indian who captured Putnam gave him moccasins. Yet, that evening, another Indian wounded him deeply in the chest with a tomahawk, then tied him, naked, to a tree and laid piles of fuel at his feet and lit them. A sudden shower of rain doused the fire, but it was rekindled and Putnam writhed at the stake in the smoke and flames.

Suddenly, Molang himself, informed by an Indian less savage than the others, rushed up and kicked aside the flaming brands. He cut Putnam loose and reprimanded the Indians for their cruelty. He then took the prisoner under his own protection until he could return him to his rightful 'owner', his original captor. To prevent his escaping, Putnam was spread-eagled on the ground and his wrists and ankles tied to young trees. Poles were even laid across his body, with Indians sleeping on the ends of them. Any unusual motion by Putnam would awake them.

After that dreary, painful night, Putnam was fed and allowed to march without burdens. At Ticonderoga, to his immense relief, he was placed under French, not Indian, guard. Montcalm questioned him and forwarded him to Montreal. There a fellow-prisoner, Colonel Peter Schuyler, replaced his rags with clothing. Putnam was later included in an exchange of prisoners.

Power see-sawed back and forth in 1758. The British, under Lord Jeffrey Amherst, captured Louisbourg, but Montcalm defeated Major General James Abercrombie at Ticonderoga. The latter had a huge force by frontier standards, 6350 regulars and 9000 colonials against 4000 French with only a week's provisions. Instead of starving the Marquis out, however, Abercrombie tried to storm the impregnable fortress and lost 2000 men, in dead and wounded, before retreating.

The foolishness of Abercrombie was balanced by the initiative of Captain John Bradstreet, back at Oswego. Though his plans were delayed by Abercrombie's failure, he built 1500 *bateaux* and with 3000 men captured and

Above: **Israel Putnam,** a general in the Revolution, first fought the French and Indians before the English. He was in command of the Connecticut troops sent to Detroit to combat Pontiac.

destroyed Fort Frontenac (Kingston, Ontario). Only 150 of Bradstreet's men were regulars; he quarreled with his provincial officers. And yet he managed to cut not only the French supply line to Fort Duquesne, and thus set up its fall, but also to break the long line of communications between the St Lawrence and Ohio Rivers.

Brigadier General John Forbes was charged with the destruction of Fort Duquesne. Although he was dying of some painful disease and had to be slung in a hurdle between two horses, the courageous, democratic and witty Scot, the very opposite of his predecessor, was determined to cut an entirely new road through the wilderness to the Ohio's Forks. He actively sought Indian help and he carefully built up an army around Montgomery's Highlanders and a detachment of Royal Americans. Although the Assemblies of both Pennsylvania and Maryland were reluctant to support the campaign with money, he put together a force of 5000 provincials from the two colonies, plus Virginia and North Carolina. Forbes was said to have overcome 'One Thousand Obstacles'. Besides penurious Assemblymen, he had to put up with the military units of the different colonies quarreling among themselves; the tardiness of his regulars and artillery train in arriving; and rivalry among his own officers.

Luckily, James Grant and Forbes's second-in-command, Henry Bouquet, were solidly loyal to him. The 39-year-old Swiss, Bouquet, had recruited troops very successfully among the Germans of Pennsylvania though he, naturally, tangled with the pacifistic Quakers. His tact and patience with the road builders during Forbes's illness were largely responsible for the ultimate success of the wearying march. Amherst could not give him Forbes's command after the latter's death because Bouquet was foreign-born. So he supervised the strengthening of the Western posts—Forts Pitt, Presque Isle and Venango—after their capture from the French. Very, very much unlike Braddock, the adaptable Bouquet taught his men mobility and open-order combat maneuvering.

Before he could move out of his base and supply dump at Bedford, Pennsylvania, Forbes found that most of his Indians, Cherokees and Catawbas, had drifted away. Washington, who found Indian auxiliaries extra-sensitive and easily offended, criticized the Cherokees for being so mercenary. Every service of theirs had to be purchased. (Naturally, for they had no concept of 'patriotism' and they received no regular soldier's pay.) Forbes tried to meet the demands of Chief Little Carpenter and his Cherokees, but did so with disgust, too, calling the warriors 'sordid and avaricious.'

General Forbes's advance was a careful one, also a slow one.

Constant rain turned the touted Forbes's Road into one long, narrow morass. He left a series of fortified camps behind him to protect his line of communications; doubtless, to insure a safe line of retreat, should it become necessary; and to indicate that his expedition was not just a foray, but a permanent conquest of territory.

The 800 Scots that Forbes sent with Grant to reconnoiter Fort Duquesne were badly battered at Loyalhanna by Indians, but they gave such a good account of themselves that many of the redmen began to desert the French. The number of deserters grew when the grapevine reported successful peace overtures by the British with the Mingos, Shawnees, Delawares and mighty Iroquois. This primitive 'psychological warfare' worked very well for the British—but at the expense of the Colonials. For the British promised that they (including the colonists) would not take Indian lands. Indeed, Forbes's chief of staff, Bouquet, issued a proclamation at Easton, Pennsylvania which prohibited settlement—even movement—by Colonials anywhere west of the Appalachian Mountains, unless with special permission. Bouquet bragged, correctly, that it was this treaty promise which 'knocked the French in the head'. Unfortunately, the Americans saw it as a blow to their own heads, and a treacherous one, to boot. It was as if the British were siding with the Indians.

The day before Forbes reached Fort Duquesne a great explosion shook the woods. The British found the fortress abandoned and gutted, occupied only by the bloody heads of Highlanders on a row of stakes, each one decorated with a piece of kilt. If this savage taunt of the French and their Indian allies was meant to intimidate their adversaries, it failed. It only made more firm the Colonials' vows to exterminate the redmen.

Forbes raised the British flag at the Forks on 25 November 1758. He was then carried back to Philadelphia to die, so ravaged by his malady that the 49-year-old soldier, to some, looked like an emaciated, 80-year-old woman.

The following September, British General James Wolfe defeated Montcalm on the Plains of Abraham at Quebec. Both officers died in battle, but it was the beginning of the end for New France.

England's great victory was diminished by unnecessary warfare against the Cherokees. Some of them, returning from Forbes's expedition, stumbled on horses running wild and, naturally, seized them. The animals' owners laid a trap and killed some of the warriors, and soon a war was dragging on. A campaign by both regulars and militia forced the Indians, at gun point, to accept a treaty which included a new boundary line and did nothing to hide the land hunger—so strange to the Indians—of the Colonials. The harshness of this treaty soon convinced the Cherokees and other Southern tribes that the Northern tribes were right. That the Colonials had no use, any longer, for Indian allies, now that the French had been driven from the West.

Pontiac's Rebellion

As usual, the Indians were largely ignored in the treaty (1760) which ended the Seven Years War in America. But the cession of France's frontier posts to the aggressive Anglo-Saxons perturbed redmen all along the frontier of the 13 Colonies. When Major Robert Rogers was dispatched with his Rangers to accept the surrender of the forts, he was met (27 November 1759) at the mouth of the Detroit River by a party of Ottawas, Hurons and Potawatomis. The sachem of the Ottawas, Pontiac, was their spokesman. He demanded to know by what right Rogers was trespassing on Indian land. When the Major told him that he was only there to remove the French, and then gave him wampum, a seemingly mollified Pontiac smoked a calumet of peace with the Ranger. He agreed to be a subordinate of the Crown, even to pay tribute in furs. But he warned Rogers that if the King should neglect him, he would close down all routes to the interior. Rogers reported to his superiors that Pontiac was anything but a conquered prince. Rather, he was like a king in his own right who demanded the respect due his rank.

The French settlers around the forts, many of whom now assumed a neutrality in the quarrel between Indians and Colonists, saw their lives changed hardly at all by the substitution of one flag for the other. But the Indians soon saw a difference. Commander in Chief Lord Jeffrey Amherst was not about to continue the old French practice of insuring Indian loyalty with lavish gift-giving. He ignored the advice of Captain Donald Campbell, commanding Detroit, even the expert advice of Sir William Johnson himself. Amherst would not tolerate a policy of 'bribery.'

The already-suspicious Indians grew more disaffected with the farthing-pinching English. The latter, when compared to the French, were aloof, maintaining a non-fraternization policy with the Indians which was broken, or at least bent, only when the officers took Indian mistresses. The Senecas were the first to become restive, sending war belts to other tribes—invitations to join them in a war against the English. These machinations were fueled by the timely appearance of a Delaware mystic who preached war as the road to heaven. God—the Master of Life, that is—told him that the route to this Happy Hunting Ground was blocked by the whites. They must be removed. A purist, he sermonized that the Indians must give up the white man's clothing, rum, even his firearms.

Thanks to traders, friendly Indians and probably some of the French *habitants*, who formed an informal intelligence network for Amherst, rumors of intended Indian warfare soon reached Lord Jeffrey. He refused to change his anti-gift position, but he sent reinforcements to Detroit and other posts by Major Henry Gladwin.

Campbell wrote Bouquet that the Indians were only awaiting an opportunity to rise in rebellion. He seemed to be no better a prophet than the Delaware. Years passed—1760, 1761, 1762—and war did not come. But frontiersmen were alarmed again in 1763 at word of circulation of new Seneca war belts among the Ottawas, Hurons, Delawares,

Above: **Pontiac's Rebellion**, which extended the French and Indian War, was also called Pontiac's Conspiracy because he put together a confederation of tribes against the whites. In 1763 he tried to infiltrate his men into Detroit with concealed weapons but was frustrated.

Potawatomis, Shawnees and Miamis. At first, Chief Pontiac of the Ottawas, about 50 years old, was only one of several conspirators, but he soon assumed a dominant role and the extension of the French and Indian War came to be called Pontiac's Rebellion, or Pontiac's Conspiracy. He called a grand council at the end of April 1763 and demanded an attack on Fort Detroit. He quoted a message delivered by God to the Delaware prophet. But Pontiac was a pragmatic pagan. He deleted all prophetic references to the abandoning of firearms, and he did not choose to lump the French with the hated British. He still had hopes that the French might be of some service to him.

Pontiac probably attended Sir William Johnson's conference at Detroit on 3 September 1761, when Major Gladwin garrisoned the post with 300 troops. He was planning to destroy not only intimidating Detroit, but all British posts, at the same time. Detroit was a village of 100 log houses within a log palisade, protected by bastions at each corner of the compound and a block-house built right over the gate. Two schooners anchored offshore in the half-mile wide Detroit River provided another field of fire and insured communication with other posts in time of trouble.

Besides the 120 soldiers remaining from his initial 300, Gladwin had some fur traders and Canadians inside the walls in 1763. Outside of the palisade was a small village of scattered French cabins where *habitants* had gardens, vineyards, and apple and pear orchards.

A league away from the fort at the Ecorse River, Pontiac led a council and war dance in May of 1763. He was not tall, even for an Indian, but was muscular, and under the war paint on his dark skin was a striking, powerful face. He had won over 18 tribes and he watched with approval as Ottawa dancers in brilliant robes were succeeded by Wyandots with painted shirts, then by Chippewas with arrow quivers slung across their backs.

Pontiac ringed Detroit with 1000 warriors disguised as ball players and spectators. As the game, a lacrosse-like game called *baggattaway*, started up in the field outside the walls, he and 60-odd chiefs came to a council inside. The gates were normally left open by day, so contemptuous of the 'Red Indians' were the British. The young men had orders to rush the gateway once they heard the signal.

But this day, Pontiac saw the gates close behind him and his party, and he found himself walking between two files of armed soldiers. His surprise attack with muskets (their barrels filed short) hidden under blankets, along with knives and tomahawks, had been betrayed to Gladwin by the major's Chippewa mistress, Catherine. The Major put his three understrength companies of Royal Americans and Queen's Rangers on the alert and now separated the plotters from their army outside by abruptly shutting the gates. Pontiac immediately called off his Trojan horsemanship. Putting on a straight face, he blamed 'bad birds' for filling Gladwin's ears with lies about him. Gladwin, when Pontiac innocently asked why all the soldiers were at the ready, replied with an equally straight face that he had ordered his men to do some exercise and drill. The Major could have seized Pontiac, but he let him carry on the farce of a pow-wow.

Pontiac later tried to get some young men inside the fort to smoke the peace pipe and then rush the guards. But Gladwin was firm. 'I will have none of your rabble in the fort'. When Pontiac gave up his plan, he was called a

Above: A great political leader, **Pontiac** (c. 1715-1769) was an Ottawa chief who first came to notice when Major Robert Rogers took the French forts in the West, including Detroit, in 1760.

coward by some of his followers. But on 10 May 1763 he put Detroit under close siege and struck at farms in sight of the fort. He first killed and scalped three civilians. When his French friends urged him to seek peace, a truce, he pretended to agree. But when Campbell came out under a white flag to negotiate, he seized him as a hostage and called on Gladwin to surrender. The Major refused. The garrison was relieved by reinforcements and supplies from Fort Niagara in July, but Pontiac continued the siege till October or November.

The Detroit plan misfired, but Pontiac's surprise attacks worked well elsewhere. Fort Sandusky, at the west end of Lake Erie, fell first. A group of Ottawas and Hurons who were admitted freely to the fort killed all 15 soldiers. The commandant was adopted by an Indian widow to replace a husband killed in battle.

Pontiac's men next defeated two boat parties unaware of hostilities and seized Fort Miami after the commander's Miami mistress, the opposite of Gladwin's fair Catherine, decoyed him into a trap in which he was killed. His 11 soldiers surrendered. Fort Ouatanon (Ouiatenin) on the Wabash River near today's Lafayette, Indiana, fell after its commanding officer was lured outside to a fake council, then seized. The garrison of 20 men surrendered. Also taken by Seneca 'conspirators' were Forts LeBoeuf at the site of Franklin, Pennsylvania, with 16 men, and Venango, with 30 defenders, at Waterford, Pennsylvania. The 27 soldiers of Presqe Isle (Erie, Pennsylvania) lined

the inside of their log blockhouse to make it extra-bullet-proof, got casks of drinking water and prepared for a siege. The blockhouse had no windows, only loophole slits for their muskets. There was a single door on the ground floor leading to the rest of the fort and a ladder between the two floors. The first floor's ceiling (the second story's floor) was perforated so that the men above could fire down at anyone storming the lower level. Senecas, reinforced by Hurons, Ottawas and Chippewas, moved up close behind log breastworks and sent flaming arrows into the blockhouse roof. The defenders tore off burning shingles and used up their water supply dousing flames. But meanwhile, some of the men dug a tunnel from under the blockhouse to the well in the fort, now occupied by Indians. They managed to get buckets of water back to the smouldering roof, but it was such exhausting work that they decided to surrender on the second day. The Indians promised to let them withdraw to Fort Pitt, then broke their word and divided the prisoners among the four tribes. But at least they were not put to death.

At Fort Michilimackinac (Mackinac), on the mainland across the strait of the same name from St Ignace (Michigan), the Chippewas told a young trader, Alexander Henry, 'Englishman, although you have conquered the French, you have not conquered us. We are not your slaves. These lakes, these woods and mountains, werc lcft to us by our ancestors. They are our inheritance and we will part with none of them.'

A French priest restrained the Ottawas, but the Chippewas decided to strike on the King's Birthday, 4 June 1763. Imitating Pontiac himself, they invited the garrison to watch a ball game between themselves and some Sac Indians on the long sandy beach outside the main gate. The latter was left open, as usual, and a large number of squaws entered the compound, all bundled up in blankets although it was a hot day. (Beneath their robes they concealed tomahawks and scalping knives.) Men and officers lounged about in the welcome sun, watching the ball players. Alex Henry had to miss the game because he had some important letters to get out by the next canoe.

Suddenly, the shouts of the Indians driving the ball across the field turned into war cries. Henry dropped his pen and picked up a fowling piece loaded with swan shot. But resistance, he saw, was hopeless. The English were being cut down everywhere and scalped alive. His only hope was for the French to hide him. 'Amid the slaughter which was raging', he later recalled without any obvious bitterness, 'I observed many of the Canadian inhabitants of the fort calmly looking on, neither opposing the Indians or suffering injury. . . .'

Henry found his neighbor, Monsieur Langlade, and begged him for help. The Canadian shrugged and turned away, muttering, '*Que voudriez-vous que j'en ferais*? [What do you want me to do about it?]' Henry was rescued from his despair when a Pawnee woman, a slave of Langlade's, led him to the garret and locked the door behind him.

Through a crack in the wall, Henry saw the Chippewas

continuing their scalping and mangling of the dead. They killed 20 of the 35 soldiers, and a trader. Ripping open bodies, they even cupped their hands and drank the blood of their victims between hoarse shouts of victory. He was horrified by the sight and terrified that he would be next.

When Indians entered the house and asked Langlade if there were any English about, the Pawnee kept her secret but the French-Canadian answered to the effect that he could not say, he did not know. Mused Henry, later, 'Langlade was . . . as far from a wish to destroy me as he was careless of saving me'. Finally, the *habitant* led four Indians, smeared with the blood of their victims and bearing tomahawks, to the garret door, found the key and bade them enter. Henry hid under a pile of birchbark vessels used in making maple sugar and the Indians missed him. But later, Mrs Langlade found him. When the Indians returned, suspicious because they missed the young trader among the corpses and prisoners, she told her husband to surrender Henry. A warrior whom the trader recognized as Wenniway, almost six feet tall and covered with a sort of war paint of charcoal and grease except for white circles around his eyes, grabbed him by the collar of his coat and brought a large knife to his throat. Henry stared fixedly at the cruel eyes and, after a few seconds of suspense, Wenniway dropped his arm and said, 'I won't kill you.'

The brave made Henry his prisoner, or slave, renaming him Misinigon, for a dead brother. Wenniway and Langlade protected Henry from the other Indians, most of whom were now drunk. Later, an Indian ordered Henry to exchange clothes with him, saying he was sent by Wenniway to fetch him. The trader had no doubt that the savage meant to kill him and did not want the European clothing bloodied. He tried to get help from Langlade but the Frenchman would not gct involved.

Some distance from the fort, the Indian pulled a knife on Henry, but he was ready for him. He seized his arm, then gave him a shove and ran back to the fort. Luckily, he saw Wenniway. The latter tried to stop the attacker, but the fellow pursued Henry around and around Wenniway, foaming at the mouth and striking with his knife. Finally, Wenniway and Henry got close enough to Langlade's house for the trader to run into it. The Indian in Henry's clothing then gave up the chase.

Alexander Henry and ten other prisoners were taken by canoe to one of the Beaver Islands in Lake Michigan and, after a debate between the Ottawas and Chippewas, handed over to the latter. The Ottawas told the Englishmen that the Chippewas not only intended to kill them but 'make broth' of them. When he had not eaten for two days, he still refused bread offered him by the brutes. It was not only cut with knives still bloody from mutilating Englishmen, but the Indians had also moistened the dried blood with their spittle and smeared it on the bread, saying, 'Eat the blood of your countrymen.'

Around 7 June the prisoners were thrown into a lodge already occupied by 14 captured soldiers, and tied two-by-two with the ropes around their necks made fast to the ridge pole.

Henry was rescued from slavery and possible death, when Wenniway and a friend of the trader's, indeed his adopted brother, Wawatam, found him in the Chippewa village. Wawatam gave him his hand in friendship, then made a speech to the chiefs and offered to buy their prisoner, his brother. The chiefs heard him out and one answered,

Opposite page: Young settlers on the Indian frontier had to grow up quickly. Any lone traveler was fair game to redmen on the warpath.

Above: Surprise attacks on isolated cabins or villages were common because of the stealth of the Indians who crept through the grass.

'We accept your present. You may take him home with you.'

After spending some time with Wawatam's family, Henry finally made his way to Montreal and a free life again.

The closer-in forts, Ligonier and Bedford, managed to hold out against Pontiac's Indians, and the Delawares who attacked Fort Pitt had less luck than Senecas and Chippewas. Although Bouquet was absent, the 338-man force was commanded by another tough officer. This was still another Swiss, a soldier of fortune named Captain Simeon Ecuyer. He rejected the surrender demand, then sent gifts to the Indians—a handkerchief and two blankets, all from smallpox patients in the hospital. The Delawares withdrew, and began to die.

Although Detroit was still holding out, so many posts had fallen that Britain decided (at least in the eyes of the Colonists) to capitulate. A Proclamation of 1763 was issued which reiterated Forbes's early policy and formalized it. White settlement west of the Appalachians was prohibited.

A Chippewa chief outside of Detroit got Pontiac to turn Campbell over to him to avenge the killing of a nephew by a patrol. He killed and scalped the Scot and threw his cadaver into the river where it drifted down to the fort. Like the decapitation of the Highlanders, this atrocity only hardened the determination of frontiersmen to rid the West of these 'fiends from Hell.'

It was up to doughty Henry Bouquet finally to turn the tide of Indian victories. He was marching from Carlisle, Pennsylvania to relieve Fort Pitt, which had been warned by Gladwin. He had 460 men, including Royal Americans and a unit of the regiment of Highlanders called the Black Watch. Bouquet was intercepted by a force of Delawares, Shawnees, Hurons and Mingos on 5 August, but repulsed them in what amounted to a draw. They made the mistake of resuming the fight the next day when he was ready for them. Bouquet now showed his newly-acquired prowess at fighting in backwoodsman fashion.

He drew his men up in a circle around his convoy, then fooled the Indians into a rash charge by having a handful of his men feign a panicky retreat. When the Indians rushed into the prepared gap in his line, his main force, in hiding, opened up at close range on them. He lost 50 or 60 men but he killed a similar number of Indians, including two Delaware chiefs, and drove the Indians away. After this battle at **Bushy Run**, he relieved Fort Pitt. The action quickly cooled the Shawnees' and Delawares' ardor for battle and won Bouquet enormous respect from all of the tribes. He later led a mixed force of regulars and provincials in a pacifying sweep to the Muskingum's forks, securing both the surrender of all prisoners in Indian hands and a general peace on the frontier. Made a brigadier in 1765, poor Bouquet died before his time. He succumbed to fever in Pensacola that very year.

Civilians suffered in Pontiac's war along with the fighting men. Probably 2000 whites were killed, and 60 'Paxton Boys' in Lancaster massacred and mutilated 20 peaceful Conestoga Indians, many of them women and children at prayer with their menfolk. The men from Paxton then marched on Philadelphia where even the Quakers took up

Above: **Ben Franklin** is not often associated with the Indians, but he did play a role as peacemaker during Pontiac's war. Villainous vigilantes began killing peaceful Christian Indians in Pennsylvania. He helped persuade the ruffians to disperse in Philadelphia and later printed a pamphlet which was a stinging rebuke of their actions.

Above: **Joseph Brant or Thayendanega,** He Who Places Two Bets, was a Mohawk chief born in 1742 who was also a friend of both Sir William and Guy Johnson. He fought Nicholas Herkimer at Oriskany and led the butchery at the Cherry Valley massacre. He was the bitter enemy of Red Jacket.

arms to defend the hapless 'tame' Indians there. Ben Franklin and a delegation persuaded the Paxton Boys to disperse after they promised them a bounty on Indian scalps. Later, Ben Franklin printed a stinging rebuke to such wicked vigilantism against scapegoats. In a pamphlet he predicted that the blood of the innocent Indians of Lancaster would cry out for vengeance.

By autumn, some tribes were ready to make peace over Pontiac's protests, and even that chief's resistance ended on 30 October when, with a price on his head since July, he asked Gladwin for peace. Although the Indians had won virtually every engagement save Bushy Run, the confederacy was falling apart. It was not in the Indian nature to amalgamate tribes for war for very long. Some war belts were later sent around by Shawnees, Delawares and Senecas, but most tribes came to terms with Bouquet or Johnson. Pontiac sulked beside the Maumee River and, with his tomahawk, hacked a peace belt to pieces.

By November of 1763, most of Pontiac's power was gone, but Gladwin in Detroit kept his men on an alert until 1764. He returned to England and never saw Detroit, or fair Catherine, again. He declined to serve against the Colonists in the American Revolution and he died in 1791.

Pontiac's last obstinate gesture of resistance was to frustrate at least five American commanders in attempts to take over France's last post, Fort Chartres, near St Louis. After two and a half years of efforts, Major Farmer finally came up the Mississippi with a strong force from New Orleans. The commandant, an old comrade of Pontiac's, St Ange de Bellarive, urged his Ottawa friend to recall all wampum belts of war and to bury the hatchet in peace.

Pontiac demanded a pardon in 1765, but finally accepted a peace belt and attended Johnson's July 1766 conference at Fort Ontario. He was murdered, shot in the back in 1769 by a Peoria Indian companion in Cahokia, Illinois. (Some said that an English trader had 'excited' the Peoria to do the evil deed.) Other stories had Pontiac killed in a drunken brawl, or murdered by two Kaskaskias.

Perhaps, because of the attention paid him by Francis Parkman, Pontiac's role in the West has been exaggerated as well as romanticized. Some at Detroit even called him 'a noted coward'. But nevertheless, he stood as the one great symbol for Indian resistance to white encroachments on the frontier between the French and Indian War and the Revolution.

Lord Dunmore's War

Lord Dunmore of Virginia ignored the Proclamation of 1763 and issued land warrants to veterans of the Indian wars to allow them to settle west of the mountains. A conflict called Lord Dunmore's War then bridged the gap between Pontiac's Rebellion and the War of Independence. Shawnees attacked the veterans' settlements and the Governor ordered out 1500 militia. Sir William Johnson died, but his nephew (and son-in-law) continued his wise policies and kept the Iroquois from joining the Shawnees. Chief Cornstalk surprised a Virginia unit at Point Pleasant at the junction of the Ohio and Great Kanawha. The Virginians rallied from a loss of 50 dead and 100 wounded to beat off their attackers. Shortly, Cornstalk made peace with the Governor to end Lord Dunmore's War of 1774.

The American Revolution

Wisely, the Indians tried not to take sides in the American Revolution which broke out in 1775 with the shot heard 'round the world' at Lexington. Even the Continental Congress asserted that it did not want the Indians to take up the hatchet against the King's men in what was essentially a family quarrel. Still, both Ethan Allen and Washington tried to recruit Indian auxiliaries.

As the war dragged on indecisively, the British general, Thomas Gage, finally instructed Guy Johnson and his counterpart in the South to bring the Indians into the war. The Mohawk chief, Thayendanega, or Joseph Brant, was lionized in London, painted by Romney and given a commission in the British Army. He fought alongside the British and brought most, but not all, of the Iroquois into the conflict on King George's side. Soon, the Iroquois were fighting each other, for the Senecas, Cayugas and Canandaiguas of Brant were opposed by Oneidas and Tuscaroras recruited by General Nicholas Herkimer to relieve Fort Stanwyx at the head of the Mohawk River.

The British stopped Herkimer at the **Battle of Oriskany** but the Patriots killed 17 Senecas and 16 other Indians besides some British. Shortly, the Oneidas and Tuscaroras helped Horatio Gates turn back British General John Burgoyne's march down the Hudson. The murder of young Jane McCrae by 'Gentleman Johnny's' Indians during the march angered all Americans, from the lowliest servant to Thomas Jefferson. Writing the Declaration of Independence, he inserted a phrase deploring 'the merciless Indian savages.'

Brant and the hated Tory, Colonel John Butler, led a mixed British and Indian force on hit-and-run raids during 1778 and 1779. Wyoming Valley, Pennsylvania was struck by Butler's Rangers and Indians on 3 July 1778. Most able-bodied men were away in Washington's army, but Zeb Butler, home on furlough, gathered the families together in Forty Fort. Unfortunately, he then led 300 men out against Colonel Butler. Outnumbered four to one, he was overwhelmed by the Indians. The Loyalist leader lost control of his redmen and they killed all of the wounded.

Above: Older men fought in Indian wars. **David Morgan,** brother of General Daniel Morgan, was 70 when he defended his family from raiders.

Above center: **The Battle of Oriskany** (August 1777) was indecisive and General Herkimer died. As a result of this battle, Indians deserted the British forces.

Above: Tories stimulated Pennsylvania Indians to massacre Patriots in 1778. One of the worst-hit areas was the **Wyoming Valley** where the weak militia was swept aside and civilians slaughtered.

Above: A great part of **Daniel Boone's** relatively long life (1734-1820) was taken up with a personal war with the Indians. His daughter was a captive; he had to fight for his son's body at Blue Licks (above); and he was, himself, a prisoner for a time. But he successfully blazed the old Wilderness Road and opened a new West – Kentucky – to settlement before he pushed on to Spanish Missouri in his last years.

Below: **The Battle of Blue Licks,** fought on 19 August 1782, took place on the middle fork of the Licking River. A band of 240 Indians who had just been rebuffed in their siege of Bryan's Station, Kentucky, were attacked by a smaller force – 182 Kentuckians. The Indians mauled the whites badly, killing or wounding 70 of them in a disorderly retreat. But the Indians' victory at Blue Licks proved to be the last gasp in Kentucky; they could never again mount such a thrust in any force. This marked the end of an era.

Sixteen of them were murdered by one woman, a half-breed who went by the name of Queen Esther Montour.

Then it was Cherry Valley's turn, in the upper Susquehanna Valley on 11 November 1778. About 30 people were massacred, their homes burned, and their cattle driven off by Brant's Mohawks and the Colonel's son, Walter (Hell Hound) Butler, even more cruel than his father.

Perhaps Kentucky suffered the most. Daniel Boone, born a Pennsylvania Quaker, came to epitomize the American frontiersman. A hunter and scout from the day his father, Squire Boone, gave him a rifle when he was 12, he first penetrated Kentucky from the Cumberland Gap in 1769. In 1775 he was employed by a company of land speculators to survey and lay out roads there. Some of his well-armed surveying party were killed in two attacks, but he established Boonesborough as the nucleus of a colony.

Indians hovered around the fort and in July 1776 kidnapped Boone's daughter, Jemima, but he pursued and recaptured her. There were two attempts against Boonesborough in 1777 and in February of the next year, Boone, now a major of Virginia militia, was captured by the Shawnees. He was quite a prize; they would not even sell him to the Governor of Detroit, Colonel Henry Hamilton, called 'The Hair Buyer', because he paid a bounty on Yankee scalps. Instead, they took him to their village at Chillicothe, Ohio where he was adopted by Chief Blackfish to fill the place of a dead warrior-son. Boone zealously played the role of a happy renegade, all the while plotting an escape.

Ironically, Boone got away while on a salt hunting expedition with the Indians. (He had been captured on a salt hunting expedition to Lower Blue Licks for the Kentuckians.) At Salt Springs on the Scioto River, he decided that the time was ripe. Some 450 warriors were gathering for an attack on Boonesborough. He escaped on 16 June 1778 and got to the fort where his appearance astonished everyone. He had been given up for dead; his wife had gone to North Carolina. Boone repaired the rickety fort and mounted and drilled 60 men as the Indians postponed their attack to await some Canadian reinforcements.

On 7 September 1778, 444 warriors led by Boone's 'stepfather', Blackfish, with Captain Antoine Dagneaux de Quindre and 11 Canadians, demanded the surrender of Boonesborough with a phrase which must have stuck in the French-Canadians' throats—'in the name of His Britannic Majesty'. Boone stalled by asking for two days to think it over. He collected all cows and horses inside the fort's walls and had the ladies fill every container with drinking water.

Dagneaux de Quindre informed Boone that Colonel Hamilton wanted the Kentuckians taken as prisoners, unharmed. He asked for nine men to come out and parley further. Boone, of course, chose to be one of them—after he first placed sharpshooters on the walls to cover his party. Dagneaux's offer seemed most liberal. The Kentuckians' freedom required only acknowledgment of British authority and an oath to King George III.

But now the Indians suggested that two warriors shake hands with each American. They explained that it was an old Indian custom. Eighteen muscular Indians came forward to grasp the 'Kaintucks' in supposed friendship. Boone knew they meant to seize his party, so he gave a signal and the Kentuckians sent the Indians sprawling in the dust. The nine then dashed for the gate. They made their escape under murderous fire from the stockade. Indian musketry had little effect on the stout fort. The defenders hoarded their ammunition and made every shot count during nine days of siege. Women loaded rifles, molded bullets, and provided food and water. The Indians set fire to the fort's roof with flaming arrows, but a young man extinguished the blazes with buckets of water, dodging arrows and musket balls all the while.

Next the Canadians showed the Indians how to dig a 'mine', apparently a trench to give them cover, not a tunnel under the fort to blow it up. Boone simply dug a counter-trench, throwing all of his dirt spoil over onto the point of the other excavation. The Indians, unused to manual labor, gave up on 20 September and pulled out. They had lost 37 dead and many more wounded. Boone had four of his men dead and two wounded.

One of the dead men was the victim of a black 'vagabond' who had been taken into the fort by the Kentuckians. He deserted to the enemy with a Kentucky rifle and became their sharpshooter. Daniel Boone bided his time and finally was able to draw a bead on the marksman, though he was 175 yards away in a tree. He let fly and the black fell to the earth. After the Indians retreated, Boone moved forward to examine the body and found that he had put a bullet hole just where he had aimed, in the center of the traitor's forehead.

In 1780 the Virginia Loyalist, Colonel William Byrd, led 800 Indians and some soldiers to smash Martin's and Ruddle's stations. His bloodthirsty Wyandots then promptly murdered the inhabitants, over his protests, and with a barbarity which shocked even the hardened soldier. To his great credit, Byrd gave up his campaign when he found he could not control his Indians; but the Wyandots, before they left, defeated a force led by Captain Estill.

In 1782, 400 Indians and a few whites, led by William Caldwell, Alexander McKee and the despised American renegade, Simon Girty, approached Bryan's Station—40 cabins near Lexington. Only a few hostiles showed themselves at the edge of the clearing opposite the gate, and they made no attempt to hide. Commandant John Craig was sure that it was a ruse. He guessed that he was supposed to make a sortie against them, allowing the main force of Indians to hit his rear wall, unobserved. He was right. Caldwell had concealed his men in the woods in the rear with orders not to show themselves till they heard gunfire from the front of the post.

Craig decided to try a couple of ruses of his own. The fort was short of water and he could not send men to the spring halfway between the fort and the woods. He asked the help of the women and children. He was pretty sure, though not positive, that the enemy would not upset their plan just to seize them. Mrs Jemima S Johnson was the first to volunteer. She took her 10-year-old daughter by the hand and let the party of 12 women and 16 children. (She left behind her four other children, including the baby—Richard Mentor Johnson, the future hero of the Battle of the Thames (1813) against Tecumseh, and later the Vice President of the United States.) With buckets, piggins (dippers) and noggins, the party laughed and chattered its nonchalant way to the spring and back. Just as Craig figured, the lurking Indians made no move. At the last moment, a few youngsters gave way to their tension and fear and sprinted for the gate, spilling precious water. But not a shot was fired at them.

Above: **Daniel Boone**, the buckskinned frontiersman, was never happier than when in the wilds of Kentucky.

Below: In 1775, Boone founded the stockaded settlement of **Boonesborough**, in the heart of Kentucky.

Now Craig planned his second trick. He quietly sent two riders out to gallop to Boone's Station for help. Once they were out of sight, he dispatched a small force, but one making enough noise and confusion for an army, to chase off the demonstrators—and apparently fall into a trap. He posted all the rest of his men and some of the women at loopholes in the back palisade. He gave them strict orders not to fire—to even move a muscle—until they heard his command.

The hullaballoo in front of the fort flushed the Indians from the rear woods. As they ran to scale the stockade, they got the shock of their lives that 16 August 1782. The wall suddenly bristled with blazing rifle barrels.

After the rush was dispersed, firing settled down to a steady pace, all day long. But only a few defenders were struck down by balls passing between the palings of the walls. However, as soon as an Indian left cover he was shot. One or two were picked off in perches in trees. Flaming arrows were launched high in the air, to land almost vertically on roofs. Little boys and big girls were boosted up to put out the fires. Because of the fort's high walls, there was little danger from direct rifle fire, only from dropping arrows. But none was hit.

Eventually, the Indians tired of taking casualties and, after killing stock and burning fields, withdrew before the relief party from Boone's Station arrived.

On the 19th of August, about 240 of the raiders met 182 Kentuckians on the middle fork of the Licking River. A rash attack by the Americans failed miserably. Seventy Kentuckians were killed or wounded in a jumbled retreat. But at least the **Battle of Blue Licks** was the last such thrust by Indians in force. An era was ending.

Britain and her allies of the Indian nations would have liked the extreme western border of the new American states to be the slanting line of the Ohio River. But a half-frontiersman, half-soldier named George Rogers Clark frustrated their hopes. With just 200 men he peeled away from Britain the Far West of that day, the North West Territory (Illinois Country) which Detroit was supposed to protect. Clark seized Kaskaskia, Cahokia and Fort Sackville at Vincennes in the summer of 1778 with no loss. He did so to let Virginia's Governor Patrick Henry beat rivals Connecticut, New York and Massachussetts in a race for this new West which reached all the way to the Mississippi. But Colonel Hamilton and 500 men from Detroit recaptured Vincennes in October.

Clark set out from Kaskaskia on 5 February 1779 to retake Fort Sackville. He led a force of 170-odd Americans and French. (The latter, like the Indians, were now fighting on both sides.) The expeditionaries marched over more than 150 miles of drowned lands, prairies swamped by overflowed rivers. Clark drove his men as if they were amphibians in one of the most daring and fatiguing marches in America's military history. Hamilton, snug in winter quarters, did not dream that anyone could attack him during the wet season.

Officers and men floundered in icy water up to their hips, sometimes to their beards. There were only a few canoes and pirogues reserved for the sick and those who gave out

Left: In the summer of 1776, Indians attacked not only **Boonesborough** but also **Harrod's** and **Logan's Stations.** The hostiles who slipped up on the latter killed three of its 16 men and wounded another (rescued by Colonel Logan) outside the walls of the fort. Logan later stole away at night to get help to relieve the siege.

Above: One of the great marches of US history was that of **George Rogers Clark** and 170 men across the flooded Wabash country in February 1779 to surprise and capture Vincennes from the British.

from total exhaustion. There were no malingerers. Clark had detailed men at the rear to shoot anyone who refused to march. Closing with Vincennes, Clark scared off Hamilton's Indians by using the old dodge of marching and counter-marching his men (in his case, slogging and counter-floundering) in a patch of prairie visible to the fort, to suggest that he had a larger force. He occupied the village and his sharp-shooters began to pick men off of Fort Sackville's works. When Hamilton wanted time to consider surrender, Clark hurried him up. Almost as brutal as his foe, he had five captured Indians executed, by tomahawk, in front of the fort. The warriors had been caught bringing white men's scalps to Hamilton. Though the Briton had five cannon, he was fooled as to the number of besiegers, too, and he surrendered on 23 February 1779. Then the hated 'Hair Buyer' was hustled off to Virginia as a

prisoner of war before some soldier or settler could murder him.

Clark wanted to take the key post of Detroit, but poor Virginia simply did not have the manpower, money or supplies to make it possible. So he checked English advances toward St Louis by reoccupying Cahokia in 1780, and, that same year, defeated Colonel Byrd and his Shawnees in Ohio. In 1782 he destroyed the Shawnee villages around Chillicothe, in one of which Boone had been a prisoner. Clark's attack was in revenge for the Blue Licks disaster.

Christopher Gist was long dead of smallpox, but a new

scout was becoming famous. Simon Kenton 'sojered' with Boone and had even saved his life. After serving with Clark's expedition to Kaskaskia, he rejoined Boone on a raid on Shawnee Town near Chillicothe, perhaps part of Clark's expedition. Kenton was captured on the Ohio while scouting and forced to run the gauntlet eight times and was tied to a stake for burning three times, but reprieved—once, inexplicably, by the renegade Simon Girty. He was taken to Detroit and held under close surveillance by the British but escaped, nevertheless, on the night of 3 June 1779. He then scouted for Clark again on the Ohio in 1780–82, served as a major in General Anthony Wayne's 1794 expedition, and closed out an adventurous career at the age of 60 by soldiering with William Henry Harrison, Commodore Perry and Richard M Johnson in the Battle of the Thames in 1813.

General George Washington decided in the summer of 1779 to retaliate against the Indians. He put together an army of 4000 men, half of them from the Continental Line and including some of Morgan's Riflemen, added 11 cannon, supplies, even pontoon boats, and gave the package to his fighting Irishman, General John Sullivan. Sullivan moved up the Susquehanna from the Wyoming Valley, where Butler's Senecas had burned men at the stake and speared them with their own pitchforks less than a year before. He burst out in the heart of the Seneca country. Unable to capture Fort Niagara, Detroit's opposite number as an outfitting point for Indian raiders, Sullivan burned 40 Iroquois towns, destroyed all granaries and crops in the field, even chopped down all orchards. His scorched earth policy, when combined with the bitter winter of 1779, all but knocked the enemy Iroquois (Senecas, Cayugas and Onondagas) out of the war. So devastated were the Senecas that, years later, they still called Washington 'the Town Destroyer' because of his surrogate, Sullivan.

Brant, Butler and Johnson all faced Sullivan at the Indian town of Chemung. Not knowing that they had experienced men of the Continental Line to meet, along with Morgan's skilled skirmishers, they tried to ambush Sullivan as if he were a civilian-soldier. The ensuing battle was a disaster for Britain's 'partisans.'

Two New Jersey officers flayed two dead Indians to make leggings for themselves. It was becoming more difficult to tell savages from civilized men. Perhaps their brutal, stupid action caused such atrocities as the horrible torturing of Colonial Colonel William Crawford to death in June of 1782, which Simon Girty so enjoyed.

By 1776 the Cherokees in the South had sided with the British and engaged in skirmishes. In 1780, Patriot Lieutenant Colonel John Sevier was ready for a Sullivan-like expedition. Though he had only 700 men even when Colonel Arthur Campbell's Virginians joined his North Carolinians, he defeated his foes at Boyd's Creek and destroyed many Cherokee settlements, even the 'city' of Chote and the Chickamauga towns.

Luckily for the Rebels, Britain bungled its handling of its Southern allies, though it spent thousands of pounds sterling on Cherokees, Creeks, Chickasaws and Choctaws who, on paper, mustered 10,000 warriors. The Choctaws were mishandled at Mobile and America's ally, Spain, captured that town in 1780. After holding Bernardo de Gálvez at bay in his first attack, thanks to 2000 Creeks, Pensacola capitulated to the Spaniard when the town had only 400 Choctaws and 100 Creeks to help its British

Above: **Simon Kenton**, when taken a prisoner by Indians, was saved from the stake by the intervention of Simon Girty. Normally, the renegade was even more cruel to scouts than the Indians.

garrison of 1500.

At war's end, most of the major tribes were identified with the English as completely as were the Loyalists, or Tories. The Colonials would not forget. A legacy of hatred would see to it. Further hostilities were inevitable and not long in coming.

In the Peace of Paris of 1783, the British made no attempt to protect their erstwhile allies, the Indians, from the vengeance of the Americans. They just clung to their forts as long as possible (1796) before relinquishing the last of them.

Spain, America's ally, feared American aggression as much as the Iroquois or Cherokees, and tried to insert a great tribal territory as a buffer between the Appalachians and the Mississippi, to protect the borders of New Spain and Louisiana. But the Yankees rudely shoved that idea aside. In victory, they now even rejected the concept of independent Indian nations.

After the war, Congress allowed the American Army—the Continental Line—to shrink. By 1785 it amounted to only one regiment of infantry and an artillery company. Small wonder that, on the Ohio, rampaging Indians killed, wounded and enslaved 1500 persons with impunity between war's end and 1790.

Post Revolutionary Battles

The new President, George Washington, meant to put a stop to the outrages of the Shawnee, Miami, Potawatomi and Chippewa confederated under Little Turtle. Washington authorized the Governor of the Northwest Territory, Major General Arthur St Clair, to raise troops. A force of about 1200 militia and 320 regulars was put together at Fort Washington, Cincinnati, headed by Brevet Brigadier General Josiah Harmar. He was a Revolutionary officer not entirely unacquainted with Indian skirmishing. He had tried, with only middling success, to expel white intruders from Indian lands north of the Ohio, and thus became half-way informed on the Indians during 1785–86, before he took over Vincennes.

Little Turtle retreated before Harmar's lumbering force,

Above: **Colonel William Crawford** was a friend of George Washington and his land agent in the West during the late 1760s and the 1770s.
Below: In 1782, Crawford's command was routed by Wyandot and Shawnee braves, and the Colonel was captured and savagely tortured to death.

with its cumbersome pack train and commissariat on the hoof—a herd of cattle. The Chief even burned some of his villages to lure Harmar deeper into a trap in the Maumee Valley. Finally, he turned on him. He first destroyed a reconnoitering party, then hit the main force. Harmar counterattacked, so Little Turtle pulled back, stringing the militiamen out in their pursuit. When he was ready he attacked the column's flanks and killed 183 men and wounded 31 more. Naturally, the General retreated. Unnaturally, Little Turtle let him extract his battered command.

Harmar claimed a victory but had to face a court of inquiry. His conduct was whitewashed, but he was replaced in command by St Clair himself. At 55, the Revolutionary War veteran suffered not only from gout but also inexperience in fighting Indians. He marched 2000 men out of Fort Washington, including 600 regulars. One critic claimed that the balance, the militiamen, were the scourings of jails and brothels, ruffians eager to sign anything—even enlistment papers—for the promise of two dollars a day in pay. (Most did not get their pay, or medicine, or sufficient food, so incompetent and corrupt were St Clair's Paymaster's and Quartermaster's officers.)

Somehow, with desertions reducing his force to about 1400, St Clair managed to establish Forts Hamilton and Jefferson, actually weak outposts, and picked a fine spot for his base on high ground on the Wabash, about 50 miles from the later site of Fort Wayne, Indiana. He was negligent in not throwing up defensive works or doubling his sentinels here in enemy country, but did send out patrols. One of them reported a large body of warriors to General Richard Butler, St Clair's second-in-command, but he failed to inform the commander.

At the next dawning, Little Turtle attacked. Some 1100 Indians scattered the Kentucky militia. St Clair was so crippled by gout that he had to be helped onto his horse by four men, but he tried to rally his troops. Butler was wounded and left to die on the field. The militiamen fired wildly, wounding some of their own comrades. The artillery-men were cool enough, but could see few targets because the heavy smoke from exploded powder hung low on the ground. St Clair launched several bayonet charges, knowing that the Indians had no stomach for that weapon. But the enemy just faded back into the woods and mowed down the advancing men, especially the officers.

When the surviving half of his army was surrounded and on the verge of absolute annihilation, St Clair ordered a retreat. It was soon a chaos of flight. The General himself later observed, 'The most disgraceful part of the business is that the greatest part of the men threw away their arms and accoutrements even after the pursuit had ceased. I found the road strewed with them for many miles.'

Prisoners were roasted, flayed or eviscerated while still alive. There were women and children among them, the army's laundresses and other camp followers. The lucky women were those who were cut in half quickly. Too busy with their slaughter, Little Turtle's warriors made no pursuit of the demoralized army.

President Washington cursed St Clair for being 'worse than a murderer'. His was the worst disaster in America's Indian wars. Out of 1400 men, St Clair had 900 casualties. Thirty-seven officers were dead, 31 wounded. Some 593 enlisted men were killed, 251 wounded.

St Clair, though the highest ranking officer in the Army, had an inquiry conducted into his conduct by the House of Representatives. Like Harmar, he was cleared and the blame for the disaster placed on undisciplined and inexperienced troops.

The debacle led to demands for a powerful force to crush the Indians, but Congress, to preserve states' rights, was content with a Militia Act. Only a token Legion was created, as a kind of nucleus of a Federal Army. It would take to the field against the Indians who had crushed Harmar and St Clair, and be led by Major General Anthony ('Mad Anthony') Wayne. He was daring, not mad. He was a disciplinarian who stamped out much of the drunkenness and malingering which had weakened the earlier forces. Wayne took command in 1792, but the Government first tried a negotiated peace in 1793, with a great council at Sandusky.

Wayne marched his army to winter quarters in Fort Greenville on the Maumee. In the spring of 1794 he raised Fort Recovery on the site of St Clair's disaster, mounting the latter's four lost six-pounders, which he found hidden by the Indians in hollow trees. Little Turtle tried an assault on the fort (29 June) and was repulsed. He now lost his nerve and advised his followers to sue for peace with 'the Chief Who Never Sleeps.'

The warriors spurned Little Turtle's advice, deposed him and made Turkey Foot their war chief. He attacked a small party which fought its way back to Fort Recovery. So Turkey Foot attacked the fort and was badly stung. He withdrew as Wayne was reinforced by 1400 mounted militiamen. With 3000 troopers, Mad Anthony was at last ready to strike. The Indians were at **Fallen Timbers** near the Maumee Rapids and the British post of Fort Miami. Nervously, Turkey Foot and Blue Jacket waited

Above: This lithograph of **Little Turtle** or Michikinikwa (1752-1812), chief of the Miamis, was made from a painting attributed to Gilbert Stuart but now lost.

for his attack. By the fourth day, 1300 Indians had left for Fort Miami, only four miles away, for provisions. Wayne was faced by only 800 Indians and some 60 Canadian militia in this undeclared war between Britain and the Young Republic.

Mad Anthony's first maneuver was a mistake. He struck with his cavalry, but they became tangled in the windfalls. He extricated them skilfully, substituted his infantry and alternated volleys, skirmishing fire and bayonet charges. He then sent his dragoons around the enemy's flanks. The Indians broke and ran for the British fort—and found the gates closed to them. In two hours, Wayne destroyed the Indian force at a loss to himself of 33 killed and 100 wounded. The Indians's losses were unknown, but large. Wayne burned cornfields just outside Fort Miami, also a trading post. He ranged the countryside, as had Sullivan, putting the torch to Indian villages and destroying 5000 acres of crops. It was a crushing defeat from which the Ohio Indians did not recover for 20 years. Wayne's subsequent Treaty of Fort Greenville, 3 August 1795, forced the Indians to cede much of the North West Territory—all of Ohio, much of Indiana—to the US, also the enclaves of Chicago and Detroit.

Samuel Eliot Morison wrote that the Indian War phase of the Revolution ended at Fort Greenville. Actually, it was

Over: Rufus Zogbaum's painting is of Mad Anthony Wayne's great victory in the **Battle of Fallen Timbers**, 1794, near the Maumee River rapids. Wayne's mounted Legionnaires avenged the disasters of Generals Josiah Harmar and Arthur St Clair and crushed the Indians of the Ohio Territory forever. It set up the Treaty of Greenville, 1795.

another 20 years before it finally ended with the defeat and death of a chief greater than Pontiac.

The War of 1812

Henry Clay's War Hawks gained control of the House of Representatives in 1810–11. They blamed Britain not only for impressment of seamen, but also laid the blame for frontier Indian raids squarely on British provocation. At the same time, the Shawnee chief, Tecumseh, began his defiance of the westward urge of the new Republic. He had lost a brother at **Fallen Timbers**; he had, himself, fought Harmar, St Clair and Wayne. He had refused to sign the Treaty of Greenville because it meant the cession of Indian lands.

A turning point for Tecumseh came from a strange direction. His brother had a vision. The Great Spirit spoke to him and demanded that the Indians abandon all of the white man's ways and return to ancient tribal traditions.

Tecumseh went only part of the way with The Prophet his mystic brother. He abominated the farm tools that well-meaning whites thrust at him. He desired to see the Indians live by hunting, forever. But he was not about to scorn either firearms or the friendship of the British. He wanted no holy war, but a confederation of tribes like Pontiac's. His vision was a secular, not a religious, one. As for the English, they were delighted to have Tecumseh as a pawn in their New World geopolitics.

A motley army of Shawnees, Wyandots, Delawares, Ottawas, Chippewas and Kickapoos gathered at the utopian capital, Prophet's Town, near the junction of Tippecanoe Creek and the Wabash. Tecumseh carried his own crusade far and wide. He also applied pressure on the white frontier by raiding isolated farms and settlements in lonely clearings.

Tecumseh's nemesis was William Henry Harrison. Harrison had enormous respect for his adversary, considering the Shawnee to be a revolutionary genius. He wrote, 'The implicit obedience and respect which followers of Tecumseh pay him is really astonishing'. Harrison had joined the Army after he failed at medicine and possibly both law and a church career, too. His father wrote of him, 'He can neither bleed, plead, or preach'. But he succeeded in politics as well as in the Army, being appointed Governor of Indiana Territory.

Taking advantage of Tecumseh's absence, Harrison summoned chiefs to Fort Wayne and traded plentiful gills of liquor, a payment of $7000 and an annuity for the cession of three million acres of Indian land. Tecumseh was furious and vehemently protested the exchange. Harrison avoided a clash by receiving the Chief and 400 warriors at Vincennes in August 1810. For three days, Tecumseh vented his grievances and Harrison patiently heard him out. But when the Shawnee scorned the Governor's talk of 'justice' and called him a liar, Harrison drew his sword to run Tecumseh through. His guard detail looked to their weapons. But the Indian quickly apologized and the anxious moment blew over. Still, the pow-wow ended in a stalemate.

In July 1811, Potawatomis killed some Illinois farmers. Harrison chose to believe that the murderers were followers of Tecumseh and his brother. He demanded that the culprits be surrendered. Tecumseh refused, then set out on one of his journeys to forge new alliances.

Above: **William Henry Harrison** became president of the US because of his narrow and costly "victory" at Tippecanoe (1811) over Tecumseh's warriors.

Once more, Harrison took good advantage of Tecumseh's absence. Using the theft of an Army express rider's horse by Indians as an excuse, he marched a punitive expedition of 1000 men up the Wabash. Before he got to Prophet's Town, emissaries from the mystic asked for a parley on the next day, 7 November 1811. Harrison agreed and camped three miles out of town, ordering his men to sleep on their arms. He sent a message to Prophet's Town by two friendly Miamis, demanding the return of stolen stock and the surrender of two Indian killers. The Miamis never returned, so Harrison must have been wary. Nevertheless, he was, quite literally, caught napping.

Although Tecumseh had ordered the Prophet to avoid a fight, the latter decided on a secret sneak attack. He convinced himself and at least some of his followers that his 'medicine' made them immune to rifle balls. He even assured his warriors that some of the whites in the camp were already dead, struck down by his power. He ordered a special party of raiders to slip through the lines and murder Harrison. Then his men would give up, said the Prophet.

For a non-military man, the Prophet did well. He sent his picked warriors slithering on their bellies through the grass, like snakes, for almost a half-mile at night—a rare time for an Indian attack—under the cover of rain. A single sentry got off one warning shot before he and the other sentinels were killed and the raiders were inside the camp. They shot into the tents and some of their musket balls kicked coals and embers from campfires. The advance party was soon backed up by the Prophet's main force. Harrison, sound asleep—the drummer had not sounded reveille; it was only 3:45—was so startled by the gunshots that he jumped on his aide's bay horse, in error, to take

Above: **Tecumseh or Tecumtha** was the great chief of the Shawnees, a gifted leader who was also a humane warrior. He was killed in 1813.

command. The aide took the General's distinctive gray mare and was shot from his saddle in a case of mistaken identity.

Harrison's coolness saved the day. Three times the Indians rushed the center of the camp and three times his green troopers drove them back. As a gray dawn broke, the Governor launched his regular infantry and his dismounted dragoons in a bayonet charge under the cover of fire from his militia. Always reluctant to face this cold steel, the Indians broke and ran. They kept up an intermittent fire all day long, but the danger to the Americans was over in the morning. So demoralized were the Indians that they did not even defend the settlement. Harrison entered Prophet's Town and, after taking what supplies from Tecumseh's stockpile that his men could carry, he put a torch to everything.

It was an indecisive, painful victory; more like a tie. Harrison withdrew with the loss of 61 dead and so many wounded, 127, that he had to burn supplies to make room for the injured men in his covered wagons, used for ambulances. The Indian loss, which must have been substantial, is unknown. But it was a terrible psychological defeat for Tecumseh, a setback to his efforts to forge a great union of tribes. And, of course, the victory, such as it was, swept Harrison into the Presidency 30 years later, when he and his running mate and successor John Tyler were to use the phrase 'Tippecanoe and Tyler too' as their campaign slogan.

Brigadier General William Hull, at age sixty a fatherly figure, moved reluctantly across the Canadian line from Detroit on 12 July 1812. His advance was unopposed and yet he was timid and vacillating. He ordered an attack on Fort Malden one day, cancelled it the next, and scooted

Above: **The Prophet** of the Shawnees, Tenskwatawa, was Tecumseh's twin brother. (This picture of him appears to have been influenced by the Swiss artist, Karl Bodmer, and his Missouri River Indians.) Urging renunciation of the white man's ways and a return to traditional Indian life, he became very influential after predicting an eclipse of 1806. The Prophet played a major role in Tecumseh's plan for a confederation of tribes till this collapsed with his defeat at Tippecanoe.

Over: In **The Battle of the Thames,** 1813, Colonel Richard M Johnson was badly wounded but was believed to have killed Tecumseh. As a result of his fame, he became a congressman, senator and finally vice president of the United States. It may well have been a case of mistaken identity; the Indians claimed to have hidden the body of Tecumseh, who *was* killed, in a hollow tree. Johnson's commander was William Henry Harrison, whose special aide was Commodore Perry. Between them they succeeded in completing overcoming the British and the Indians in the Midwest, opening up new territory for settlement.

back to Detroit to go on the defensive. Hull was plain scared, frightened by the idea of Tecumseh cutting off his retreat to Detroit.

Tecumseh, wearing now the uniform of a brigadier general in the British Army, proposed to the dashing British General Isaac Brock at Malden that they mount an attack on Detroit. He drew a map on birchbark. The two officers easily encircled Hull, then terrified him by playing on his fears of massacre. (His daughter and grandchildren were in the fort.) They boasted of Tecumseh's '5000' warriors. Tecumseh's 600 warriors marched around and around as George Rogers' Clark's men had done at Vincennes, and fooled the Governor. Over the violent objections of his officers, Hull abjectly surrendered Detroit without firing a shot except a few token rounds from his cannon.

Hull's disgrace in surrendering to a force half the size of his own was on a par with the debacles of Harmar and St Clair and altogether typical of officers seemingly chosen not for merit but by politics, wealth, family, etc., a practice made worse by Jefferson's insistence on unpreparedness via his pacifistic 'neutrality.'

But Hull's ignominy was not yet complete. When Fort Michilmackinac fell, he ordered the evacuation of Fort Dearborn (Chicago). Although a friendly Indian warned him not to leave the safety of the stockade, Captain William Wells had his orders from Hull. Soldiers and civilians, including women and children, left the fort on 15 August. There was no Tecumseh there—compassionate and disciplined. (There was no massacre at Detroit.) But at Fort Dearborn, 500 Indians fell on the evacuees and killed half of them and made slaves of the rest. Wells was beheaded and had his heart cut out and eaten.

The West forced the Federal Government to name William Henry Harrison a brigadier general in command of a 10,000-man army to recapture Detroit that fall. But rains turned the countryside into a bog and Harrison had to winter over at Fort Defiance on the upper Maumee River. Sickness and desertions reduced his force to about 6500 men, but he nevertheless ordered General James Winchester to move down the Maumee with 1200 men. Winchester's men dragged sledges through the snow until rain turned it to slush and rotten ice, then fought mud and flooded prairies. Winchester fortified his camp near Fallen Timbers and the Maumee's rapids, but answered a call for help from the Americans living in Frenchtown on the Raisin River (Monroe, Michigan). Seven hundred Indians and 50 Canadians were in town, threatening the inhabitants. Although Frenchtown was closer to the British at Fort Malden than to the rapids, Winchester decided to risk a relief effort. He sent Colonel William Lewis and 550 men, who speedily cleared the town of its invaders. Winchester followed with 300 reinforcements. Then, with incredible foolishness, Winchester put his main force on the north bank of the **Raisin River** and his headquarters on the south bank. And he ordered out no extra patrols or night sentinels.

The British under Colonel Henry Proctor, with 1200 men, half of them Indians under Walk in the Water and Roundhead, struck Winchester in a snowstorm before dawn on 22 January 1813. The Americans did not have a chance. In minutes, 100 were scalped and Winchester was a prisoner. Only Major George Madison's 400 fought well until a British officer under a white flag reminded him that Winchester had surrendered his *entire* command. Madison would not agree to give up until Proctor guaran-

teed the safety of all prisoners. He reminded him that it had been customary for the Indians to massacre American wounded and prisoners after a surrender. Proctor was furious at his impertinence, but agreed.

Proctor, afraid that Harrison might come after him, withdrew. He kept his promise by marching his unhurt prisoners under British guards. But he left the wounded without guards or medical help. He joked, cruelly, as he left them, 'The Indians are excellent doctors.'

As soon as Proctor left, the Indians—now drunk—scalped some of the prisoners and set fire to the log cabin used as a temporary hospital. When the wounded tried to crawl out to escape the flames, the Indians drove them back in with their tomahawks.

Harrison reached the rapids a week or so after the Raisin River massacre. He built stout Fort Meigs there as a base to attack Detroit and nearby Fort Malden in Canada. But again weather—snow and ice—made the roads impassible in February and the advance was postponed. By spring, Harrison's force had shrunk to about 1000, but 1200 reinforcements were on their way from Kentucky.

Proctor and Tecumseh attacked Fort Meigs, their cannon pounding the log walls when the Kentuckians were only two hours upriver. To raise the siege, Harrison concocted a daring plan. He rushed the battery on the south side of the river while the arriving Kentuckians spiked the cannon on the north bank. But the overzealous Kentuckian, Lieutenant Colonel William Dudley, then led his men on a charge which chased the Indians back to Proctor's camp. The British counter-attacked and the Indians flanked the Americans. Some 600 were killed or captured and Dudley was tomahawked to death.

Only the belated presence of Tecumseh prevented a repetition of Raisin River. The Indians had taken 20 scalps of prisoners when he rushed up, knocked one warrior sprawling with the flat of his sword, grabbed another by the throat, and menaced a third with the point of his sword. 'Are there no men here?' he shouted. He demanded of Proctor why he had allowed the Indians to murder prisoners. The craven Englishman said, 'Your Indians cannot be controlled, cannot be commanded.'

Tecumseh contemptuously told the Colonel 'You are not fit to command. Go put on your petticoats!'

On 9 May with his Indians deserting and his militiamen muttering about the need to plant crops, Proctor abandoned the siege and returned to Malden.

On 20 July Tecumseh tried to take the fort with his Indians alone, by a ruse. He put on a sham battle in the nearby forest, but Colonel Greene Clay, in Harrison's absence, refused to be lured into a sortie.

Harrison built his army up to 4500 and prayed for a miracle. It came on Lake Erie. On 10 September 1813, Commodore Oliver Hazard Perry broke the war in the

Opposite page: A 1776 portrait of **Colonel Guy Johnson** by America's first great painter, Benjamin West, forms a part of the Andrew W Mellon Collection of the National Gallery in Washington, DC. Johnson (c. 1740-1788) was the son-in-law of Irish-born Sir William Johnson and his successor as the Crown's Superintendent of Indian Affairs in the Colonies. Like his namesake, he was responsible for all tribes during his tenure of office (1774-1782), but particularly the powerful Iroquois. Just as Sir William kept them on Britain's side in the French and Indian War, so the Loyalist Guy Johnson held their allegiance during the American Revolution. From headquarters at Niagara he sent out raiding expeditions of Indians against the Patriots and must be held partly responsible for the bloody massacre in the Wyoming Valley.

Below: **General Winfield Scott**, eventual commander-in-chief of the American Army, was one of only a handful of officers who distinguished themselves in the War of 1812. A Johnson, Fry & Company engraving pictured him as he ordered the charge of McNeil's battalion at the Battle of Chippewa in 1814.

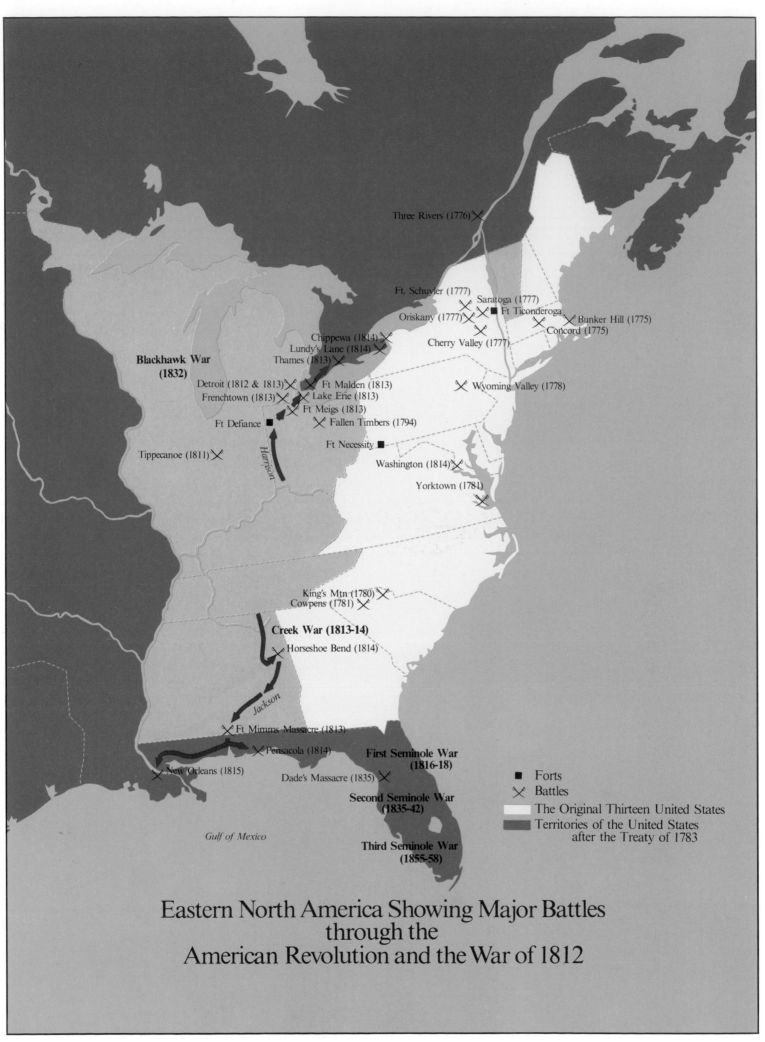

Three Rivers (1776) ✕

Ft. Schuyler (1777) ✕
Saratoga (1777) ✕ ■ Ft Ticonderoga
Oriskany (1777) ✕ ✕ ✕ Bunker Hill (1775)
Concord (1775) ✕
Cherry Valley (1777) ✕

Chippewa (1814) ✕
Lundy's Lane (1814) ✕
Blackhawk War Thames (1813) ✕
(1832) Wyoming Valley (1778) ✕
Detroit (1812 & 1813) ✕ ✕ Ft Malden (1813)
Frenchtown (1813) ✕ ✕ Lake Erie (1813)
✕ Ft Meigs (1813)
Ft Defiance ■ ✕ Fallen Timbers (1794)
Harrison
Ft Necessity ■
Tippecanoe (1811) ✕ Washington (1814) ✕
Yorktown (1781) ✕

King's Mtn (1780) ✕
Cowpens (1781) ✕

Creek War (1813-14)
✕ Horseshoe Bend (1814)

Jackson
✕ Ft Mimms Massacre (1813)
✕ Pensacola (1814) **First Seminole War**
✕ New Orleans (1815) **(1816-18)**
Dade's Massacre (1835) ✕

Second Seminole War
(1835-42)

Gulf of Mexico

Third Seminole War
(1855-58)

■ Forts
✕ Battles
The Original Thirteen United States
Territories of the United States
after the Treaty of 1783

Eastern North America Showing Major Battles
through the
American Revolution and the War of 1812

Above: The daring General Mad Anthony Wayne proved himself to be a skilled Indian negotiator as well as a distinguished soldier in 1795. He followed up on his smashing victory over the Indians at the Battle of Fallen Timbers with the tough **Treaty of Greenville** that secured the Northwest Territory – Ohio and the Lakes – to the US.

Below: Oddly, a naval officer turned American fortunes around on the Indian frontier during the War of 1812. Although he had to abandon his wrecked flagship, **Commodore Oliver Hazard Perry** conquered the British fleet on Lake Erie, then joined William Henry Harrison in the defeat of Tecumseh and the British Army at the Thames in Canada in 1813.

Above: Charles Willson Peale, a student of Benjamin West, painted this portrait of the old Indian-fighter, **George Washington**.

West wide open with his smashing of the British fleet. Tecumseh saw the fight from a distant canoe, but could not tell who was winning. Perry used some of Harrison's Kentuckians as marine sharpshooters, and among his prisoners he found two Indians who had been doing the same duty on a British war vessel. Perry's note to Harrison signaled the invasion of Canada—'We have met the enemy, and they are ours.'

The Commodore quickly converted his warships into troop transports and ferried Harrison's army across Lake Erie. Detroit fell on 26 September and Proctor, disheartened by Perry's victory—and fearful of Kentuckian revenge for the Raisin River massacre—abandoned Fort Malden after having promised the Indians to hold it. Tecumseh now compared him, to his face, to a whipped dog running with his tail between his legs. But he accompanied him on his withdrawal up the Thames River. Harrison hurried in pursuit as did Perry, with his smaller craft going up the river as far as they could. Then the Commodore attached himself to Harrison as an aide, unwilling to miss the final fight.

Proctor finally halted near Moravian Town, probably because of Tecumseh's goading. He chose a good battlefield. The road narrowed as it passed a bog between the river and a large swamp. The British made a defensive line between river and bog while the Indians held the area between bog and swamp, and took to the swamp itself.

Tecumseh had a premonition of death and gave his sword to someone to pass on to his son, when he should become a noted warrior. He forgave Proctor his poltroonery and said goodbye by touching hands with his fellow-officers and saying a few words in Shawnee.

On 5 October 1813 Harrison cancelled a frontal infantry assault when his scouts reported the British in open order and the Indians scattered as skirmishers in the swamp. Instead, he split his dragoons into two battalions, one under Richard Mentor Johnson and the other under his brother, James Johnson, because of the narrow space for a cavalry charge. Harrison later admitted, 'It was not sanctioned by anything I had seen or heard of, but I was fully convinced it would succeed.'

James Johnson's squadron, swinging tomahawks like sabers, broke the British line. In only 10 minutes, the redcoats were in retreat. Proctor jumped into his waiting coach and ran away, escorted by 40 dragoons. On the other flank, Tecumseh's men had emptied 20 saddles and Richard Johnson ordered his men to fight dismounted, in hand-to-hand combat. Colonel William Whatley and an Indian shot each other to death. Some whites thought that the Indian was Tecumseh. Richard Johnson, on the ground and wounded several times, shot an attacker through the head before he passed out. Many believed that his victim was Tecumseh. Johnson never claimed to have killed the chief, but his friends said that he had, and got him elected Vice President of the United States in 1836 on the basis of that boast. Brutal Kentuckians flayed—skinned—the corpse of a big warrior for 'souvenirs', assuming that it was that of Tecumseh. It was another case of mistaken identity,

Above: British General Proctor and Tecumseh tried to take Harrison's 1813 strongpoint, **Fort Meigs,** by storm and by siege, but failed.

probably. Tecumseh was killed, but it is believed that his warriors hid his corpse in a hollow log where it was never found.

Harrison took hundreds of prisoners, a million dollars in munitions and supplies, and 'Gentleman Johnny' Burgoyne's cannon, recaptured by the British from Hull at Detroit.

British-Indian power was crushed forever. The entire Midwest, from Ohio to Minnesota, was thrown open to American occupation, and Indiana and Illinois became states in 1816 and 1818, respectively, all because of the teamwork of William Henry Harrison and the wilderness commodore, Oliver Hazard Perry, who refused to concede victory to the Royal Navy when he was, seemingly, whipped on Lake Erie.

Above: **Richard M Johnson** assassinating **Tecumseh** at the Battle of the Thames. *Left:* Fort Wayne, Indiana, in 1812. William Henry Harrison met here with Indian chiefs to make a trade for Indian land, which angered Tecumseh.

Below: Americans used propaganda – political cartoons – against George III's **Detroit hair buyers** who put a bounty on Yankee scalps.

A Scene on the FRONTIERS as Practiced by the HUMANE BRITISH and their WORTHY ALLIES

Bring me the Scalps and the King our master will reward you.

Reward for Sixteen Scalps

Arise Columbia's Sons and forward press,
Your Country's wrongs call loudly for redress;
The Savage Indian with his Scalping knife,
Or Tomahawk may seek to take your life,

By bravery aw'd they'll in a dreadful Fright,
Shrink back for Refuge to the Woods in Flight;
Their British leaders then will quickly shake,
And for those wrongs shall restitution make.

MANIFEST DESTINY

1816-1849

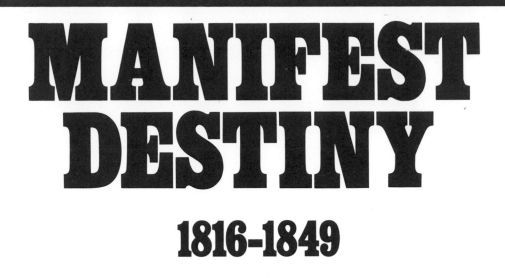

Having won the War of 1812, its second 'war of independence,' the new nation turned its attention to settling the western frontier, its 'manifest destiny.' The nature of the conflict between the white man and the Indians changed from one of skirmishes centered around static settlements to one which found the white man plunging headlong into the once guaranteed Indian land, and the Indians were fighting back.

The Creek War

The Creek War of 1813 led to the First Florida War, or Seminole War (1817–18), and the more drastic Second Florida or Seminole War of 1835–42. This dramatic conflict proved to be a rehearsal for the Mexican War, training both regulars and volunteers so well that they performed creditably in Mexico, in marked contrast to their general incompetence during most of the War of 1812.

One of Tecumseh's converts was Chief Little Warrior. He led a detachment of Creeks north and participated in the dastardly Raisin River massacre. En route home, he murdered some families on the Ohio. When the American government demanded that Chief Big Warrior and his Creek elders surrender the killers, the Creeks executed the culprits themselves.

Just as feuds would eventually split the Cherokee Nation

Opposite page: Thomas Sully painted a portrait of Indian-fighter Andrew Jackson in 1845 that is now in the nation's National Gallery.

Below: A detail of George Catlin's painting of an 1830s **buffalo hunt** on the snow covered plains of the Upper Missouri country.

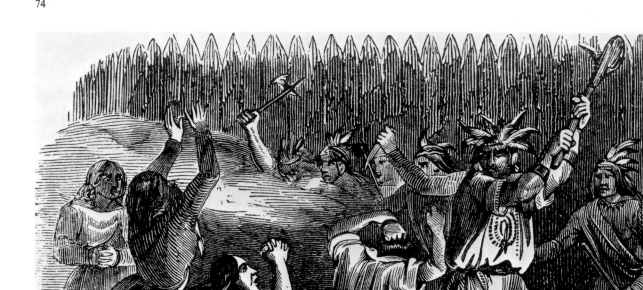

in two, Big Warrior's drastic action led to a civil war in which his 'loyal', or pro-white Lower Creeks (White Sticks) were pitted against the hawkish Upper Creeks, or Red Sticks, so called because of their distinctive war clubs.

The 24,000 Creeks were civilized Indians who practiced farming and lived in 100 towns. They intermarried with whites so much that a number of their chiefs were half-breeds. William (Billy) Weatherford was one of them. He called himself Red Eagle, but he was only one-eighth Creek, the rest being a mixture of Spanish, French and Scottish. He was kin of the rich and respected chief, Alexander McGillivray, who pretended friendship for the US and was made a brigadier general in the American Army, but who remained a foe, secretly, until his death in 1793. Weatherford liked to brag that there coursed in his veins 'not one drop of Yankee blood'. He and another half-blood, Peter McQueen, led the Red Sticks.

After drubbing a company of settlers in a skirmish, Weatherford's 800–1000 Red Sticks advanced on Fort Mims on the Alabama River 40 miles north of Mobile. This was actually just the fortified home of a half-breed, Sam Mims, but it was crammed with 550 refugees. There were Creeks, halfbreeds, blacks and whites, all under the protection of two half-breed rivals of Weatherford, Major Donald Beasley and Captain Dixon Bailey, and their Louisiana militiamen.

Beasley boasted that he could hold the fort against any number of Indians, but he was singularly unprepared for Weatherford. Although blacks warned him of Indians lurking in the tall grass nearby, he left both gates open (one could not even be closed because of a mound of sand in its path), and there were no sentinels on duty when the drummer tapped out mess call at noon of 30 August 1813. The Red Sticks used the drumming as their signal to attack.

Above: Conflict spread to the South during the War of 1812. On 30 August 1813 a large force of Indians led by a half-breed Creek, William Weatherford, made a surprise attack on unprepared **Fort Mims.** The temporary stockade, near the junction of the Alabama and Tombigbee Rivers, fell in a bloody massacre of perhaps 500 people.

Beasley was clubbed or tomahawked as he ran to a gate. The militia fought back under a hot sun, but the fort was soon set afire. About 36 people escaped the ensuing massacre, besides most of the blacks, who were spared to become Creek slaves. At least 350 people were massacred. A sense of guilt or compassion led Weatherford to try to stop the savagery, but he was unsuccessful.

The Fort Mims massacre shocked the United States. A committee of public safety called on Andrew Jackson, sick in bed at his home, The Hermitage, near Nashville. He was suffering agony from a gunshot wound in one shoulder, received in a fight with Thomas Hart Benton and his brother. Andy cursed himself for squandering his strength on a personal vendetta when his country needed him. The Tennessee Legislature voted money to outfit 3500 citizen-soldiers, so Jackson ordered volunteers to gather in Fayette-ville on 4 October promising to lead them, personally, a few days later.

Jackson would face only 4000 Red Sticks at most, and probably never more than 1000 warriors together for any one battle. Many would not even own muskets, but would fight effectively with tomahawks, bows and arrows and their famous war clubs. But their sacred country, which they called The Hickory Ground, at the junction of the Coosa and Tallapoosa Rivers in Alabama, was so remote that Georgians and Alabamans would strike at it with little success. Jackson had to make a difficult move across mountains and through dense forests, yet he carried out forced marches of 20 and even 30 miles a day. All the while, he was thin and pale, his arm in a sling because of the painful slug still lodged in his shoulder muscles. Shortly, he would come down with dysentery, too. But he was tough as hardwood, hence his new nickname, Old Hickory, and he never succumbed to defeatism.

Andy Jackson sent his closest friend, Colonel John Coffee, and his 500–1000 dragoons ahead of his own force. This mounted detachment drew first blood, 3 November 1813, at the **Tallushatchee River**. Coffee lured the Red Sticks into a circle of his troops and closed it on them. He killed 180 warriors while losing only five dead and 41 wounded. The frontiersman, Davy Crockett, chortled, 'We shot them like dogs.'

It was Jackson's turn a week later when he relieved the siege of friendly Creeks by Red Sticks at **Talladega**. When the Creeks saw Jackson's column, instead of crying out 'Huzza!' or 'Hooray!', shouted simply, in their relief, 'Howdy-do, brothers, howdy-do!' According to Crockett, the hostiles rushed Andy's force like a cloud of locusts led by a devil (Weatherford). But it took only 15 minutes to force them back. Only 290 of the 700 enemy Creeks finally got away. Jackson lost 15 dead and 85 wounded.

But the campaign then inched on through November and December with no more battles. Bored and grumbling militiamen began to demand their release. Jackson argued that their terms of service were not yet up (though they were), and bluffed them with a rifle, saying that he would shoot the first 'deserter'. Still, the strength of his force sagged downward from musterings-out, desertion and sickness till he had barely 500 effectives. Some said that he had only 150 men ready for battle at the low point of the campaign.

Even Governor Willie Blount of Tennessee despaired of success and suggested a withdrawal. Jackson lectured him, ending his diatribe, 'Save Mobile, save the Territory, save your frontier from being drenched with blood! . . . What, retrograde under these circumstances? I will perish first.'

Reinforcements arrived, but many of them were to serve only 60-day enlistments. But, finally, when he received the 39th Regiment of regulars in February of 1814, Jackson was on the move again. He took 2000 men, including Cherokees and Creek White Sticks, to attack the 800 Red Sticks 'forted up' at **Horseshoe Bend** in eastern Alabama. They had built a zig-zag barricade of double logs, like a snake fence, all the way across the narrow peninsula of the Tallapoosa. On the beach they had a whole fleet of canoes for a getaway, if necessary.

Since his cannonballs simply bounced off the logs, Jackson sent Coffee's horsemen across the river to cut off the canoe retreat. But Coffee was discontent with this maneuver; he attacked the rear of the Creek position. So Jackson ordered a frontal assault. The major leading the regulars in the charge was killed, but sword-waving Ensign Sam Houston took over. The Red Sticks fought desperately until Jackson's flaming arrows set the barricade afire around dusk. Houston was carried off the battlefield, wounded twice, but the Tennesseans overran the blazing breastworks and won the day. Some 550 of the Red Stick Creeks died in the fort and perhaps another 200 in and on the river. Jackson lost 49 dead and 157 wounded.

Weatherford was away from the fort when it was attacked, 27 March 1814. He left Minewa in command. Jackson ordered the Scots-Indian found and brought to him in chains. Only a few days after the fight, however, a

Above: **The Creeks** of Alabama and Georgia were led by Tecumseh to go to war. It was a disaster; Jackson beat them and drove them west.

manly, impressive fellow in ragged clothes walked into camp. 'I'm Bill Weatherford', the erstwhile Chief Red Eagle announced himself.

Jackson either forgot the Fort Mims massacre or remembered his visitor's attempts to stop it, for he told Weatherford that he was not a prisoner. He pardoned the Chief. But he dared Weatherford to lead his remaining Creeks on the warpath. The saddened and humbled man answered, 'I cannot animate the dead. My warriors no longer hear my voice'. He was surrendering, he said, relying on the generosity of a brave man. And he would enforce Jackson's terms of peace.

If Weatherford really expected magnanimity from Old Hickory, he was in for a rude shock. The Treaty of Horseshoe Bend at Fort Jackson offered on the battle site (9 August 1814) demanded 23 million acres of Creek land. That was almost half of Alabama and one-fifth of Georgia. Big Warrior protested on behalf of the peaceful White Stick Creeks, but Jackson lumped them with the hostiles. And the chiefs, some of them so hungry that they scrambled for kernels of corn spilled on the ground by Jackson's feeding horses, signed.

Andrew Jackson wrote his wife that it was disagreeable business to rob a fallen nation of half of its territory. But he believed that such stern measures were necessary to pacify the Southwestern frontier.

Only a few Creeks resisted, and they fled to Florida to join their relatives of the Seminole tribe.

In the summer of 1816, US soldiers, backed by the Navy, attacked a fort of rebellious—or, at least, runaway—black slaves on the Apalachicola River in West Florida (claimed

Over: **Meriwether Lewis** and his close friend, **William Clark,** proved in their Lewis and Clark Expedition of 1804-05 that diplomacy worked better than warfare in westward exploration, although the lesson was lost on later explorers and Army officers. In 1897, Charles M Russell painted Clark's pow-wow with Northwest Indians toward securing the Upper Missouri country of the Louisiana Purchase and access to the sea via Oregon Territory.

by the United States as part of the Louisiana Purchase) where 300 men, women and children were holed up. A hot cannonball from a bombarding gunboat touched off the fort's powder magazine, and only 50 people survived the explosion. The two rebel leaders were executed; the slaves returned to their masters.

The Seminole War (First Florida War)

The Seminole troubles resumed with raids into Georgia by the Mikasuki band, then a counter-raid across the Spanish line into Florida by Captain David E Twiggs and 250 men, against the village of Fowlstown. Jackson was back in the area at the beginning of 1818 on orders from Secretary of War John C Calhoun to pacify the Georgia border with 800 regulars, 900 Georgia volunteers, and a contingent of Lower Creek scouts under half-breed Chief William McIntosh. By March, Old Hickory was burning Seminole villages. He captured the town of Chief Boleck, alias Billy Bowlegs, on the Suwanee River and, though bothered by short rations, pursued the Indians right into West Florida, their Spanish sanctuary, assuming that he had the President's tacit blessing. After he seized the old Spanish fortress-town of St Marks on 29 April, he executed two Creek chiefs and two British traders, Alexander Arbuthnot and Robert C Ambrister, for aiding and abetting Seminole marauders. He again took over the Spanish fort-town of Pensacola (which he had also captured in 1814) and this time, expelled its governor.

Jackson's high-handed conduct created an international incident which enraged both Madrid and London, just as the United States was entering the so-called Era of Good Feeling with the Mother Country after two wars of independence. Some politicians in Washington wanted Jackson's resignation, but President John Quincy Adams not only supported the public's new folk hero, he used the raid as leverage to demand that Spain either control the Seminoles or give up its territory. Spain gave up all of its possessions east of the Mississippi, selling East Florida (the peninsula) to the US in 1819 for five million dollars and a promise by the United States to honor the rights of the Indians. The cession was completed in 1821. In addition, Madrid recognized the United States border as the 42nd Parallel along the top of New Spain, or Mexico, and extending all the way through Oregon Territory to the Pacific. Thus, a major European capital acknowledged the US as a continental, two-ocean power after just 43 years of independence.

Perhaps this Spanish action was the spark which led to the eventual editorial by John O'Sullivan in the New York *Morning News* which coined the phrase (December 1845) which symbolized the ongoing westward expansionism, the 'Manifest Destiny' of the United States to occupy the entire continent.

Manifest Destiny was long preceded by another frontier philosophy, however, Indian removal. Congress's 'final answer' to the Indian problem was the Indian Removal Act of 1830; move all of the tribes across the Mississippi to an Indian Nation, or Indian Territory, but not to the kind of which Pontiac and Tecumseh had dreamed. It was a distant and, presumably, worthless prairie which would not attract white settlement beyond a line of forts keeping apart, forever, the two antagonistic peoples.

Opportunistic white settlers, 'Crackers', infiltrated

Above: **Davy Crockett** (1786-1836), who died in the defense of the Alamo during the Texas Revolution, was a backwoodsman, a judge and state legislator, and a teller of tall tales who soldiered with Andrew Jackson against the Creeks. He was also a mighty hunter who once killed 17 bears in a week, 105 of them in just two months.

behind Jackson's army in Florida, of course, to fill the vacuum left by ousted Seminoles. They took the good land while the Indians were left a poor reservation in the center of the peninsula. When the annuity, food and farm tools proved slow in arriving, bands drifted away and resumed their raiding of settlers.

Second Florida War

To implement Indian removal and to quiet petitioning settlers, James Gadsden pressured some Seminole delegates to sign the brutal Treaty of Payne's Landing, Florida in 1832. This became the bridge between the **First and Second Florida Wars**. It required all Seminoles to be out of Florida in just three years, moving to the Creek area of the Indian Territory, Oklahoma in exchange for one blanket (or a frock, for women) for each man, woman and child, and—for the entire tribe—a pittance of $15,400. And this would be reduced by an assessment of $7000 if 'stolen' (ie, runaway) slaves were found in the Seminole country. The Army aided slave catchers, of course, and the Seminoles retreated deeper into their swamps and the great 'river of grass', the Everglades. They had to; because of intermarriage, there were many part-black Seminoles who were to be segregated from their Oklahoma-bound kinfolk and treated as black slaves.

When the appointed time was up, not one Seminole had

Above: The Second Seminole War began on 28 December 1835 when Seminoles led by Micanopy, Jumper and Alligator fell on **Major Francis L Dade's** command, marching from Fort Brooke to Fort King, Florida. Although they had a six-pound cannon and took shelter in a log breastwork, only three of 102 soldiers survived, but died soon after.

been moved west. But Indian Agent Wiley Thompson, in the spring of 1835, presented to a similar group of chiefs almost a carbon copy of the original treaty. Seven chiefs reluctantly, sullenly, signed the paper with their marks. Others signed the next year, but when the government tried in April 1835 to get unanimous support for removal, a warrior (not yet a chief) leaped up and dramatically plunged his hunting knife through the document, as if killing the hated agreement.

Thompson put the man, 30-year-old Osceola (Black-Drink Singer), one of the Creeks who had fought Jackson before joining the Seminoles, in irons. At first, Osceola had helped the government with the reservation idea, but after Payne's Landing he not only refused to go west himself, he swore to stop other Seminoles and Creeks from going. After only one day in manacles, Osceola agreed to sign. He was released—and immediately disappeared in the swamps to organize a resistance movement. He recruited followers and began to raid settlers. Both whites and peaceful Indians now begged Washington for help, but little was done until after Christmas.

A Seminole band of 180 warriors under Chief Alligator waylaid an Army column on the military road out of Fort King, Tampa. Two unsuspecting companies of 112 men of the 45th Infantry and 2d and 3d Artillery regiments, with a six-pounder, ammunition caisson and ration wagon under Brevet Major Francis L Dade, were annihilated in a sneak attack in an undeclared war. Deadly fire came from the cover of a palmetto grove at a distance of only 35 yards. Just three soldiers escaped to bring the word to Fort King. The fourth man, Luís, Dade's black guide, was actually a Seminole spy who set up the ambush.

The Second Seminole War continued with an assassination. Osceola, humiliated by his one day in irons, took his revenge on Wiley Thompson. The Indian Agent was dining with friends in a house near Fort King. Osceola shot Thompson and four of his companions from the window, and then melted into the grass and palmettos.

Next, on New Year's eve, Osceola defeated a force of 300 regulars and 500 Florida militia on the Withlacoochee River. He killed or wounded 63 of the soldiers, but was himself wounded and lost many braves. In the future, the Seminoles would avoid open battles almost entirely, and stick to the guerrilla tactics which they perfected in their peninsular jungle.

Finally, Washington was roused to action. Following General Edmund P Gaines's ineffective expedition of 1836, President Jackson replaced him with General Duncan Clinch as commander. Clinch was equally ineffective, so Jackson picked the best soldier of the War of 1812 (except for himself), Winfield Scott, though he disliked the man. But even the redoubtable Scott could not do very much against a few hundred hit-and-run partisans who insisted on avoiding pitched battles. Jackson recalled Scott. Scott faced a court of inquiry, but was exonerated of all blame for the Army's failure to end the Seminole War.

Florida's governor, Robert Call, tried next. His campaign failed, so General Thomas S Jesup took over. Even with such excellent Indian fighters as William S

Harney of the crack Second Dragoons and Colonel Zachary Taylor, he accomplished almost nothing in a year of marching and skirmishing. Finally, in October of 1837, he stooped to treachery. His excuse was that the Seminoles often broke their promises. Jesup asked Osceola to come to a parley under a flag of truce and then blatantly violated it. He seized the chieftain and threw him into a dungeon of ancient Fort Marion, the Spanish Castillo de San Marcos, in St Augustine. Osceola died on 30 January 1838 of malaria and a throat ailment.

Jesup's unconscionable act of treachery, when combined with his experiment with bloodhounds to track down Seminoles, was denounced by most Americans. His reputation bespattered and his inability to close out the war continued by Billy Bowlegs and other chiefs, made it inevitable that he, too, would be replaced.

The new commander, Zachary Taylor, 'Old Rough and Ready', abandoned large operations and tried to fight the Seminoles more nearly in their own backwoods fashion. He plotted the entire peninsula into a grid of 20-mile squares, then posted garrisons to patrol their areas constantly.

With 1000 men, mostly regulars of the 1st, 4th and 6th Infantry regiments and the 4th Artillery, the rest mounted Missouri infantry, and a huge baggage train of pack mules and 80 wagons, Taylor marched from Tampa to Lake Okeechobee and there enticed the Seminoles into their second, and last, orthodox battle. On Christmas Day of 1837 he attacked Chief Alligator's excellent defensive position, a hammock (a mound or hummock of dry ground, wooded with cypress and palmetto) above the five-feet tall sawgrass of the great marsh surrounding it.

Taylor had to dismount his horsemen as the animals bogged down in the marsh. When his dragoons, turned foot soldiers, advanced, the first Seminole volley cut them up badly and killed their colonel. They withdrew. Old Rough and Ready then had his regular infantrymen close in on the high ground. After a charge, the Seminoles stole away silently and gave Taylor the victory. But it was a costly one. He lost 28 killed and 111 wounded. The Indians lost some of their property to Taylor but their casualty count was probably much, much lower than his. (One estimate of Seminole losses had only 100 warriors killed and 2900 captured in the war by May 1838).

Even Zachary Taylor was recalled by Washington, but this victory at Lake Okeechobee started him on the long road to the White House (1849). He was replaced by the conciliatory generals, Alexander Macomb and Walker K Armistead. The latter imported Seminole chiefs from Oklahoma to try to talk their dissident people into migrating. They had no luck, so the government abandoned its 'Quaker' policy and substituted the military stick for the carrot. They appointed a man like Harney and Taylor, General William J Worth. In the spring of 1841 he began a methodical war of attrition, a scorched earth policy in a swampland. He burned all crops, all canoes, all shelters. When he captured a few warriors, he held them as hostages. Ultimately, the hungry Seminoles tired of fighting and

Above: Colonel Zachary Taylor attacked the Seminoles in a defensive position in the sawgrass of **Lake Okeechobee**, Florida, on Christmas Day in 1837. He won the field in a battle, but suffered a total loss of 26 men dead and 112 wounded.

began to straggle in. The war itself was dying as Chief Coacoochee, Wildcat, emerged from the Everglades with two aides, all dressed in Shakespearian costume from the looted trunks of a captured theatrical company.

About 4000 Seminoles were eventually removed to Oklahoma. Some hid out in the Everglades to fight a Third Florida War (1855–58) which was put down by Colonel Harney. A few of their descendants are there today, proud of never having signed a treaty.

On this small tribe the United States spent somewhere between $20 million and $60 million for warfare, using 30,000 regulars and volunteers, including virtually all of the Army, plus the Navy and some Marines, over a period of six years. The war cost the government a minimum of 1466 and a maximum of 2000 dead (estimates vary), of whom 215 were officers. Thousands of men were wounded or felled by fever. Perhaps 1500 Seminoles, on the outside, were killed.

The Removal of the Cherokees

Although the Seminoles had crops and slaves, they were definitely poor compared to the numerous wealthy Cherokees of the Georgia-Tennessee border. Not only the richest, but the most advanced of all American Indian tribes, the Cherokees owned fertile farmlands on 40,000 acres of the Tennessee River country. They ran 22,000 cattle and 7200 horses, kept many black slaves, owned 2900 plows, many wagons and 10 sawmills. They built improved roads and ferries. The Cherokees had an alphabet, devised by Sequoyah; they read books and published a newspaper, the *Phoenix*, until it was suppressed by whites. They even had a constitution (1826), the only one possessed by an Indian nation. They were on relatively good terms with their white neighbors. They lived not in tents but in log cabins and frame houses. The principal chieftain, John Ross, resided in a fine brick plantation home until he was arrested. He

Opposite page: In 1838, the year of the chief's death, Catlin painted a portrait of the Seminole, **Osceola.** He led the young anti-treaty warriors who refused to move west from Florida. Osceola murdered the Indian Agent, Wiley Thompson, and paid for it by being seized while under a white flag in 1837. He was imprisoned in Ft Moultrie, where he died.

Over: A detail of Charles M Russell's 1905 watercolor painting of **Captain Meriwether Lewis** and **Lieutenant William Clark** meeting with the Indians in log canoes on the lower Columbia River a century earlier. The explorers conducted another in the series of *wa-was* or pow-wows that kept the peace and permitted continued exploration.

84

was soon released, but his home was seized.

The Cherokees were accommodating neighbors of the Georgians, but they did not reckon on the land greed in the latter's nature. Local politicians wanted nullification of their land titles and removal of the tribe to the west of the Mississippi. Naturally, the Indians resisted. Georgia had no right to extend its laws over the Cherokees, defined by the Supreme Court as people of a 'domestic, dependent nation'. There was violence, but the Cherokee Nation took its case to the Supreme Court and won it in 1832. Cynically, President Andrew Jackson said, 'John Marshall has made his decision. Now let him enforce it.'

In 1830 the Indian Removal Act, Jackson's pet legislation, was passed. It barely squeaked through a shame-faced Congress by one vote. In 1835, Georgia pressured 500 Cherokees—not one of them an elected chief—to sign a treaty involving the sale of all of their lands for five million dollars and seven million acres in the West, plus an option to buy another eight million acres for only $500,000. Some 16,000 Cherokees signed a petition repudiating the treaty. Andy Jackson was adamant. He ignored the petition. He had decided that the only solution to the problem of white-versus-Indian hostility was the complete removal of all redmen beyond the Mississippi—even if the ridding of the South of its Indians involved the sacrifice of the Five Civilized Tribes and a gigantic land-grab by covetous whites.

The deadline for removal was set for 23 May 1838 and

Above: At **The Battle of Tallapoosa**, or Horseshoe Bend, Jackson met the Creeks on 27 March 1814. Though the Red Sticks had breastworks as defenses, he crushed them. 'The carnage was dreadful,' said Jackson.

Generals Scott and John E Wool, later a Mexican War hero, were Jackson's reluctant agents. Both were ashamed of their roles in the despicable scheme. Wool found the evacuation a heart-rending scene. He was for removal *only* if it would get the Indians 'beyond the reaches of the white men who, like vultures, are watching, ready to pounce on their prey and strip them of everything they have.'

Scott told the 7000 soldiers assigned to escort duty to show every kindness to the 16,000 Cherokees. About 2000 had gone ahead, 'voluntarily', and a small band hid out in the North Carolina mountains and was never moved. He promised swift and sure punishment for any insult or injury done to a Cherokee. As a result, there was little violence, though incidents of robbery, rape and even murder were not unknown.

President Jackson wanted the Indians moved out quickly, but Scott waited for cooler weather, to make for healthier traveling. The evacuees were penned up in camps that hot summer, where they suffered from dysentery and fevers. The moment they left their cabins and fields, of course, their property was looted by white settlers. In the fall of 1838 they were put on the road in the long trek of from 700 to 1200 miles to Oklahoma. We still call it The Trail of Tears.

Above: En route to his victory over the Creeks at the Tallapoosa River, Andrew Jackson had a run-in with them at **Emuckfaw Creek**, Alabama, on 22 January 1814. It was a close call, but the Indians pulled out.

The Cherokees were preceded to Oklahoma by the Choctaws in November 1831; the Creeks, some in irons, in 1836; and the Chickasaws in 1837. The Seminoles refused to budge from Florida until after the Second Florida War. Probably 4000 Cherokees died on the road, mostly of disease and hardships, and the tribe was torn by vendettas and civil war for years.

The Black Hawk War

While the South was rent by war and forced migration, the North was quiet for quite a while after the War of 1812. But another of the men who had listened attentively to Tecumseh's oratory was Black Hawk, actually Black Sparrow Hawk (*Ma-a-tai-me-she-kia-kiak*.) He was a Sauk (Sac) and chief of the closely-allied Sauk and Fox Indians of the Rock River country of Illinois. He took his first scalp at the age of 15 (*circa* 1782) and, by the time he was in his 30s, was a chief of war parties against Osages and Cherokees. He became angered by an 1804 treaty in St Louis, the capital of northern Louisiana Territory, just delivered to Meriwether Lewis by the Spanish. In the treaty, William Henry Harrison took much land from the allied tribes. So Black Hawk fought alongside Tecumseh

in the War of 1812, at Frenchtown (Raisin River), Forts Meigs and Stephenson and at the culminating Battle of the Thames.

Black Hawk looked almost classically Indian with his high cheek bones, 'roman' nose and shaved head, except for its roach, or scalplock. But he was an articulate orator as well, whose autobiography became a popular book and is now a classic of Western Americana.

Black Hawk was an old veteran by Indian standards when he protested to Indian agents, in the late 1820s and early 30s, against the theft of his people's cornfields by white squatters. This was in violation of the 1804 treaty provisions. He did not believe in the right to buy and sell land, in any case. Land, to him, was like the air—put there by the Great Spirit for everyone to enjoy. The whites not only occupied his village in 1831, but they also took over his home, ignored his demands to leave and plowed up the Indian graveyard as cropland.

Even when the General Land Office illegally put his property up for sale, Black Hawk continued to return there from his hunts to the west, in order to plant and harvest corn. The last time that he came back was in 1832, against the wishes of the conciliatory rival chief, Keokuk, with

Over: A detail of an 1821 group portrait by Charles Bird King (1785-1862), commissioned by Thomas L McKenney. The subjects were members of a Pawnee delegation from the Platte-Arkansas River plains, in Washington to see the Great White Father. The tribe was usually friendly, though there was a minor Pawnee War in 1859.

Above: Artists of the War of 1812 period sometimes took liberties and, seemingly, transported Creek or Seminole Indians northward to William Henry Harrison's country as depicted in this engraving called *The Defense of Fort Harrison.*

500–1000 followers. Black Hawk's bitter hatred of whites led him to burn a few squatters' cabins to get them to pack up and leave. This action caused the governor of Illinois to ask General Gaines to deal with him.

Gaines came by steamboat to talk to Black Hawk. He ordered the chief to move his people west of the Mississippi. Some went, but Black Hawk and others refused to budge. He told Gaines, who really did not want to start a conflict, 'Provoke our people to war and you will learn who Black Hawk is'. But when 700 militia came up, Black Hawks's braves deserted him for the right bank. Gaines made a few concessions, but the settlers were uncooperative and Black Hawk's people were reduced to stealing food from their own cornfields.

The Chief tried, like Pontiac and Tecumseh, to put together a confederacy. His was to be composed of Sauks, Foxes, Winnebagos, Potawatomis and Kickapoos. (The powerful Sioux were enemies.) But it was too late. By April 1832 the only help to 500 Sauk braves came from 100 Foxes.

White refugees exaggerated the number of warriors and the danger from Black Hawk, and General Henry Atkinson was faced with the (non-existent) uprising. He was both slow and timid, but his second in command was Zachary Taylor and he had 1800 volunteers, many of them mounted, and 400 regular infantry.

Black Hawk kept insisting that he only wanted to plant his usual corn crop, but the whites would not listen. He was intercepted by a party of 270 men under Major Isaiah Stillman. When the Chief sent messengers to him, the Major seized them. When Black Hawk sent five men to look for his missing emissaries, Stillman's men attacked them and killed two of them. So Black Hawk was forced to respond, though he was separated from his main force and may have had as few as 40 braves with him. He prepared an ambush into which the blundering Stillman marched. To Black Hawk's surprise, the volunteers ran like deer all the way back to their base camp, 25 miles distant. Even their comrades called this shameful engagement **'Stillman's Run.'**

General Scott took over an expanded army but only to have it ravaged by cholera. It was reorganized for a third time in June and handed back to Atkinson. Abraham

Lincoln was a lieutenant under Zachary Taylor, as was Jefferson Davis, later President of the Confederate States of America. (Without her father's permission, Taylor's daughter married Jeff Davis.) Albert Sidney Johnston, the Civil War general, also served, as did Daniel Boone's son, Nat.

Lincoln saw no action, but was horrified when he stumbled on five cadavers from Stillman's Run. He never forgot the frightening, grotesque scene—the red light of the sun seeming to focus on the darker red circles on the dead men's heads where scalps had been ripped away.

Black Hawk kept retreating into southern Wisconsin where the 65-year-old warrior chief went on a rampage of burning farming settlements and scalping families. Newspapers called for a war of extermination so that the only Indians left in Illinois would be dead and scalped.

On 28 July 1832 General James D Henry's volunteers defeated Black Hawk in battle. He lost 68 braves of his shrinking band. But the end did not come until 3 August 1832, when Black Hawk was forced back to the Mississippi near the junction of Bad Axe River. Scott had the steamboat ('fire canoe' to the Sauks) *Warrior* outfitted with cannon. When Black Hawk tried again to negotiate, perhaps surrender, troops fired upon his envoys. Small wonder; he sent a body of 150 men! Met with fire again under a truce flag, Black Hawk finally lost his patience and attacked the canister-spitting steamer with musket fire. The *Warrior* retreated after she almost ran out of firewood for her boilers.

Black Hawk lost 23 men to the floating battery that was the *Warrior).* But it was only the beginning of the end. Atkinson rushed 1300 reinforcements overland to Scott. The Army overran the Indians as they tried again to surrender. Atkinson's attack turned into a reversal of Raisin River, an eight-hour massacre of Indians. Only 30 warriors were taken prisoner. Some 200 Indians died, including women and children, clubbed or stabbed to death. The loss to the soldiery was just 20 men. Some 200 Sauks and Foxes managed to flee to the far bank of the Mississippi—where the Sioux, or Lakotas, waited like wolves. The Lakota pounced on them, scalping or enslaving the remnants of Black Hawk's pathetic 'army.'

Black Hawk escaped, but was seized by Winnebagos who surrendered him at Prairie du Chien for a reward of $100 and 20 horses. He was taken as a prisoner of war by Jeff Davis on the *Winnebago* for a year's imprisonment in Fort Armstrong on Rock Island and at Fortress Monroe. President Jackson then summoned him to Washington for a talk. Black Hawk told him, 'I took up the hatchet . . . to revenge injuries which my people could no longer endure'. The President did not quite know what to do with him. He was imprisoned again, then released and sent as an exhibit on tour. Old and quite tame now, he suddenly became a celebrity, a romantic and antique memento of a vanishing frontier east of the Mississippi. Only in the Sioux country and in Detroit, where he was burned in effigy because of long memories of massacres, did he have to be protected by guards.

When Jackson recognized Keokuk as the only chief of the Sauks and Foxes, the old Black Hawk's pride was hurt

Opposite page: Seminole chief **Micanopy** wore a peace medal when he posed for this portrait by McKenney and Hall. The circumstances surrounding the award of this medal are ironic, because Micanopy was a warrior, not a peacemaker.

Above: A detail of George Catlin's oil-on-canvas painting of **Chief Keokuk** in 1834 portrayed a great warrior with his hair in a savage-looking red roach. Actually, Keokuk was the pro-peace chief of the Sauks and Foxes. It was his rival, Black Hawk, who sided with the British during the War of 1812 and then fought the Americans (1832) in the Midwest. Keokuk had the bearing, wisdom and eloquence of a chief and was an influential man. The US government usually dealt with him and invited him to Washington in 1833 and 1837.

Opposite page: The Pennsylvania-born George Catlin (1796-1872) was one of the earliest, one of the most accurate, and one of the most talented of all the artists who pictured America's Indians. He practiced as a lawyer for two years in Philadelphia before trading his shingle for a palette. He became a New York portrait painter, but a turning point in his life came when he went west in 1832 on an expedition to study the Indians and paint them in their natural surroundings. **Horse Chief** was a typical Pawnee plains warrior that he met in 1832.

and he became depressed. But the government sent him on another barnstorming tour in 1837–38. He died after this grand tour, in Iowa. Even in death, the proud Black Hawk continued to be humiliated. White ghouls vandalized his grave to exhibit his decapitated head in one last tent side-show for the warrior-chief.

The Early Battles on the Plains

Washington, DC was reminded of its Indian wards not only by the vaudeville-like procession of Black Hawk, but also by a series of visits to the capital by tribal delegations. They were expected to report back home about the kindly feelings of the Great White Father toward his Indian children, after seeing the power and sheer numbers of the white man's world. The emissaries were wined and dined; their portraits painted by Charles Bird King such as the Pawnee delegation pictured on pages 86–7 (in later years they were photographed, instead), their greasy buckskins replaced with surplus Army officers' uniforms.

In the new West that lay beyond the Mississippi, the Army was faced with an impossible task, guarding a frontier stretching 6000 miles from Canada to Mexico, its horizons extending toward a sunset somewhere out in infinity. Half a continent was to be patrolled and policed by a few under-strength regiments of infantry and dragoons (cavalry) from a few strategically placed forts. Luckily—*very* luckily—for the soldiers, the trans-Mississippi Indians were not generally hostile until well after the California Gold Rush of 1849, for the entire Army totalled only 16,000 men and officers in 1860 and only 37,000 as late as 1870. And not all of the Army was in the West to face 75,000 plains Indians. These included 16,000 people of the power-ful Lakota (Dakota) tribe, alone. Even with their cannon, mostly howitzers, with rifles replacing smoothbore muskets, and (*circa* 1855) with .69 caliber conical and hollow minié balls improving the range and accuracy of their weapons, the soldiers were overwhelmed in most actions. Western author Emerson Hough estimated that there were 200 pitched battles (more likely skirmishes, though bloody affairs) between 1869 and 1875 alone.

The plains tribes, which lived by hunting buffalo, con-stituted about a fifth of the 360,000 trans-Mississippi natives. California and the Pacific Northwest were popu-lous areas. The 12,000 Navajos of Arizona and New Mexico were warlike people until crushed by Kit Carson in 1864. Small in numbers, the Apaches of Arizona and New Mexico were even more ferocious than Sioux, Kiowas or Comanches. They dominated the Southwest from the 1860s through the 1880s. Unlike the High Plains Indians, they were largely guerrilla 'infantry', skilled at hiding in the moun-tains and fighting on foot, though they had horses.

The Indians of the High Plains continued their age-old tradition of warring against one another after the whites arrived on the scene. The war-bonneted Sioux—Oglalas, Tetons and other bands—dominated the High Plains from the Mexican War through the 1870s. They were the arche-types of all warriors of these steppes and indeed, finally became the symbols of all American Indians. The 4000 fighting Sioux warriors were surpassed as horsemen only by the Comanches, dubbed the 'Lords of the South Plains'

Left: By 1847 photographers like Thomas M Easterby were making daguerreotype pictures of the Sauk chief **Keokuk**.

because they were superb natural cavalry.

The Sioux's friends and allies were Cheyennes and Arapahos, also Comanches and Kiowas to the south, though they had driven the Kiowas from their original range in the Black Hills. Enemies of the Sioux were the Crows or Absarokas (Bird People), the Pawnees and the Shoshones. Their other old rivals, the more sedentary Arickaras and Mandans were no longer a threat because of their reduction by warfare and white man's diseases, especially cholera and smallpox. The Five Civilized Tribes of Oklahoma's Indian Territory were numerous, 84,000 souls, but posed no danger to the whites.

Frontier posts varied from miserable, feverish Fort Gibson, nicknamed 'The Graveyard of the Army', to such cozy quarters as Fort Leavenworth, an early rival in terms of creature comforts to the choice quarters of San Fran-cisco's Presidio and San Antonio's Fort Sam Houston. The best of the posts introduced civilization to the Indian West in the shape of grainfields, vegetable gardens, hay camps, sawmills, cattle herds, improved roads, fords, ferries and bridges. The Army interpreted the West to curious Eastern-ers by means of its artists, like Captain Seth Eastman, and its scientist-officers, John C Fremont, Dr Elliott Coues and John Gregory Bourke.

The first trans-Mississippi skirmish occurred in 1829, between the minor Winnebago War (1827) around Fort Crawford and Prairie du Chien, and the Black Hawk War. It involved Kiowas and Comanches. Major Bennett Riley, later military governor of conquered California, took a battalion of the 6th Infantry from Fort Leavenworth to escort a New Mexico-bound wagon train of 60 men and 36 vehicles, under plainsman Charles Bent. A war party of 100 cut off the train's herd of cattle just as Riley rendez-voused with the traders at Round Grove on 11 June. The Indians surrounded both caravan and troopers until Riley planted a round shot in a knot of warriors. The survivors of this cannonball scampered away and Riley dismissed the rest with a few rounds of 'grape' or grapeshot. Only one soldier was killed, but he had 13 arrows imbedded in him.

Riley escorted the caravan a short distance across the line, the Arkansas River, into Mexico, then fell back to the river to await the return of the wagons. The train was harassed, but made it safely to Santa Fe, then returned under an escort of cavalry, either lancers or dragoons, to the crossing of the Arkansas.

While bivouacked, Riley was the victim of Indian forays. He lost stock, four men, and his temper. Because he had only foot soldiers, and could not pursue the raiding horse-men, he growled, 'If we had been mounted, we could have beaten them to pieces'. He returned to Fort Leavenworth on 8 November after a long, difficult, but generally success-ful mission.

William Becknell had pioneered the Santa Fe Trade in 1821. While traders complained of being molested by Indians, no fort was placed at the Great Bend of the Arkansas or at the mouth of the Little Arkansas, as sug-gested. In 1827 far-off Fort Leavenworth was supposed to do the trick. However, Riley's expedition was an experi-ment not repeated for years. Escorts were not really neces-sary on the Santa Fe Trail between 1829 and 1843. Probably the Kiowas and Comanches left travelers alone, at least north of the Arkansas ford, in order to continue receiving presents from the whites, including precious arms and ammunition.

Opposite page: At Fort Union on the Missouri River, George Catlin spied – and painted – **Buffalo's Backfat.** He was a Kainah or Blood, a representative member of the three-tribe Blackfoot confederation that was composed of Bloods, Piegans or Pikuni, and Blackfeet proper or Siksika. All were closely related Algonquian-speaking peoples with a range from the Rockies to the Yellowstone River and on up to the North Saskatchewan. The Blackfoot bands were often very hostile to whites – and to other Indian tribes, for that matter. For example, the only serious trouble that Meriwether Lewis encountered in all of his 1804-05 expeditionary travels was a clash with Blackfoot raiders.

Left: **Mint** was the name of this Mandan woman painted in 1832 by Catlin. The Mandans were an important sedentary tribe on the upper Missouri River until disease, especially a deadly smallpox epidemic of 1837, annihilated them. The few survivors sought refuge with other tribes. Culturally, they were much closer to the Hidatsa and Arikara than to the Sioux, their enemies, though they were, themselves, of Siouan stock. Lewis and Clark, Catlin, and Prince Maximilian were all intrigued by these villagers and wrote a good deal about them.

Below: Catlin was impressed by the stockaded Mandan villages near the Junction of the Knife River and the Missouri. They had elaborate ceremonies like the **Bull Dance** (below); the self-torturing Okeepa, a sun dance; and, like the Pueblos, a corn dance. They were farmers who raised beans, maize, squash, pumpkins and tobacco. They also hunted buffalo, fished, and gleaned roots and berries. Their distinctive dome-shaped lodges were of packed earth supported by poles and were partly underground. Because of their brown hair, hazel and gray eyes and light complexions, some whites took the sedentary Mandans for a tribe of long-lost, wandering Welshmen.

B-4621

Opposite page: **Sam Houston** lived with Cherokees as a young man. Like Crockett, he served under Old Hickory in the Creek War. When Major Montgomery was killed in the Battle of Horseshoe Bend, Ensign Houston led a charge, jumping over log barricades with an arrow imbedded in one thigh. He had it pulled out, but lost so much blood that Jackson sent him to the rear. He returned to the fray only to be shot twice in the right arm, nearly losing it. One ball had to be left in the arm.

Right: **Bent's Fort**, alias Fort William, was built in Colorado on the Arkansas River near the mouth of the Purgatoire in 1833 by Charles Bent and Ceran St Vrain. It immediately became a center for trade with the Indians and Mexicans and was visited by almost all travelers bound for either the Far West or the Southwest via the Santa Fe Trail. Charles' brother and partner William, sole owner in 1849, blew up the fort when the US Government offered him too low a price for the post.

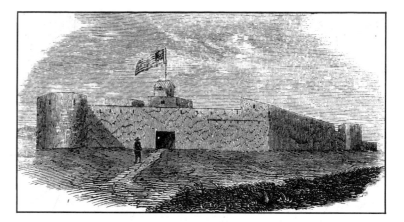

The Army's Corps of Rangers was reorganized into the 1st Dragoons in 1832. The regiment attracted first-rate officers like Colonel Richard Dodge, Captains Stephen W Kearny, Nathan Boone (Daniel's son), Philip St George Cooke and E V Sumner. Its enlisted men also were a sort of elite which a British traveler, Charles J Latrobe, contrasted with the American 'scum' and 'worthless' Irish and German immigrants who filled the ranks of the infantry.

To carry out what Congress called, optimistically, 'the more perfect defense of the frontiers', Dodge took the Dragoons on an 1834 expedition to the villages of the so-called Pawnee Picts, actually Wichitas, in hopes of rescuing white captives while 'showing the flag' to Pawnees, Kiowas and Comanches. Although Dodge's sick list was swollen by the excessive heat of that summer, the expedition—which had no trouble with Indians—was a success. It impressed the Indians with the mobility of mounted troops, as compared with the 'walk-a-heaps', or infantry. So did an even more ambitious expedition by Dodge in 1835, all the way to the Rocky Mountains.

Texas, a Republic from 1836 to 1845, had plenty of Indian troubles particularly from the Comanches during its independence and its early years of statehood.

Closely allied to the Comanches were the Kiowas and the Kiowa-Apaches. The latter were actually Apaches, as the Lipans of Texas were also. The Kiowa-Apaches kept their language, but otherwise merged into the South Plains Kiowa horse culture.

The public was particularly enraged by the Comanches because of their tradition of enslaving Anglo as well as Mexican captives, including young women. Most of the other hostile tribes of Texas by the 1840s were weak from years of fighting—the once-cannibalistic Karankawas, the Wichitas, the Caddos, and the offshoot of the Jicarilla Apaches, the Lipans. The sedentary Alabama-Coushattas of East Texas and the Pueblo-like Tiguas of the El Paso area were peaceable. As for the Tonkawas, or 'Tonks', they were friends of the whites and scouted for them against a common enemy, the Comanches. Chief Placido, their leader, used to brag that he had never shed a white man's blood.

Because Texas had disbanded its army in 1835, the campaign against the Comanches was led by the newly formed Texas Rangers. Drunkenness and lack of discipline were the twin curses of the early Texas Rangers and, with their 'greenness' as Indian fighters, led to such debacles as the 1837 pursuit of Comanches in which the Indians turned on them and killed more than half of them. The next year saw the **Council House Fight**, in which the Rangers killed 35 Comanches and captured 29, but only because of treachery which recalled Jesup's seizure of Osceola in Florida.

Chiefs brought 65 warriors and one captive white girl to a parley in San Antonio. The Texans took the chiefs hostage in an effort to regain other captives—which the Indians said they did not have. A fight broke out. The Council House affair led directly to Buffalo Hump's sweep down the Guadalupe Valley, all the way to the coast. At Linnville, the townsfolk fled to their boats in the Gulf. But two dozen citizens were too slow and were killed. In their retaliation for Council House, the Comanches also burned Victoria. But on their return northward, they were intercepted by a volunteer force at Plum Creek, near Lockhart. The Texans lost only one man and estimated (probably too optimistically) that they killed 100 Indians.

Cherokees came to East Texas, then Mexican Territory, before the Trail of Tears to Oklahoma. They settled in the 1820s around the Trinity, Neches and Angelina Rivers.

Above: An unknown hack artist transformed **Sam Houston** into a bearded Sam Grant look-alike though he fought Creeks at age 20.

Above: George Catlin's **The White Cloud**, a chief of the Iowa Indians, showed the facial painting and bear-claw necklace of a typical 'wild' warrior. By 1820 the Iowas had been pushed out of the area that became a territory named for them in 1836 and a state in 1844 by more aggressive tribes like the Sioux and Potawatomis.

Principal Expeditions and Trails into the Frontier

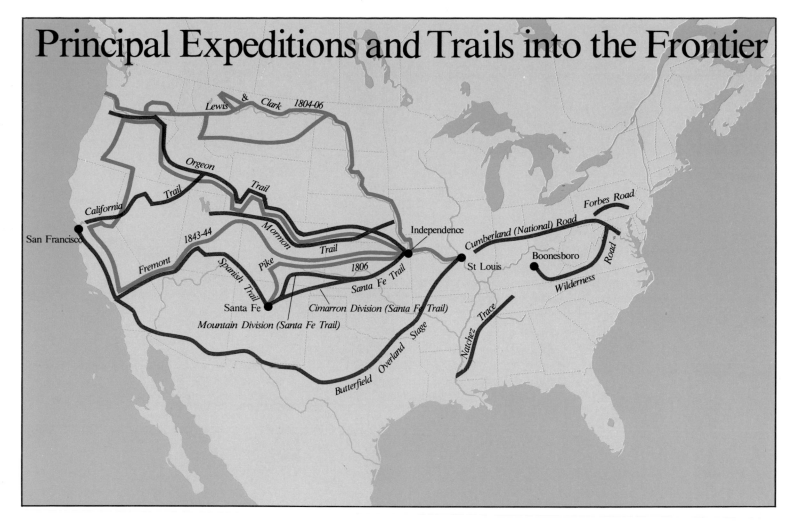

Chief Bowles remained neutral in the Texas Revolution because of a treaty with the Anglos guaranteeing Cherokee lands. The treaty was rejected by the Republic's Senate, however, in 1837. Sam Houston, the first President of Texas, was a friend of the Indians, but not so his successor, Mirabeau Lamar. He said that 'The white man and the red man cannot dwell in harmony together. Nature forbids it'. He sent his army to attack the Cherokees in 1839. Chief Bowles was defeated and killed, 16 July, on the Neches River west of Tyler. The survivors were driven from Texas.

Fortunately for the Texas Rangers, John Coffee Hays, an ex-surveyor, joined the corps in 1840 and improved morale considerably. He was a disciplinarian, a natural leader and one of the most skilled Indian fighters in Western history. He armed his men with the new Colt (Walker type) six-shooters. These, with the later Spencer, Henry and Winchester repeating rifles, evened the odds, somewhat, between Indians and outnumbered whites. More than any other man, Jack Hays was responsible for the glorious legend of the Rangers. Hays went to the California Gold Rush in 1849 via the Gila Trail and later became Sheriff of San Francisco and Surveyor General of California. But there were other great Rangers—Ben McCulloch, W A A (Bigfoot) Wallace and John S Ford.

The line of 13 forts spotted across West Texas by the Army between 1849 and 1852 could not repel Comanche raids into the Lone Star State. Luckily, another man of Hays's caliber appeared in the Rangers. Governor Hardin Runnells decided to help out the Seminole War veteran, Colonel David Twiggs of the 2d Dragoons, by mustering five companies of Rangers under 'Rip' Ford. On 11 May 1858, Ford and just 100 Texas Rangers swooped down the

Above: **See-non-ty-a** was an Iowa medicine man who posed for Catlin. He was not a chief but a priest or sorcerer, usually called a shaman, although the term is of Asian, not American, origin.

Canadian River Valley on a Comanche village of 300 braves near the Antelope Hills of Oklahoma. After seven hours of desperate combat, the Indians fled the scene, leaving 76 dead. Ford burned their village and headed south, back to Texas.

The most famous of all Indian captivities in Texas was that of Cynthia Ann Parker, captured 19 May 1836 by Caddos who misrepresented themselves as friendlies at Parker's Fort near Mexia. They fell on the settlers, killing four men and a boy, wounded others, and took five prisoners. All but Cynthia were returned; she was sold to the Comanches. She married Chief Peta Nocona and among their three children was the great half-breed Comanche war chief, Quanah Parker. Cynthia Parker was reluctantly 'rescued' during the Battle of Pease River in 1860, but, after 24 years as a Comanche, she was unhappy in her new environment and died in 1864.

The last of the classic captivities was that of Olive Oatman, seized in 1851 on the Gila River in Arizona by Yavapai Indians after her Mormon family was massacred. (For years, the Tonto Apaches were blamed for the atrocity.) She was traded to the Mojaves and finally ransomed at Fort Yuma, California in 1856.

The Mexican War

In 1846 President James K Polk, a protege of Andrew Jackson, turned the Government's attention from the Indians to the problems with Mexico. They would provide hardly a sideshow during the Mexican War. The Tennesseean was elected on a political platform whose widest plank was the idea of Manifest Destiny. In endorsing the philosophy of territorial expansion westward, Polk annexed Texas in 1845 and secured a compromise joint occupation of Oregon Territory with Great Britain. He then got Zachary Taylor to draw Mexico into a war by ordering one of his old Seminole War dragoon companies to scout in the disputed no man's land alongside the Rio Grande.

Indians played only minor roles. The Comanches did not impede Taylor's invasion of northern Mexico from Texas. Only in one remote theater of the war was there Indian trouble. Colonel Stephen Watts Kearny, leading his Army of the West over the Santa Fe and Gila Trails to conquer California in a truly magnificent march, accidentally stirred up a revolt reminiscent of Popé's rebellion of 1680, which drove the Spaniards from New Mexico. And, again accidentally his troopers got themselves involved in difficulties with the Navajos.

On 5 August 1846, with his scout, Tom (Broken Hand) Fitzpatrick, by his side, Kearny promised the people of New Mexico protection from raids by Navajos and Apaches. His words did not even win the affection of the *Hispanos*, much less the Navajos. Instead, the former combined with the supposedly gentle Pueblo Indians of Taos in a January 1847 revolt, after he left Santa Fe. Colonel Alexander W Doniphan, left in command, had no trouble in the capital. But he learned that the Mexicans of San Fernando de Taos and the *Taoseños* of the adjacent pueblo, 70 miles to the north, had murdered the first American governor of New Mexico, Charles Bent. He was scalped while still alive and then killed. Others of his associates were killed, too.

Doniphan responded to the murders by sending Lieutenant Colonel Sterling Price with 400 dragoons and

infantry, plus Lieutenant Alexander B Dwyer's six-pounder and four 12-pound mountain howitzers. Price found the road blocked at La Cañada by 800 Taos Indians and Mexicans. He cleared them out with his artillery, despite their attempts to cut off his force from its ammunition and supply wagons in the rear. By nightfall, the village was in American hands. They lost two dead and eight wounded to their foe's 36 dead and 50 wounded. Price waited for the arrival of another six-pounder and ammunition, then resumed his march at the end of January, brushing aside more skirmishers in the mountain passes.

Price's men arrived at **Taos Pueblo** nearly exhausted and half-frozen from marching through snow in bitter cold weather and camping for three nights without tents. But tired as they were, they went into action immediately. The artillery pounded the multi-storied, apartment-like pueblo and the Spanish mission church. But the cannon fire barely

Above: The Spaniards gave the name of Pueblos to people of four different language stocks who lived in adobe or stone houses. **Taos**, New Mexico, was both a typical and an atypical Indian pueblo. It resembled others in its architecture and sedentary life-style but differed in that it attracted successive waves of outsiders – Spaniards, Mexicans and *Yanquis* – to build up an adjacent village. The latter bustled with activity in the heyday of the Southwest fur trade. Tucked between the Rocky Mountains and the Sangre de Cristo Mountains at 7000 feet, Taos has managed to preserve its cultural integrity in spite of the presence of the nearby *Anglo* town.

Left: The **Taoseños** and other Pueblos were generally peaceful after the 1680 revolt that drove the Spanish from New Mexico. General Stephen Kearny captured Santa Fe in 1846 without a fight and pushed on to conquer California. He left Charles Bent as governor of the new territory. In January of 1847, the resentment of the **Taos Indians** at Bent's trading with their enemies led them to join Mexicans in a revolt. Among Americans killed and scalped at Taos and Mora was Bent. Colonel Sterling Price battered the Pueblo's church (turned into a fort) with his cannon, put down the uprising and executed the ring-leaders.

dented the massive walls of adobe brick, so Price retired to San Fernando de Taos to rest and warm his men.

Come morning, the artillery opened up again. Once more, the Colonel saw that the fire had little effect. He fired a second barrage, but as a diversion, a cover under which he moved his infantry in. They came under sharp fire from both church and pueblo. Several men dropped as they unsuccessfully tried to rush the heavy doors of the mission. Then Dwyer somehow managed to get one of his heavy guns within close range, 60 yards, and blasted a hole in the church wall. The artillerymen dragged the piece forward and, from only 30 yards, filled the opening with grapeshot to clear the immediate interior. Soldiers scrambled their way through the breach and stormed the church. Its surviving defenders fled toward the hills, but many were picked off as they ran. With the church fallen, the pueblo now begged for mercy. Price let them have it, but he quickly tried and executed the ringleaders in Bent's murder. The 650 defenders lost 150 dead and many more wounded.

Now it was the Navajos' turn to be dealt with, as Kearny had promised. They would be accused of stealing more than 3500 horses, almost 13,000 cattle and about 300,000 sheep from New Mexican or Pueblo settlers between 1847 and 1867. No accurate count of enslaved children was made. (It must be noted that the *Hispanos*, in counter-raids, also enslaved Navajo children for household servants.) The

toll exacted by the Navajos would have been much greater, were it not for the presence of the Army.

Colonel Doniphan first tried to stop Navajo marauding in a winter campaign in 1846. His three columns of 330 men found few Indians to chase, but they covered a lot of difficult unknown territory in bad weather with inadequate clothing, food, forage and firewood. In fact, they were lucky to make it to the rendezvous of Bear Spring. The Navajos were impressed by this kind of tough campaigning, even if it only involved the Army making its presence known without fighting. The tribe signed a worthless treaty, probably to keep the Army from invading the inner sanctum of its homeland, the deep gash of Cañón de Chelly near the Arizona-New Mexico line. The agreement was voided by the Indians quite soon, and an intermittent Navajo War, or series of campaigns, continued until the Civil War. During that larger conflict, Colonel Kit Carson (1863–1864) raided right through the heart of Navajo country, including Cañón de Chelly, destroying hogans, cornfields, sheep and peach trees in a scorched earth campaign that whipped the Navajos into becoming peaceful Indians, forever.

In a program like the Cherokee removal, the Navajos were exiled from their homeland to a reservation at Bosque Redondo, near Fort Sumner, on the Pecos River. The 300-mile march, which recalled the Trail of Tears, was called The Long Walk. The Navajos lived in misery until

Below left: George Catlin's imaginative brush caught a Comanche, at a gallop, about to lance to death an Osage warrior. The *Comanches* were the 'Lords of the Southern Plains.'

Above left: **Little Bluff** was head chief of the Kiowas (1834-1864). The Kiowas were buffalo hunters, Plains nomads almost the equal of Comanches as natural horsemen.

Above: Catlin's portraits of such Indians as **The Light** (1831) re-established the notion of native Americans as 'noble redmen' just before the westward push to the Pacific.

Above: **Charles A May** of the 2nd Dragoons was an earlier version of the 7th Cavalry's George A Custer. He was the Indian-fighting Army's *beau sabreur* 20 years before Custer. The historian of the Regiment, T F Rodenbough, described young May – 'the youthful and impetuous subaltern' – as having literally vaulted into his second lieutenant's commission. President Jackson gave him an appointment to the crack new dragoons after seeing him perform feats of horsemanship. May came to national attention in the Mexican War. At the Battle of Resaca de la Palma, 9 May 1846, General Mariano Arista made excellent defensive use of a *resaca* or old river bed to block the narrow Matamoros road through mesquite and chaparral thickets. General Taylor ordered his gunners to manhandle their cannon aside to let May through. He was 30, a colorful figure like Custer, but the Captain's long wavy hair was black, not blond, and he wore fierce moustachios and a full beard. He got his troopers in a column of fours and led a wild saber charge. (Jealous critics said that May's horses ran away with him.) But he penetrated to the *resaca* and temporarily drove the Mexican artillerymen from their guns. May lost nine men killed and 10 wounded and had 18 horses killed and others hurt. He got the rest of his men out safely and brought along that *rara avis* to an untried American army – a captured Mexican general, R D de la Vega. His success – de la Vega was the subject of popular prints – was hardly overnight. His apprenticeship was in the Second Seminole War. He did well on numerous scouts or reconnaissances of the Florida peninsula and several bloody skirmishes in the saw grass and palmettos or pine barrens. In 1837, at the Battle of Welika Pond, May captured the Seminole chief, King Philip, father of warrior Coacoochee or Wildcat. And when Colonel Worth forwarded officers' dispatches on operations in 1841 to superiors, he solicited a 'particular examination of those of Captain May.' The gallant cavalryman was honored with three brevet promotions during the Mexican War for Palo Alto, Resaca de la Palma and climactic Buena Vista. At Buena Vista, Lieutenant Colonel May's squadron escorted General Taylor and then routed the Mexican cavalry to send Santa Anna in retreat.

the government took pity on them in 1868 and let them return west to the large reservation they now hold.

Skirmishes in the Pacific Northwest

Far from New Mexico, a minor Indian massacre of 1847 led to an era of war in the Pacific Northwest. Trouble had been brewing for years around the missionary compounds near the end of the Oregon Trail. It was inflamed by increasing numbers of immigrants after 1846 to the Willamette and Columbia River valleys. These new whites were not the easy-going mountain men with whom the Indians got along. They were farmers who came to stay, and to spread out; or they were missionaries. Catholics like the Jesuit Father Joseph De Smet were tolerated because they were less disruptive; they accepted the 'pagan' ways of the Indians better than their Protestant peers. The latter, Presbyterians, not only proselytized and converted the Indians, but also acted as propagandists for Oregon settlement. They also meddled in Indian customs and traditions.

Marcus and Narcissa Whitman were the most 'successful' (that is, aggressive) of these. Brusque and judgmental was Marcus's paternalism; Narcissa was aloof and critical. They tended to divide Indians into only two categories, the devout (Christian) and the heathen, regardless of tribal affiliations.

Resentment of the meddling Whitmans became hatred when they were blamed for the measles epidemic which was brought to the Cayuse Indians by American immigrants. On 29 November 1847, Chief Tilokaikt and a warrior, Tomahas, asked Dr Whitman for medicine. As he stooped to get it for them, the Chief tomahawked him repeatedly. Other Indians now entered the mission at Waiilatpu on the Walla Walla River. They shot Narcissa to death along with a dozen men. Five men, eight women and 34 children were taken as hostage-prisoners.

Father Jean Baptiste Brouillet found the bodies. He warned other missionaries, the Spaldings, and they fled their Lapwai Mission. (Even so, because he was not harmed and because he was a rival of the Protestants, Brouillet was blamed by bigots for the massacre.)

Peter Skene Ogden, agent for the Hudson's Bay Company, was able to negotiate the captives' release with a ransom of blankets, shirts, guns and ammunition.

With one hand, the Provisional Oregon Legislature now created a peace commission, led by the able Joel Palmer. But with the other it put into the field a punitive party of 550 citizen-soldiers. It was led by an early example of that frontier phenomenon, the fighting parson.

This fire-and-brimstone preacher *cum* Indian fighter, Cornelius Gilliam, was as inept as he was fanatical. He destroyed a camp of Cayuses in February 1848, but they were peaceful Indians, not involved in the Waiilatpu tragedy. Joel Palmer now resigned from the peace commission in disgust. Soon, 250 Palouses entered the war and defeated the hot-head, Gilliam, driving him back to the mission.

Before he killed himself accidentally, Gilliam narrowly missed uniting the major upper-Columbia tribes—the Nez Percés, Walla Wallas and Umatillas, as well as the Palouses and Cayuses—against the whites. But the Cayuses wasted away and in 1850, six leaders, including Tilokaikt and Tomahas, surrendered. They were given a hasty trial at Oregon City and hanged. However, that same year, the

seeds of future wars were sown by the Oregon Donation Land Law, which opened Indian lands to homesteaders.

Conflict in California

Indian conflicts erupted in California shortly after the discovery of gold in 1848, although most tribes there were rather peaceful. The 49ers disrupted the gleaning of seeds and roots by the so-called Digger Indians, as well as their hunting of deer and other game. Malnutrition turned to starvation and brought on resistance and violence. Soon, whites were shooting Indians on sight, and the natives replied in kind. Shootings probably accounted for only 10 per cent of the Indians' casualties, however; the rest were killed by disease—especially malaria, cholera and smallpox —and by starvation. The number of Indians dropped from 100,000 in 1846 to barely 30,000 in 1851, when the governor of California predicted—practically preached—a war of extermination against them.

The only conflict on any scale in California, besides the later Modoc War, was the **Mariposa Indian War**. It was caused by gold-hungry 49ers, but did not break out until the end of 1850. Chief Tenaya led some 350 Miwoks, Chowchillas and Yokuts against miners and burned the trading posts of James D Savage, called The King of the Tulare Indians. Appointed major of the Mariposa Battalion of state militia, Savage led a Sierra Nevada expedition which killed few Indians, but which made the first effective discovery of Yosemite Valley in 1851.

Trouble also occurred far to the south of the gold mines. The Yumas and Mojaves controlled the Colorado River crossings of the Gila Trail to California. They tangled with Spaniards, Mexicans, mountain men like Jedediah Smith and, finally, gold-seekers. The commandant of Fort Yuma, Major Samuel P Heintzelman, was criticized for failing to

Top: Scalping was practiced in Europe, Asia and Africa as well as in North America by the Indians. White men in North America also exercised this custom, often to receive bounties. *Above:* Conflicts with the Indians continued in the southwest. *Over:* Scalp dances were part of the ritual that celebrated the transferral of power from the dead enemy to the victor, which actually took place during the act of scalping. The dances were not a celebration of the taking of war trophies.

try to rescue Olive Oatman, a captive of the Indians, in 1851. His excuse was that she might be across the Gila in the Mexican state of Sonora.

But there were some officers of a different sort at Fort Yuma. One was Lieutenant Thomas W Sweeny, a New York Irishman from Cork nicknamed 'Fighting Tom'. He was one-armed, like the more famous Phil Kearny, having lost a limb at Churubusco in the Mexican War. Once he took only 25 men into the Baja California desert against the Yumas. He burned villages and crops and forced 150 hostiles to surrender. Later, he was active in the first (1855–56) Sioux campaign.

WAR CLOUDS
1850-1865

In the 1850s the Army was installed across the frontier as a peace-keeping force, and for much of the time there were no major campaigns since the Army was consumed with the War Between the States. The period was marked by the wars in the Pacific Northwest and lesser skirmishes, often provoked by overzealous and brutal Army volunteers, as Indians were being pushed into allocated territories. In 1864 the famous scout, Kit Carson, brought about the largest Indian surrender in history, in Cañon de Chelly.

Gold-hungry emigrants did not tarry on the plains west of the Missouri River. They hardly paused to curse the country's heat, their thirst and the Indians as they hurried toward their promised land of El Dorado. But they left behind them a wide swathe of destruction. For hundreds of miles along the so-called Coasts of the Nebraska, the banks of the Platte, they stripped away the grass and firewood and collected every dried-up buffalo chip for kindling cookfires. They killed all game, especially the Indians' staff of life, the buffalo. They fouled campgrounds with animal and human waste and polluted springs and streams all along the deep-cut, braided ruts of the Overland Trail.

The Plains Indians, with a patience so strong as to invite caricature, stoically put up with greedy and intolerant white travelers. They hardly interfered with the tidal wave of humanity rolling toward California. Hostilities were usually limited to thefts of livestock for food or pilfering of property, often out of sheer curiosity. Begging by Indians for hand-outs of beef and beans sometimes deteriorated into bullying, but violence was rare. Murder was confined almost entirely to the Humboldt River of Nevada, where Paiutes picked off stragglers.

The worst effect of the Gold Rush was the splitting in two of the vast buffalo herd of the Plains. This was accelerated by the building of the trans-continental railroad in the 1860s. By the mid-70s the herds of bison were declining to extinction.

In 1851 Indian Agent Tom Fitzpatrick joined his boss, Superintendent of Indian Affairs David D Mitchell, in a treaty-making council at Fort Laramie, Wyoming. The Arapaho chief, Little Raven, described Fitzpatrick as the one really fair agent that his people had ever known. Fitzpatrick was best known as Broken Hand because an exploding rifle had blown off several fingers. He was also

Opposite page: Unable to get 'action' shots of **Paiutes** in 1872, John K (Jack) Hillers resorted to posing three braves in costume.

called White Hair because a scare thrown into him by a band of Gros Ventres was said to have bleached his hair overnight.

To Fitz's amazement, 10,000 Indians camped around the post. The entire Army, stretched from Maine to California, totaled only 10,000 men, and that was on paper. Its actual strength was probably closer to 8000.

The dominant Sioux were present in force, accompanied by their loyal allies, the Northern Cheyennes and Arapahos. The Hidatsas and Mandans came to the Big Talk, too. Enemies of the Sioux—the Crows or Absarokas, the Gros Ventres, Arikaras, even Assiniboines from far-off Canada— also dragged their *travois* to the Laramie Fork of the North Platte. The Pawnees were too hostile to the Dakotas (Lakota), or Sioux, to show up. Curiously, the Kiowas and Comanches, friends of the Sioux, chose not to come. They told friendly whites that there would be too many horse thieves, meaning both Crows and Dakotas. But the wary Shoshones made an appearance, led by their friend and protector, Jim Bridger. Jim, nicknamed Old Gabe, promised to make sure that the Sioux were peaceful.

Several times during the proceedings, inter-tribal rivalries almost boiled over into violent clashes. But they were averted by the prompt actions of the 270 troopers who policed the Big Talk.

Earlier, the US Government had promised the tribes a vast country of their own—one great reservation beyond the Missouri and the so-called Permanent Indian Frontier. But now that promise was abandoned as a result of the California Gold Rush and the growth of the Concept of Manifest Destiny, which held that it was ordained by God that the persistent westward drive of white Americans should, rightfully, fill the continent from sea to sea.

By Fitzpatrick's 'Treaty of Horse Creek', the Indians not only guaranteed travelers the right of safe passage through Indian country and permitted the building of roads and forts, but they also accepted their own allocation to specific tribal 'territories', reservation-like tracts, with boundaries as fixed as those of the states of the Union. And they promised to abstain from warring on each other. The Federal Government guaranteed that the Indians' lands would be theirs forever. Weary of debate, the chiefs x'd their signatures to the document so that Broken Hand would give out the presents that he had promised them.

In 1853, at Fort Atkinson near the later site of Dodge City, Kansas, Fitzpatrick carried out a similar treaty-signing with the southern tribes that had refused to have anything to do with the Sioux at Laramie.

Broken Hand knew that intertribal warfare would continue. It was ingrained in the Indian's nature. Prowess in combat was ten times as important as skill in hunting. Indians would fight to gain territory, plunder or revenge, but most of all to gratify their lust for personal glory. And the greatest glory of all came from counting *coups* in hand-to-hand combat. He also knew that chiefs, in peace or war, had no authority to speak as sovereigns for all of their people. This idea was a conceit of functionaries in Washington who found it convenient to treat with Indian chiefs as if they were European princes or Asian potentates.

But Fitzpatrick was not banking solely on Indian Bureau paperwork to keep the peace. He put most of his faith in the string of forts in the West, weak as they were. The Army's strength had sagged to a dangerous low after the Mexican War's end in 1848. Its effective power was reduced further by epidemics of drunkenness, disease and desertion. Most of the rank and file was composed of the greenest of soldiery. Many were Irish and German immigrant boys, down on their luck and ready to try anything after the abject squalor and grinding poverty of Eastern tenements.

The ink was hardly dry on the two optimistic treaties when hostilities broke out between the Army and the powerful Teton Sioux. On 18 August 1854, six months after Fitzpatrick died of pneumonia in Washington while seeking approval of his treaties, a Miniconjou Sioux, High Forehead, visited his Brulé relatives and Oglala friends. Needing some cowhide, he left the 4000 Indians camped on the North Platte to receive their annuities, and shot an arrow into a Mormon's footsore cow. Probably the owner was on the point of leaving the beast behind, but he complained to Fort Laramie's commanding officer, Second Lieutenant Hugh B Fleming. Fleming was willing to negotiate for recompense, but was hesitant about arresting or punishing Indians without an Indian agent being present.

One of Fleming's subordinates, Brevet Second Lieutenant John L Grattan, begged permission to deal with the Sioux. He was just out of West Point and had not even received his commission. But he had frequently stated that his greatest desire was to fight the Sioux.

The cocky Grattan took only 30 volunteers. He was convinced that all Sioux were cowards. As for the Cheyennes, he bragged that, with ten good men, he would beat them. With an added ten, he would thrash all of the Plains tribes! As he left the post, he postured with absurd naivete, dramatically promising to 'conquer or die.'

The brevet lieutenant drew up his small force in a battle line in the camp of Conquering Bear's Brulés in the North Platte Valley west of Ash Hollow. Through a drunken interpreter, Grattan lectured and abused the Sioux. The chief offered horses in payment for the cow, but would not deliver up the Miniconjou. The drunkard now tried to throw a scare into the Sioux. He told them that the Army was coming for them and 'would eat their hearts, raw.'

Conquering Bear tried to calm the hotheads on both sides of the quarrel, but someone opened fire. Possibly it was all an accident—a nervous private discharging his musket by mistake. But musket firing came from both sides

Right: Artist Charles M Russell documented a familiar incident on Montana's grassy plains – an Indian scouting party on a bluff awaiting the approach of whites unaware of their presence.

and the cannoneers with Grattan's two menacing howitzers took the first shot as a signal. One of them dropped a round almost on top of Conquering Bear, mortally wounding the chief as he cried out to his people not to shoot.

Now the village turned into a hornets' nest, even before other Sioux rode up to join the fray. The foolish Grattan tried to fall back to the fort, but the Sioux easily cut off his retreat. The combat came to be called **Grattan's Massacre** because the Indians destroyed his command to the last man. (One soldier made it to Fort Laramie but died there of his wounds.)

Older men prevented the angry young braves from attacking the fort, where Fleming had only 42 men. After stripping the warehouse of the annuity goods, the Tetons broke up into small bands.

The Commissioner of Indian Affairs decreed that the Army had exceeded its authority. Grattan's action was illegal; he had no right to arrest Indians for thefts. But Secretary of War Jefferson Davis called the Grattan affair part of a deliberate plan by the Sioux to loot all annuity and trade goods in their area. And he wanted to make an example of the Sioux for giving the Army such a black eye.

Jeff Davis had just the man for the job of avenging Grattan. Colonel William S Harney, born in 1800, was a steel-hard soldier still, tempered by Seminole and Mexican War service. The fiery-tongued, profane six-footer was said to have hated all Indians with a passion ever since he had been obliged to run ignominiously for cover—and for his life—in his underwear during the Second Florida War. Cowering in palmetto and sawgrass, scratching mosquito welts, he had had plenty of time to work up a lasting hatred for all redskins, not just Seminoles.

Harney led 600 infantry, cavalry and artillery out of Fort Kearny, Nebraska to **Ash Hollow**, on 24 August 1855. For some reason, fatalism perhaps, Conquering Bear's successor, Chief Little Thunder, made no attempt to avoid Army retribution. Or possibly he was paralyzed with indecision. He waited Harney's coming with only the 250 braves who had destroyed Grattan's unit. For once, the Army outnumbered its opponents.

Harney gave the Brulés a token ultimatum on 3 September. When he left the fort, he had said, 'By God, I'm for battle. No peace'. Not surprisingly, he did not wait for an answer but fell on the village. His infantry and cavalry advanced in a quick pincers movement of two columns. The fury of their charge so surprised the Sioux, overconfident after their easy victory over Grattan, that they fled after only a slight resistance. Revenge was complete. Harney killed 85 warriors. Counting women and children, the dead totaled more than 100. He took four braves as prisoner-hostages and rounded up 70 women and children. His own losses were but five dead and seven wounded. Small wonder that the Sioux, ever after, called Harney 'The Butcher.'

After this Battle of Ash Hollow, actually fought at Blue Water Creek west of that Emigrant Trail camping ground toward Grattan's battle field, Harney moved up the California-Oregon Trail to talk to the Sioux at Fort Laramie. He told them to stay away from the White Man's Road—or else. He demanded that Indian robbers and murderers surrender. Several chiefs and warriors, including Spotted Tail, gave themselves up and were locked away in Fort Leavenworth.

The bellicose colonel suspended all trade with the Sioux, then marched smack through the heart of the Dakotas'

country, inviting a brawl. But there were no takers. He circled the Sioux holy land, the Black Hills, and descended the White River to winter at Fort Pierre. In March of 1856 at that old fur trade 'factory' he exacted a peace treaty from the Tetons that reiterated and confirmed Fitzpatrick's document of 1851.

Harney had punished only the Tetons. The Cheyennes continued to annoy Overland Trail travelers. So the Army called upon another tough old soldier to lead a company against them. He was 60-year-old Colonel Edwin Vose Sumner.

Ironically, the veteran Indian fighter, commanding officer of Fort Leavenworth, was Harney's worst enemy or, at least, rival. Made a brevet colonel in 1840 for distinguished Florida service, Harney was promoted to Colonel of the Second Dragoons before the Mexican War, making him the nation's ranking cavalry officer. However, he clashed with General Winfield S Scott, Commanding General of the Army. Scott thought him too impetuous; for his part, the dragoon sized up Scott as weak-willed.

Scott replaced Harney with his own favorite, Sumner. Harney refused to step down and appealed to higher-ups. Finally, Harney won and Sumner lost. The former was restored to command of the 2nd Dragoons. But the latter performed well in the Mexican War, earning the brevet of brigadier general and the nickname of Bull, or Old Bull. Originally, it was Bull Head. The name was awarded him after his thick skull turned back a spent Mexican musket ball at the Battle of Cerro Gordo.

Sumner's two-pronged expedition caught the Cheyennes on the **Solomon River** of western Kansas on 29 July 1857. So overconfident were the 300 warriors that they waited in a European-type line of battle. This rare choice of tactics, an open encounter, was the result of a medicine man's assuring them that, after bathing their hands in a sacred lake, the warriors would be immune from bullets.

Old Bull Sumner had exactly the same number of fighting men as the Cheyennes. He had his men sling their carbines and led them in what was probably both the first and the last saber charge in Indian wars history, movies to the contrary. Either the soothsayer's super-natural vision was cloudy or the warriors had broken a taboo, for their spirit allies failed them. The spell was no more effective against musket balls than saber cuts. Nor was there suitable magic in the medicine bundles, or the buffalo hide shields with their religious talismanic and heraldic symbols, or the war paint well known to give courage to fighting men. The shaken Indians broke and ran for their lives, so fast that they lost only nine braves in a major psychological defeat. Only two of the cavalrymen, who pursued them with hacking sabers for the first seven miles of a headlong retreat, were killed. Sumner had ten enlisted men wounded and one officer, who was to become the Civil War's legendary J E B (Jeb) Stuart.

On balance, the brutal measures of the rivals, Harney and Sumner, probably saved both red and white lives in the long run. Their prompt and thorough punishment ended the Indians' contempt for the Army, fostered by Grattan's debacle. The conflict of cultures was so acute that war was inevitable, but for seven years there was a tacit ceasefire, an uneasy truce on the Great Plains. This shaky peace even survived the arrival of yet another wave of pioneers, those heading up the Smoky Hill Trail to Colorado, with 'Pike's Peak or Bust!' lettered on the canvas tops of their wagons.

Wars in the Oregon Country and in the Pacific Northwest

However long before the Pike's Peak Gold Rush of 1858, the infection of war spread all the way across the continent to Washington Territory. Isaac I Stevens, its young (35 years of age) and ambitious governor, doubled as superintendent of Indian affairs. He held a council in May and June of 1855 in the Walla Walla Valley. There he tried to persuade, then to pressure, the natives into peacefully abandoning much of their overlapping land claims for reservations of their own choosing around permanent villages or salmon fisheries.

The Nez Percés, always friendly to whites since they first shook Meriwether Lewis's hand in 1805, came in. So did their opposites, the Cayuses. The Yakimas, Walla Wallas and Umatillas showed up, too.

Old Peo-peo-mox-mox, chief of the Walla Wallas, told the governor that his people would not eat the white man's food in the great dining hall. Stevens, disappointed by the failure of his gustatory diplomacy, was shortly surprised by the general obstinacy of his guests. Though he promised chiefs annual salaries and homes, horses, cattle and even schools for their people, the Indians refused to give up their ancestral hunting and fishing grounds in exchange for the smaller sites that he was ready to assign them.

The governor then threatened them. Old Chief Joseph of the Nez Percés signed. To Stevens's satisfaction, the other chiefs followed suit. He was annoyed when Looking Glass of the Nez Percés, a late arrival, exclaimed, 'My people, what have you done! While I was away, you have sold my country!' But Stevens was able to cajole most of the tribal leaders by assuring them that they would not have to move for two or three years, since the Senate would debate that long before ratifying the treaty. The Indians misjudged the slippery Stevens badly. Stevens was a deceptive negotiator, indeed an outright liar—the type of individual that Indians would refer to as one who spoke with a forked tongue. He did not wait two years as he promised, but hardly two weeks, before declaring the Indian lands open to white settlement.

The Yakima War

Some Yakimas protested that Kamiakin had had no right to speak for them in accepting a reservation and giving up claims to land beyond its limits, or in permitting whites to build roads across their lands.

A Yakima War broke out in September of 1855 after exasperated young braves, including Kamiakin's nephew, Qualchin, murdered prospectors heading for British Columbia's gold fields. Next, they brutally murdered their well-liked agent, A J Bolon, when he investigated the killings. The Indians feared that he was fetching the Army to punish them.

Kamiakin was a pro-peace chief, though he wanted the whites to stay west of the Cascades. But he was easily able, with 500 warriors, to turn back a reconnaissance in strength from Fort Dalles. Major Granville O Haller lost five dead and 17 wounded on 6 October, then had to fight his way back to the fort after burying his howitzer and burning baggage and supplies to keep them from Yakima hands. Major, alias 'General', Gabriel Rains's Yakima Expedition did little more in November than burn a Catholic mission

Above: Even before they acquired firearms, America's Indians made use of a varied armory of weapons of war. These included bows and arrows, the latter which were either flint or obsidian-tipped until the white man introduced steel to the redmen; buffalo-hide shields, which were hung with feathers; and lances, which were favored by the Comanches who often had to charge Mexican *lanceros* similarly armed. The Indians also made skilful use of fire in warfare; burning arrows and torches were effective means of destroying many settlements.

when they found gunpowder buried in its garden. But Colonel James Kelly's volunteers, by seizing Peo-peo-mox-mox during a parley, guaranteed the spread of war from Yakimas to Walla Wallas, and even Umatillas and Cayuses, for they killed the chief and sent his scalp and ears to the Oregon settlements to be put on display.

By now, whites were shooting Indians on sight, as if they were predatory animals, and braves fell on the nearest settlers, usually innocent of wrongdoing, in their blind retaliation. Bewildered Army regulars, expecting to guard settlers from attack, often found themselves protecting

Above: **Jefferson Davis** is commonly remembered only as president of the Confederate States of America during the Civil War. But he enjoyed a long career in United States government service before he played a leading role in states' rights and Secession, especially between 1861 and 1865. He was born in Kentucky in 1808 and educated at Transylvania University in Lexington. He graduated from West Point in 1828. Davis served for seven years at various frontier Army posts and saw action in the Black Hawk War with the Sauks and Foxes in 1832. He left the Army in 1835, the year that he married Zachary Taylor's daughter (who lived only a few more months), for the life of a Mississippi cotton planter. Davis entered Democratic politics in 1843 but in 1846 resigned from the House of Representatives to lead a volunteer regiment of Mississippi Rifles in the Mexican War from 1846 to 1848. Colonel Davis distinguished himself at the Siege of Monterrey and the Battle of Buena Vista, then returned home to his Mississippi plantation to recover from his war wounds. His interest in the West – both positive and negative – continued. He fought the admission of California to the Union as a free state. As Secretary of War for President Franklin Pierce he was the prime mover behind the important Pacific Railroad Surveys of 1853-54 and the subsequent building of a transcontinental railway (1869) that connected California with 'the States' but split, forever, not only buffalo herds but also Indian tribes into two great north and south segments. Naturally, he preferred and recommended the southern route, along the 32nd degree of latitude, and favored the Gadsden Purchase of 45,535 square miles for ten million dollars and cancellation of some Mexican claims against the US. This secured the Mesilla Valley of New Mexico and added the Gila River country to Arizona Territory in 1853. Davis was modest, fearless and honest and he always thought of himself as a soldier.

peaceful Indians from bloodthirsty militiamen. Naturally, the embittered settlers preferred to muster their own militia companies to deal, decisively, with the Indians. They felt that they could not count on the ambivalent Army. They considered its commander virtually a traitor to his country.

Feisty General John E Wool, commanding the Department of the Pacific, was a veteran of 42 years service. He had not liked the indecent Cherokee Removal of the 1830s, which he had been forced by duty to supervise, and he would not tolerate now the machinations of the supposedly patriotic 'war governors', Stevens of Washington Territory and George Curry of Oregon Territory. He disliked the latter, but detested the former, considering Stevens to be a scoundrel. And he said so, publicly, openly sympathizing with the Indians and condemning the white citizenry as hot heads who wished to exterminate the natives. Wool ordered his subordinates not to fight Indians unless forced to do so, but to persuade all tribes to be peaceful.

Stevens blasted Wool for 'locking up' the regulars in their forts while hostiles killed citizens with impunity. He demanded the General's removal from command for incapacity and criminal neglect of duty.

Wool retorted that both 'war governors' were covetous men provoking needless bloodshed in order to prosper not only from Indian plunder, but from looting the US Treasury of militia pay and supplies and, eventually, reparations for war losses, real or imaginary. He was also profoundly disgusted, he said, by the brutal, disgraceful behavior of the volunteers against the two territories' peaceable Indians. Reluctantly, in order to protect innocent victims of war, white and red alike, Wool was forced to send Colonel George H Wright, the veteran now commanding Fort Dalles, to the front with 500 regulars. It was a bloodless campaign; all hostiles had scattered by mid-June of 1856. But Colonel B F Shaw's volunteers on 17 July thrashed 300 of the allied hostiles in the Grande Ronde Valley. He killed 40 and destroyed the village while losing only five dead and four wounded.

Peace in the Columbia Basin was more the work of Wright than Shaw, however. He persuaded Stevens to pull out his vengeful volunteers and the Indians ceased their disavowal of treaties, relinquished tribal lands and ceased hostilities. The Yakima War, or at least its beginnings, seemed to fade away in November 1856. Forts Simcoe and Walla Walla were established to keep the peace in the Pacific Northwest. However, Stevens had the last laugh on Wool. He won his fight, getting the General reassigned in May of 1857.

To the south, trouble had broken out in Oregon as early as 1851. The ten founders of Port Orford on the south coast had hardly waded ashore in July before they were attacked. They holed up atop an unusual, whale-shaped, offshore 'stack', Battle Rock. A hundred braves charged the rock at low tide, clambering up its steep sides as their friends filled the air with arrows. J M Kirkpatrick and his men struck back fiercely with a round from their antique ship's cannon. An estimated 20 warriors were killed and 17 more wounded. But since the defenders had only two more charges for the gun, they hoarded them for 14 days of siege, then sneaked ashore at dark and cut through the woods to Portland.

Rogue River War

Hostilities shifted inland to the Siskiyou Trail area of the

Rogue River in southern Oregon, named for the villainous Indians who had a reputation for ambushing travelers. Captain Andrew Jackson Smith commanded a solitary troop of dragoons at Fort Lane to keep the Rogues in subjection in 1855. In October, when rumors of war spread Smith moved some peaceful Indian men up to the fort for their own protection. Before the women and children could follow them, their camp was raided by a volunteer company. The amateur soldiers killed 23 people, mostly women, children and old men. On the very next day, the young warriors took their revenge, but they fell on the wrong persons, butchering 27 innocent Rogue River settlers.

Newspapers and the public joined in a clamor for Indian scalps. In fact, they wanted the complete destruction of the 'bloody fiends'. Just as Wool had predicted, the raid-and-retaliation cycle in Oregon blazed up into a full-scale war of extermination by both sides.

When Wool reluctantly sent regulars to reinforce the volunteers in the spring of 1856, the Rogues agreed to surrender to Captain Smith, whom they trusted. But they changed their minds and decided to destroy him. Some 200 Rogue Rivers attacked Smith's 50 horsemen and 30 foot soldiers at **Big Meadow** on the Rogue.

Fortunately for the captain, two Indian women wanted no part of the upcoming bloodbath. They warned him of the treachery of chiefs Old John, Limpy and George. Smith had time to dig in atop a hill before the attack came on the morning of 27 May 1856. His howitzer and the infantry's musket fire did considerable damage but his dragoons' short-range musketoons or carbines were less effective. The regulars appeared doomed by the great discrepancy in strength between themselves and the Indians. Old John sensing victory cursed the whites in his own tongue and his lieutenants shook hangman's nooses at them. The two Indian women dutifully translated Old John's fiery speech for Smith.

Just in the very nick of time, Captain Christopher C Augur's company of regulars came up on the double. The Rogues, pressed between two forces, ran. Smith's men, though almost out of both ammunition and water, managed a gallant and spirited counter-attack as Augur came in view. When the warriors lit out, they took their dead and wounded so their casualties could not be known. But Smith lost nine killed and 17 wounded, Augur two dead and three wounded.

A month after Big Meadows, completely dispirited, the Rogues surrendered and allowed themselves to be herded like sheep onto the coastal Siletz Reservation, protected by Siletz Blockhouse, a satellite of Fort Hoskins. There they nearly starved in the next months. Old John was exiled to the military prison at Fort Alcatraz in the middle of San Francisco Bay.

The Coeur d'Alene War

The Yakimas were not yet ready to move onto a reservation for good, as had the Rogues. Some of their belligerents picked off farmers and Colville District miners while Kamiakin secretly sought alliances with the Palouses, Coeur d'Alenes and Spokanes against the 'white-eyes.'

The Army became exasperated in 1858 by the murder of miners, so in May, Lieutenant Colonel Edward J Steptoe marched from Fort Walla Walla to pacify the recalcitrant Yakimas and Coeur d'Alenes, hence the alternative name

Above: **Winfield Scott** was long lived for his day. Born in Virginia in 1786, just after the American Revolution, he died 80 years later in 1866, just after the close of the Civil War. The career soldier attended William and Mary College and began his military career as a militia officer, but in 1808 he was commissioned a captain of light artillery in the Regular Army and served on the Louisiana frontier. In the War of 1812, Scott distinguished himself at Queenstown Heights (1812) but was taken prisoner. He was exchanged and won fame in the Battles of Chippewa and Lundy's Lane in 1814 and was made a brigadier general. Congress and his home state of Virginia gave him medals and he was made a brevet major general. After he studied military tactics in Europe, he wrote a manual of infantry field exercises and maneuvers. He then served in the Black Hawk War (1832), commanded the forces in the Second Seminole War, and supervised the exile of the Cherokees from the south in 1838. Scott became Commanding General of the Army in 1841 on the death of General Alexander Macomb. In the Mexican War he was at first shunted aside as a Whig by the Democratic administration. Finally, Old 'Fuss and Feathers,' as his troops knew him from his love of showy uniforms, was given his head. He not only struck at the capital from Vera Cruz, he did so with many soldiers 'borrowed' from rival Zachary Taylor's force in the North. He captured Mexico City but was recalled in 1848 in another political squabble. Lieutenant General Scott was a national hero in the 1850s, though his presidential run was unsuccessful in 1852. The able Scott helped settle a San Juan Islands boundary dispute with Great Britain in Washington Territory's Puget Sound in 1859, but was really too old when the Civil War broke. He organized the defenses of Washington, but retired in 1861, to be succeeded by General George B McClellan.

for part two of the Yakima War, the Coeur d'Alene War. (It was even called the Spokane War by some.) Steptoe took three dragoon companies, reinforced by an infantry unit and a few Nez Percé scouts, plus an artillery battery of two howitzers. He had only 164 men and each carried only 40 rounds of ammunition.

The Coeur d'Alenes were traditionally friendly to whites but, punished by white diseases, Stevens's treaties and the rush of aggressive miners to Colville, they walked into the waiting arms of the Spokanes and Yakimas in 1858.

Steptoe was bound for Colville. He never made it. To his shock, he found the grassy-hilled country called The Palouse (for its Indians) to be aswarm with war parties. There were 1200 Yakimas, Spokanes, Palouses and Coeur d'Alenes, all mounted.

When chiefs rode up to his camp one evening and ordered him away, Steptoe meekly—and wisely—obeyed. But his prudence went unrewarded. The Indians fell on the rear of his column as he turned back on 17 May 1858. All morning long they drew blood. He took up a defensive position on a hill, **Steptoe Butte**, from which he had to fight his way down to a ravine and back for water. Surrounded and pinned to his position, Steptoe fought well but, by dark, he had lost six dead, two of them officers, and a dozen men wounded. There were only three rounds of ammunition left per man.

Steptoe wanted to fight to the death but younger and cooler heads persuaded him to live to fight another day. Burying the dead and forfeiting the howitzers, the soldiers slipped away in the darkness and got themselves and their wounded comrades safely back to Fort Walla Walla.

The Army, smarting from the humiliation of Steptoe's aborted campaign, now sent Wright into action again. The Indian allies awaited him at Four Lakes on 1 September 1858. He chased some of the 500 warriors out of the pines with howitzer fire, then gave them a dose of musketry in the open. His men were armed with the new 1855 model 'rifled muskets' (that is, rifles), not smoothbores. They took the new hollow, conical, Minié balls which extended their effective range from 600 yards to almost 1000 yards. And the new slugs were capable of tearing through the toughest —and most sacred—buffalo-hide shields.

Now Major William Grier shouted 'Charge the rascals!' and his four companies of dragoons tore into the Indians, who fled with a loss of 60 dead and many more wounded. Incredibly, Wright did not have a man even hurt in the **Battle of Four Lakes**.

On 5 September at **Spokane Plain**, or Great Spokane Prairie, Wright repeated his bloody lesson. The grass fire started by the Indians provided a handy smoke screen for his yelling dragoons to charge and scatter 500 hostiles. Their loss could not be determined, but Wright had only one man wounded and a number of soldiers completely exhausted.

As the several whipped tribes made peace overtures, Wright policed the area, slaughtering 900 Palouse ponies. He then went after the ringleaders, hanging 15 of them and putting others in irons. For years, the pile of whitening horse bones on the Spokane River served not only as a landmark but as a reminder of Army retribution for Steptoe's defeat.

Kamiakin was badly injured at Spokane Plain by a tree limb dropped on him by a howitzer round. He got across the line into Canada, however. In 1861 he sneaked back into southeast Washington Territory and lived quietly near Spokane. He died at Rock Lake in 1877.

Kamiakin's brother-in-law, Owhi, came in to make peace and was forced, under threat of death, to summon his son, Qualchin, whose murders had started the war. Wright had him summarily hanged. Owhi tried to escape by lashing a lieutenant in the face with a horsewhip, but the officer shot him three times in the body and a sergeant gave him the *coup de grace*, a fourth shot in the head.

Wars on the South Plains

During the pre-Civil War decade, Kiowas and Comanches continued their old tradition of raiding Mexicans, but largely left Arkansas River and Santa Fe Trail travelers alone. They did not wish to jeopardize their presents of arms and ammunition ('for hunting', of course) from the *Anglos*. But they eventually strayed from the Great Comanche War Trail to Mexico and stole livestock from West Texans.

A new governor in 1858, Hardin R Runnels, admitted that it would be cheaper for the state just to pay raided frontiersmen for their stolen cows and jackasses. But he was determined to rebuild the Texas Rangers after a decade of decline, and used the border troubles to justify his call-up of new men.

Runnels chose the best man available since John Coffee

Far left: The Army's General John E Wool did not want a fight with the Northwest Indians in the 1850s, but violence came anyway. Colonel **Benjamin F Shaw** took his 2nd Regiment of Washington Territorial Militia on a march to Walla Walla against allied tribes. The campaign of 1856 was largely bloodless till July, when Shaw struck in Grande Ronde Valley in northeastern Oregon Territory and defeated them.

Above left: A photo panorama, circa 1856, of the **Yakima Valley**.

Above: **Lieutenant Colonel (later Brigadier General) Silas Casey**, CO of Fort Steilacoom during the Indian troubles in Washington Territory.

Hays, the greatest of the Rangers, had migrated to California in the Gold Rush. Senior Captain John S (Rip) Ford was told to cooperate with General David E Twiggs's regulars and with US Indian agents. But in typical Texan fashion, Runnels also instructed him to brook no interference from them or anyone else. His orders were clear, simple and specific: 'Follow any and all trails of hostiles or suspected hostile Indians you may discover and, if possible, overtake and chastize them, if unfriendly'. He wanted the most summary punishment for the enemies of Texas.

Ford intended to strike the Comanches hard. If he did not secure a telling victory, he was prepared to accept a disastrous defeat. But half-way measures were unthinkable. And he would not be restrained by the supposedly sacrosanct Indian Territory border.

On 29 April Ford left Texas by crossing the Red River. One day, some of his Keechi, Tonkawa, Shawnee and Anadarko scouts from the Brazos Reserve, led by the Indian Agent's son, Shapley P Ross, killed a buffalo with fresh Comanche arrows in it. On 11 May 1858, they spotted

a small village near the Canadian River and Oklahoma's Antelope Hills. At seven o'clock the next morning, Rip Ford loosed his scouts. They demolished the five lodges, mounted the Comanches' horses and joined the Ranger pursuit of two braves for three miles. From there, the Tonks and Texans could see the conical white lodges of a much bigger village three miles away on the Cherokee side of the Canadian.

Chief Iron Jacket, who wore an old coat of Spanish mail, was alerted and ready for the Rangers. Trusting to his armor's medicine, he led the force bearing down on Ford. But a half-dozen musket balls dropped his horse, and Shawnee and Anadarko guides riddled the chief on the ground. A number of individual fights occupied an area of six by three miles. Mostly, Rangers and reservation Indians made futile chases of Comanches who only occasionally would halt and fight. When the chief replacing Iron Jacket was also shot down by the Captain of Ford's Shawnees, the Comanches gave up the field. Ford recalled, 'Our red allies sent up a wild shout of triumph'. Only the weakened condition of their horses prevented a pursuit by the Texans.

When Comanches rallied from another camp a few miles up the Canadian, Ford let his allies handle it. He described the colorful scene: 'With yells and menaces and every species of insulting gesture and language, they tried to excite the Reserve Indians into some act of rashness by which they could profit. . . . Shields and lances and bows and headdresses, prancing steeds. . . . When the combatants rushed at each other with defiant shouts, nothing save the piercing report of the rifle varied the affair from a battlefield of the Middle Ages.'

The 100 Rangers grew tired of the pageant after a half-hour of this cavorting without damage to either side. They moved in and drove the Comanches from the field. All fighting was over because Ford's tired horses could not manage an attack on Buffalo Hump's big village, only a dozen miles away. Ford engaged 300 warriors in the drawn out and intermittent seven-hour battle. He killed 76 warriors, captured 300 horses, and took 18 prisoners, mostly women and children. His force suffered only two dead and two wounded.

Above: Charlie Russell was as skilled with pen and ink as with brush, as this sketch of a family moving on with a **dog travois** hauling all its worldly goods, wrapped in buffalo robes, indicates.

Ford commended Agent Ross and also his own four captains. Of the latter he said, 'They behaved under fire in a gallant and soldier-like manner, and I think they have fully vindicated their right to be recognized as Texas Rangers of the old stamp.'

Runnels was pleased when First Sergeant Robert Cotter sent him a souvenir of Ford's victory, accompanied by a note—'I send you . . . a small part of the Comanche chief's coat of mail. It covered his body and each piece lapped over like shingles on a roof. It is all I could get, as it was eagerly taken and divided by the boys.'

That summer, the Army followed the Rangers' example and went on the offensive after too long a time on the defensive in a line of 13 forts spaced for 400 miles across West Texas. Secretary of War Jeff Davis's favorite Indian fighter was appointed leader of the expedition. Captain (Brevet Major) Earl Van Dorn was brave, gentle, and kind, but he was also a hard-drinking, boastful adulterer, according to California's Judge Charles Fernald.

Van Dorn's column, the **Wichita Expedition**, was composed of four companies of the 2nd Cavalry, 135 Indians and a guard detachment of infantry to watch over campsites. Oddly, the commander of the Indian scouts was the Agent's 20-year-old son, Lawrence S (Sul) Ross, home on vacation from college. Van Dorn set up a supply base, on Otter Creek near the Wichita Mountains and, once he located Comanches, made a 90-mile march in 37 hours.

Van Dorn reconnoitered the little valley of Rush Creek and found Buffalo Hump and 500 of his followers in 120 lodges at the springs. At sunrise, 1 October 1858, Van Dorn's 350 men struck. His surprise attack was perfect; he separated braves from their ponies and he got men in among the teepees. But the **Battle of Rush Springs** was a ferocious one, for the Comanches stood to defend their families.

In the series of desperate hand-to-hand engagements, Sul Ross fell with a bullet in his side. A Comanche grabbed at him to lift his scalp, but a lieutenant planted a charge of buckshot in the Indian's spine. Van Dorn was shot in the

Above: After apprenticeship-like explorations of Minnesota with the French scientist, Nicollet, and a survey of the lower Des Moines River, **John Charles Frémont** was sent to explore the Rocky Mountains or, rather, the headwaters of the Platte River in 1842. From South Pass, he headed northwestward into the Wind River Mountains of the Rockies and climbed **Fremont Peak** in Wyoming, at 13,730 feet one of the highest peaks in the entire chain. When his report and map were published by Congress, the public began to be aware of the 'Pathfinder.'

Right: **Frémont** was a split personality, a splendid scientific explorer, but a failure as a soldier-politician. He reached the Rockies in 1842, the Great Basin and Oregon in 1843, and made a rash midwinter crossing of the Sierra Nevada into California. His reports of his great circuit excited much popular interest. He was back in California in 1845 but retired 'growlingly' to Oregon before a Mexican force. Surprised by Indians there, he retaliated against the wrong tribe. Frémont joined the Bear Flag rebels against Mexico and in the Mexican War formed his company, plus mountain men, into a California Battalion of 'horse marines' under Commodore Stockton rather than the Army. He accepted the surrender of California, to the annoyance of his superiors, and sided with the Navy in its controversy with General Kearny as to who was in supreme command. Kearny took him East for court martial for disobedience of orders. Found guilty, he was pardoned by the president but angrily resigned his commission. His private winter expedition to the San Juan Mountains for a railroad route was a disaster. Frémont later operated gold mines in California, ran for president, was a mediocre Civil War general, and Governor of Arizona Territory.

Above: Artist James E Taylor and engraver Charles Spiegle titled this engraving **Sam Cherry's Last Shot**. It should have been *Sam Cherry's Next-to-Last Shot*, for he saved the last pistol ball for himself, to save himself from death by hellish tortures. Colonel Richard I Dodge was Adjutant when the Army established Fort Davis in West Texas in 1855 with six companies of the Eighth US Infantry. From October 10-30, Dodge was out with a tiny patrol, only a single non-commissioned officer, three privates and the scout, Cherry, to find timber suitable for saw logs. They found Indian signs everywhere but not of large parties, so the men were careful but not uneasy. At the end of the month, Dodge was replaced on muster day by Sergeant Love. That night the party did not return. An infantry company hurried out and found the soldiers, riddled with bullets and disfigured. At the entrance to the *cañón* of the Limpia River, called Wild Rose Pass, about 30 mounted Indians had apparently cut them off from any retreat to the fort, driving the troopers into a trap from which Cherry tried to escape. He was found, pinned to the ground by his dead horse, but unscalped and not mutilated, his pistol still in his hand. Dodge immediately understood why. Indians feared suicides and would not scalp – even touch – one. When Cherry's horse broke its leg and fell on him, Sam Cherry shot five of his pursuers but put the last lead slug into his own head.

wrist and stomach with arrows.

The Army killed 56 warriors (and, accidentally, two women) and dispersed the rest in the hour-and-a-half battle. Some 300 horses were captured and all 120 lodges burned. Van Dorn had five dead and a dozen men wounded, including himself. No wonder General Twiggs crowed that it was 'a victory more decisive and complete than any recorded in the history of our Indian warfare.'

Van Dorn was not expected to live although the army surgeon extracted the arrow from his abdomen. But he was as tough as he was vain, and was back in the saddle in only five weeks. On 13 May 1859 he surpassed his Rush Springs fight by trapping a Comanche war party at **Crooked Creek** near the Cimarron River. He utterly destroyed the Comanches who, he reported, fought till not one was left to bend a bow. Not one brave escaped; 49 were dead and the five wounded and 32 women became prisoners. Van Dorn lost two troopers and four Indian scouts; two officers and nine enlisted men were wounded.

The Paiute War

The last major campaign in the West before the Civil War broke out was the Paiute War, or Pyramid Lake War, of 1860 in that part of Utah Territory then called Washoe rather than Nevada. The discovery of Comstock silver led to the murders of miners around Virginia City which were blamed on both Washoes and Paiutes. But war did not blaze up until two Paiute girls were brutally raped by whites at Williams Station. Paiutes rescued the girls, killed the rapists and burned the stage station.

This **Williams Station Massacre** led to the formation of a citizens' army under Major William Ormsby. He was a poor soldier and led his rag-tag army of miners into a trap at the Big Bend of the Truckee River just south of Pyramid Lake. This trap was set by Numaga, a pro-peace chief dragged into belligerence after a fast against violence. As a Sacramento *Union* correspondent wrote about Ormsby's force, 'They had charged through an open gate into an Indian corral.' Numaga let the terrified volunteers retreat in a wild run that turned into a sagebrush gauntlet. Some historians, such as Ferol Egan, have likened the rout to a bloody rabbit drive.

California rushed militia units to the rescue of its underpopulated neighbor. The **Carson Valley Expedition**, a handful of regulars, joined them, and ex-Texas Ranger Jack Hays took command of a provisional Washoe Regiment. His skirmish at Big Meadows near the Big Bend of the Carson River was inconclusive. But he pushed across Ormsby's battlefield and struck the Paiutes at Pinnacle Mountain. Hays killed 25 warriors and captured 20 ponies before scattering the Indians to the desert winds. They never regrouped for resistance after Fort Churchill was established at the Big Bend of the Carson to keep a watchful eye on them.

Arizona Territory had been surprisingly quiet in the 1850s. Apaches continued to raid their age-old enemies, the Mexicans, but hardly ever took on the better-armed Americans. In fact, for three solid years, the Butterfield Overland Mail Line's Concord coaches of the Mesilla-Tucson run passed through the very heart of the Chiricahua country, the defile of Apache Pass at the north end of the Chiricahua Mountains, without problems. Indeed, some Chiricahuas regularly traded firewood for supplies at the mail station.

The situation in Arizona changed almost overnight in 1860 because of the stupidity of a single army lieutenant. In October, Apaches hit the adobe ranch house of a roughneck settler, John Ward, on Sonoita Creek. They not only stole his cattle, they abducted one of his children, his stepson and adopted son, Félix Téllez. Félix was the 12-year-old son of Ward's Mexican wife and an Apache father, born while she was a captive.

Ward was away at the time of the raid, but on his return he firmly identified Cochise, chief of the Chiricahuas, as the guilty party from descriptions by eye-witnesses. The chief was hard to miss; neat and well-mannered, six feet tall with muscular shoulders, a barrel chest and arrow-straight posture. One settler described him as 'As fine a looking Indian as one ever saw.'

Ward complained at Fort Buchanan, 40 miles south of Tucson, and the courageous but reckless Second Lieutenant George N Bascom of the 7th Infantry was ordered to restore the kidnapped boy to him. He took 54 men on mules and pitched his tent near the Apache Pass stage station where Cochise often camped. Bascom invited the chief to a talk on 4 February 1861.

Cochise assumed that it was a routine meeting, so he brought five members of his family—a brother, two nephews, a woman and a child. At first he thought that the short-fused lieutenant must be joking when he demanded the return of the boy and the livestock. Cochise denied any complicity in the raid and guessed that Coyoteros, or White Mountain Apaches, were responsible. He offered to help ransom the boy and recover the animals. But Bascom would have none of it; he had convinced himself of the chief's guilt. He bluntly advised him that he was under arrest and that the tent was surrounded by a dozen soldiers. Cochise barely waited for the interpreter to explain Bascom's treachery before he had his knife out. But he did not kill the lieutenant; instead, he slashed his way through the tent's wall. His kin were seized as hostages but Cochise escaped.

122

Cochise quickly took several whites prisoner on the Butterfield Trail, for bargaining power. He did not bother with the Mexicans he despised. When he captured eight teamsters, he just tied the Mexicans to the wheels of their wagons and set the vehicles afire.

Reinforced by White Mountain warriors and the Warm Springs braves of his giant father-in-law, Mangas Coloradas, Cochise appeared under a flag of truce. Bascom suspected treachery—and he was right. He would not budge, but three stage employees walked out to talk with their old friend, Cochise. The Indians tossed aside their white flag and seized one of them, James F Wallace. The other men ran. Both were hit, and one later died. Bascom's troopers returned the Apache fire.

On 6 February Cochise shouted an offer to trade hostages. Bascom was willing, but wanted the Téllez lad and the livestock thrown in. Cochise repeated his offer of a trade, this time in writing. He attached a note, written for him by Wallace, to a stake that he drove into the ground in view of the stage station.

When Bascom took no action, Cochise lost his temper. He had his men pile up heaps of tinder-dry brush in the canyon road to halt and seize the stages. But before he could light it, the westbound stage crashed through, ahead of schedule.

Cochise turned his attention to the eastbound coach. His men wounded the driver and killed one of the lead mules. The passengers cut the carcass from the harness and headed for the station. The Apaches had stripped the planking from the stringers of a small bridge, but the mules dragged the protesting stage over the span on its axles. At the far abutment, the wheels found purchase and, miraculously, the seemingly doomed stage clattered up to the besieged station.

Cochise ran off Bascom's mules, but paid a price. Riflemen wounded up to a dozen of the rustlers. Bascom's courier brought a medical unit which, surprisingly, captured three Coyoteros. The arrival of two dragoon companies from Fort Breckinridge sent Cochise flying towards Mexico. Patrols searched the mountains around the re-opened pass, but encountered no hostiles.

But the handiwork of Cochise was everywhere. The charred corpses of the Mexican wagonmen were cut away from the wheels and buried. The horrible remains of Cochise's six American hostages were found, repeatedly lanced in Comanche fashion, and so butchered that

Wallace, Cochise's particular friend, could only be identified by gold fillings in his teeth. About 16 Mexicans and Americans were tortured to death by Cochise between 4 and 11 February.

Keeping the woman and child in detention, Bascom, with the approval of his officers, on 11 February hanged the six Apache men to the limbs of scrub oaks over the graves of the murdered whites. And he refused to bury their remains. The corpses hung there, dessicating in the hot desert winds for months, a warning to all Apaches.

The warning was not heeded. Cochise and Mangas Coloradas terrified the territory. Within two months, more than 150 Americans and Mexicans were dead. On 10 August 1861 the *Arizonan* newspaper lamented that most of the territory's male population had been killed or run off and that most ranches, farms and mines had fallen to the Apaches. Even conservative estimates put the final cost of these Apache depredations at more than 4000 lives and hundreds of thousands of dollars in property losses.

When the echoes of Fort Sumter's bombardment rolled across the plains and mountains, Indians were not slow to fill the vacuum left by departing regulars. But militiamen rushed to fill the breach in the frontier's defenses. By war's end, 1865, the Volunteer Army in the West grew from 11,000 to almost 20,000. Officers varied widely in ability, just as in the Regular Army, but the militiamen were a surprise. Most were healthier specimens, and true patriots, who made better soldiers than those who clogged the ranks of the so-called peacetime Army. Even Confederate prisoners, 'Galvanized Yankees', volunteered to fight Indians. The civilized Indians of Oklahoma fought on both sides, but mainly in Arkansas, not in the Far West.

Wars in the Rockies and the Southwest

Two of the best leaders of citizen-soldiers of the Civil War in the West were Colonels Patrick Edward Connor and James H Carleton. The former, a pugnacious Irish immigrant, had been an 18-year-old enlisted man in the Seminole War, then a captain of volunteers in the Mexican War. In 1861 Governor John Downey of California appointed Connor colonel of the 3d California Infantry, to patrol the US mail route between Salt Lake City and California, protecting travelers and the new telegraph line as well as the mails with his 750 men.

But it was the Carleton who first drew blood. He had

Left: This warrior is typical of the **Apaches** who, with little armament – or clothing – held off the American Army in Arizona for decades.

Opposite page: Right after Adobe Walls (1874), scout **Amos Chapman** protected a wounded comrade in the Buffalo Wallow fight.

Fillmore had been abandoned because of the Army's fear of their warriors, not the threat of Rebel invasion. So Mangas, supported by Cochise, planned an ambush for Carleton, now a brigadier general, in the bottleneck of Apache Pass. The giant Mangas Coloradas, who towered over his tall son-in-law, Cochise, at six-foot-six, had been friendly with whites for years. But now annoyed by American miners at Silver City and Pinos Altos, he threw in his lot with Cochise's hostiles.

On 15 July 1862 Captain Thomas L Roberts led Carleton's lead company into the trap set by 'Red Sleeves'. Roberts was fired on from both slopes but had to press on to the spring because of his parched troopers. His two howitzers could lob a 7-pound shell 1000 yards, shrapnel 800 yards, and deadly canister shot 250 yards. The artillery shells cleared Apaches from the breastworks they had erected around the springs, but there were still perhaps 500 Indians in the pass. Roberts sent a warning message to Captain John C Cremony's supply train and cavalry escort, which were behind him. Mangas Coloradas and 50 warriors took off after Sergeant Mitchell's five couriers, who now rode for their very lives. Every man was hit, but none was shot from his saddle. Three of the horses were shot, throwing their riders. Two men were picked up, but Private John Teal was left behind, alone, to fight off the greatest war chief of the Southwest and his 50 picked warriors.

The Californian dropped down behind the carcass of his horse and commenced firing carefully with his breech-loading, repeating carbine. The Indians were puzzled, awed, by the rapid fire that the one soldier maintained. Repeaters were new to them. Instead of rushing him, they circled for an hour, not daring to come to close quarters. Recalled Teal, 'I got a good shot at a prominent Indian, and slipped a carbine bullet into his breast. He must have been a man of some note because, soon after, they seemed to get away from me.'

The 'man of some note' was Chief Mangas Coloradas. Unconscious, he was rescued by Cochise who did not trust his own tribal *curanderos* but took him all the way to Janos, Chihuahua, where a Mexican surgeon was forced to operate on him, under penalty of death if he failed to cure the chief. Mangas was out of action for months with his chest wound and was a strange sight when he returned to Arizona in a Mexican sombrero, serape and leather leggings—and Chinese sandals.

Carleton's main column reached Apache Pass ten days after the gutsy Teal hiked back to his comrades, not forgetting to carry his saddle so that his pay would not be docked. To protect his exposed lines of communication and deny the area to Cochise and Mangas, Carleton founded Fort Bowie in Apache Pass.

Mangas returned to raiding but did not live long to enjoy his depredating. The Army resorted again to treachery to entrap and kill him. Such action was justified, in army eyes, by his record—'the most atrocious cruelties, the most vindictive revenges and widespread injuries ever perpetrated by an American Indian'. He was lured into an army camp near Pinos Altos on 17 January 1863 by the promise of a

soldiered in Maine's hardly-bellicose Aroostook 'War' of 1838 before beginning a 20-year career in the regulars, where he rose to the rank of major of dragoons. He was the Governor's choice in 1861 for colonel of the 1st California Infantry.

Contemporaries called Carleton selfish, ambitious, tyrannical, aggressive, abrasive. He had thick moustache, eyebrows and sideburns, and liked to pose for photographers in Napoleonic posture. But he was a zealous and able officer, who replaced General E R S Canby as departmental commander in New Mexico and Arizona in 1862.

Early that year, Carleton led his California Column all the way to Fort Davis, Texas, retaking the Rio Grande forts for the Union. But Mangas Coloradas and Cochise mistakenly believed that Forts Buchanan, Breckinridge and

parley with Captain E D Shirland.

Mangas Coloradas was held at old abandoned Fort McLane on the Mimbres River. There, Private Clark Stocking overheard General Joseph R West, who looked like a pygmy alongside the chief, tell two sentries that the old 'murderer' had left a trail of blood for 500 miles. 'I want him "dead or alive", tomorrow morning. Do you understand?' he asked the guards, 'I want him *dead*.'

That bitter-cold night, a prospector, Daniel Conner, saw sentinels heat their bayonets in a campfire and stick them into the chief's legs and feet as he lay, rolled up in his blankets, by the fire. When he jumped up, the guards shot him, point blank, with their muskets and finished him off with six-shooters. One soldier scalped Mangas and, later, before he was buried, another cut off his head and boiled the flesh off to sell the skull to a phrenologist in the East. The wretched General West 'investigated' the incident. He claimed that the Apache was shot during his third attempt to escape and that the affair in no way compromised the good faith of the US Army.

The Shoshones (Shoshoni) of the Pacific Northwest had been friendly to Lewis and Clark and American mountain men, but relations with whites deteriorated and hit a low in 1862 when the Indians boldly marched down the street of Franklin, a hamlet in their winter camping grounds just above the Idaho line on Bear River. They wanted the settlement abandoned.

Colonel Connor was called in to discipline the Shoshones. He used a norther to hide his movements, leading 250–300 Californians through the blizzard. But Bear Hunter was ready to receive him on Bear River, 140 miles north of Bear Lake. In fact, he had added rock parapets to the natural defenses of his steep ravine.

On 27 January 1863, just as Connor's skirmishers deployed, they were dumbfounded to see a chief ride up and down in front of the gulch, brandishing a spear and chanting in quite recognizable English—'Fours right, fours left, come on you California sons of bitches!' Connor's men were more amused than intimidated by this strange performance and they speedily flanked the Shoshones' position, then swept through the village in the face of obstinate resistance as braves defended their wives and children.

Casualties were high for an Indian fight. Some of the braves had to be killed in their hiding places. Bear Hunter was one of 224 Indians killed, by Connor's count. But a Mormon tallied 400 bodies on the snow-covered field, many of them women and children.

The Battle of Bear River, almost forgotten today, won Connor his general's star as well as command of the Department of the Plains in 1865. And doubtless it saved the scalps of many prospectors. Connor was able to report that fall that all roads out of Utah could be traveled with safety. The Shoshones signed treaties in 1868 and 1873, went on the Fort Hall Reservation, and stayed there peacefully, except for a few young men who joined in the Bannock War of Chief Buffalo Horn in 1878.

War with the Santee Sioux

When trouble came from the Sioux again, it arrived from

an unexpected quarter. The sedentary Eastern Sioux, or Santees, were the least warlike people of that Indian nation. Some were Christians, all seemed submissive wards of government, accepting fatalistically reservation life on a strip of land along the Minnesota River. In 1851, by treaty, they had acknowledged the extension of US jurisdiction and had sold away their hunting grounds.

After the war, there would be no shortage of explanations for the savage uprising of a presumably peaceful native people. Some whites blamed the cutworms that ruined the Indians' spring corn crop and left them nearly starving. Others blamed the incessant pressure of settlers, both aggressive Anglo-Saxons and stolid, phlegmatic, Swedish and German immigrants who occupied one-time Santee land. Then there was the indifference or corruption of Indian agents, the meddling of missionaries and the chicanery of Indian traders. All these factors galled the Santee Sioux into deeper discontent.

As the Civil War wore on, rations fell short or were spoiled, unfit for human consumption. Blankets were cut in half to double their number. The monopolistic Indian trading posts, like company stores, got the Dakotas into debt, honestly and otherwise. When a war-distracted Washington was tardy in sending annuity payments to the agent at Yellow Medicine the Sioux feared that the traders would ask the Army to collect on these debts. Fort Ridgely tried to reassure uneasy Santees that its soldiers were not collection agents. But traders put signs on their counters advising their red customers that no more credit would be extended until the annuity should arrive and all outstanding debts were paid. When an interpreter protested that the Sioux might starve while waiting for Washington's bureaucrats to act, trader Andrew Myrick quipped, callously, 'If they're hungry, let 'em eat grass, or their own shit.'

The very day that elders sat to discuss their plight, 17 August 1862, four hungry hunters were making their way back to the reservation, disgusted at having shot no game. One of the frustrated youths dared another to prove his bravery by killing a white man. Before they were through with their senseless test of courage, five harmless settlers

Opposite page: Peace-loving **Chief Numaga** of Nevada's Paiutes was driven to war in 1860 by white violence. At the Big Bend of the Truckee River near Pyramid Lake he destroyed Major William Ormsby's militia.

Below: **Bear River**, in southern Idaho's Cache Valley, looked strangely peaceful some years after California's tough Colonel Patrick E Connor

struck at Shoshones (camped on this site) in a bloody battle that resulted in a large number of Indian losses.

Above: After Colonel John Coffee (Jack) Hays and his Washoe Regiment scattered the Paiutes, **Fort Churchill** was located on the Carson River to keep the peace in western Nevada.

of Meeker County lay dead.

Little Crow, who had been the Santee chief since 1834, was a cautious man. A long-time peace advocate, he was held largely responsible by whites for the lack of hostilities ever since the 1851 treaty. But he was weak-willed, as easily swayed to war as to peace, though he had firmly placed his feet on 'the white man's road'. (He lived in a house, ran a farm, and had visited Washington while wearing a plug hat.) He was an opportunist without the courage of his convictions. Deep inside him remained some of the old irresponsibility and arrogance of his misspent youth. As a young man, he had been alcoholic, mendacious and adulterous. He had finally been 'invited' by cuckolded husbands to leave his own village, Pig's Eye, on the site of St Paul. His father described him then as a young man with very little sense. True, when he became chief, he changed his ways, at least in terms of drinking and womanizing.

In a stormy, all-night council, tribal elders heard Little Crow warn that war with the powerful whites was futile, then persuade himself that it was inevitable because of the murders. He took over the rebellion from the militant youngsters even though his initial strategy, an attack on Fort Ridgely before it could be reinforced, was overruled.

The Santees instead attacked small towns and Indian agencies. Their first victim was a clerk at the Redwood Agency, shot in cold blood although he was married to a Sioux. Stores and homes were burned as the raiders tried unsuccessfully to wipe out **New Ulm**. A small (46 man) party of volunteer soldiers from the fort then blundered into the Sioux. Only half of them escaped back to Ridgely.

At midnight of 18 August the first day of the undeclared war, Indians were looting their own stores at Yellow Medicine Agency as the blood clotted on the last of their 400 victims, murdered in unsuspecting settlements. As many as 300 refugees crowded into Fort Ridgely, the vanguard of perhaps 30,000 people who would choke the roads in their flight from an area 50 miles wide by 250 miles long.

Finally, Little Crow and his 800 war-painted warriors moved against the fort, which was crammed with non-combatants but held by only 155 volunteer infantry. Other war parties ranged widely about, killing all settlers that they found. At Lake Shetek, they massacred a party completely; there was not one survivor.

Minnesotans were praying for help from the bastion of the Old Northwest, St Paul's Fort Snelling. But Fort Ridgely was not counting on prayer. It sent Private William Sturgis for help. His dash of 125 miles in 18 hours would not be surpassed until the fabled ride of Portugee Philips, four years later.

While the alarm was being spread, Fort Ridgely had to hold against two assaults of several waves of Indians on 20 and 22 August. It did so only because of an accident, a fluke of circumstance. Though seriously undermanned in 1862, the fort had once been an ordnance depot. It retained a 24-pound cannon and a 6-pound and a 12-pound mountain howitzer.

Luckily, the artillery had been looked after by Ordnance Sergeant John Jones, who had also taken the time to train gun crews. Jones's canister shot at close quarters tore attackers to rags, while the big 24-pounder devastated Little Crow's headquarters in a ravine. The Sioux were demoralized by the cannon, saying that, given such 'wagon guns', they could rule the world. The Santees lost 100 men in the siege, mostly to the gun battery.

Colonel Henry Hastings Sibley was the choice of the governor of Minnesota to put down the uprising. The 51-year-old, Detroit-born, former fur trader was the Territorial Delegate to Congress who organized the Minnesota Territory and brought about the Santee land cession in 1851 and was, in 1857, the state's first governor.

Sibley took a relief column out of Fort Snelling as soon as possible. But he knew that it was inadequate. While in the village of St Peter, he received a cry for help from New Ulm, being attacked again. But he could not spare any men till reinforcements should arrive. On 23 August the Santees hit New Ulm, dashing through the streets to plunder and fire buildings till one-third of the town was gone. But citizens of other settlements made common cause with the Germans of New Ulm and repulsed the Sioux by nightfall.

Once reinforcements brought his troop strength to 1600, Sibley marched to Fort Ridgely, which was full of sick, wounded and dead. He had to bury the corpses outside the fort for reasons of sanitation, but the graves detail was

Opposite page: **Little Crow, the Younger**, also known as The Hawk That Hunts Walking, was the leader of the Sioux Indians in the Minnesota Uprising of 1862.

Over: In 1862, Anton Gag painted a realistic view of the Sioux attacking **New Ulm** from the German colony's surrounding cornfields.

Above: **Abraham Lincoln**, the railsplitter-president, was born in a Kentucky log cabin but was not a frontiersman like Daniel Boone and only once was in an Indian war. (However, as president, 1861-65, he was Commander in Chief of the Army that had to pacify the Indian country.) Abe was dragged along by his impoverished father, a 'grasshopper' homesteader always seeking greener pastures. He lived near Hodgenville and Knob Creek in Kentucky, Spencer County, Indiana, and Macon and Coles Counties, Illinois, frontier areas then. He called Indiana 'a wild region, with many bears and other wild animals still in the woods.' In 1831 Abe settled in New Salem, Illinois, but in 1832 was caught up in the excitement of the Black Hawk War. A Galena paper, for example, demanded a war of extermination in which 'there shall be no Indian (*with his scalp on*) left in Illinois.' He was elected captain of his local company of militia. Much later, he observed that the election was 'a success which gave me more pleasure than any I have had since.' Some encyclopedias state that Lincoln's company saw no service. This is incorrect. The rawboned, strong six-footer soldiered for 80 days. He confessed he never saw 'any live, fighting Indians. . . . But I had a good many bloody struggles with the mosquitoes and although I never fainted from loss of blood, I can truly say I was often hungry.' He did not joke, however, about his coming across victims of Stillman's Run. Abe, a lieutenant, like Jeff Davis, under Zachary Taylor, never forgot the morning light on the corpses. 'Every man had a rough, red spot on the top of his head about as big as a dollar, where the redskins had taken his scalp. It was frightful . . . it was grotesque; and the red sunlight seemed to paint everything all over. I remember that one man had on buckskin breeches.'

attacked. All but one of the horses drawing the wagons were killed. The burial party fought back from behind wagons and dead animals, but 23 men were killed before a relief column drove off the Santee Sioux.

Fort Ridgely was badly battered, but its brave defense closed the door on any Sioux advance down the Minnesota River to threaten St Paul itself. Chief Big Eagle later observed that if the Santees had crushed the fort, nothing could have stopped them short of the Mississippi River.

Already, some Santee chiefs were arguing whether to flee westward, surrender, or stand and fight. Some wanted to kill all white prisoners, too. The decision was to fight, but to spare the hostages.

Sibley started up the Minnesota River Valley for Yellow Medicine and on 23 September, when in sight of the agency, was attacked at **Wood Lake** by Little Crow and 700 men. Once again the Sioux showed that they had no stomach for artillery. Little Crow later said that he was ashamed to be a Dakota because the 'wagon guns' of the whites, whom he contemptuously called 'cowardly women', dispersed his warriors. He could not account for his defeat at Wood Lake, even with the cannon, unless (he said) it was caused by traitors in his army.

For all of his brave talk, Little Crow had lost his will to fight and was on the run for Dakota Territory with other chiefs. There he holed up at Devil's Lake. The old villain wanted to torture all captives to death, in revenge for his defeat at Wood Lake. Chief Red Iron successfully argued against this sordid action. However, Indians guarding the makeshift prison camp raped some of the women captives. (Contrary to frontier belief, this was not the inevitable consequence of Indian captivity.) Still, the Santees released 400 prisoners only three days after the battle. Within a month or so, 2000 Sioux surrendered.

The Minnesota Uprising took the lives of about 700 whites at a time when the North was used to casualty figures in the thousands. But the Civil War did not harden the nation to the horrors of senseless torture and murder of housewives and little girls and ribbon clerks and farm hands by these barbaric 'wards' of the government. Americans everywhere were shocked. Minnesotans developed a burning hatred for Indians and a demand for prompt vengeance. This hatred stoked fiery reprisals by militiamen on campaigns and led to a mass execution that is unique in the Indian Wars and, in fact, in all American history.

Sibley selected the 400 most guilty Indians to clap in irons and another 60 or 70 to place under close surveillance. The military commission that he set up sentenced 303 men to be hanged. Sibley sent the names to the President for confirmation.

In some areas of the country, sympathy still remained with the Indians, in spite of their atrocities, because of the many wrongs done them, for years, by whites. Abraham Lincoln was convinced that inflamed passions were trying to make a right out of two wrongs in Minnesota. He appointed two commissioners to review the evidence and determine, objectively, the various degrees of guilt of the Sioux charged with war crimes.

The Indians were marched first to a stockade at Fort Snelling and then to one on the Mankato River. Settlers lined the roads to turn them into gauntlets, striking at the passing Indians with stones, clubs, even garden hoes. They injured 15 of the prisoners and snatched one infant from its mother's arms and dashed it to death on the ground.

There was confusion over Sioux names and identities. The worst culprits were in hiding in Dakota Territory or Canada. No wonder that Lincoln set aside all but 38 sentences.

On the day after Christmas, 1862, the 38 condemned Sioux in Mankato were made to stand in four rows around the edge of a platform with nooses fitted around their necks and hoods over their heads. Ingeniously, the cutting of a single rope sprang all of the gallows trapdoors at once. Hangman William Duley (Dooley?) enjoyed his grim task. He had seen the Santees kill and scalp two of his children. The bodies were dumped in a mass grave but, in a final act of ignominy, they were disinterred by ghouls for laboratory experiments.

Little Crow, after trying without success to secure British support at Fort Garry (Winnipeg), foolishly returned to his old haunts with a few followers in the summer of 1863 to raid settlers in McLeod and Meeker Counties. On 3 July a settler killed him when he caught him on his farm picking raspberries. His scalp, taken as a trophy, was given to the Minnesota Historical Society. But his body was not buried, just left in the field as offal.

Among the insurrectionists who fled westward were the four young murderers who caused the awful war. They poured out their hatred of whites amongst the Teton Sioux of Dakota Territory and their Cheyenne and Arapaho friends.

Sibley, made a brigadier general in thanks for the Wood Lake victory, made expeditions into the Dakotas in the summers of 1863 and 1864 with 3000 men. He engaged in several skirmishes but it was General Alfred Sully, son of the famous painter, Thomas Sully, who hurt the Sioux. He was too late to link up with Sibley, but campaigned westward from Devil's Lake to the Yellowstone River with Iowa, Nebraska and Dakota citizen-soldiers.

At Whitestone Hill, North Dakota, on 3 September 1863, Sully slammed into a huge force of Sioux, 4000 people, of whom a thousand were warriors. The chief was Inkpaduta, who had carried out the Spirit Lake Massacre of 1857, a

Above: In a pen and ink sketch, Charles M Russell pictured Montana Indians, with horse-drawn travois, dropping down to **Fort Union** on the Missouri River near its junction with the Yellowstone.

preview of the Santee uprising. (Ironically, Little Crow had helped the whites against Inkpaduta in 1857.) The battle was a catastrophe for the Sioux; they lost 300 braves and had 250 children and women captured at a cost to Sully of 22 dead and 50 wounded. After establishing Fort Rice on the upper Missouri to restrain the Tetons 'infected' by fleeing Santees, Sully took 2200 men against the Sioux again at **Kildeer Mountain**. He lost only five killed and ten wounded, and the Indians admitted a loss of 35. (Sully figured that their losses were closer to 100 or even 150.) The main thing was that they fled in the night, leaving all of their provisions. Sully said, 'I would rather destroy their supplies than kill 50 of their warriors'. The Teton Sioux were far from crushed, but they were whipped by Sully into an inclination for (temporary) peace.

The Yankton Sioux tended their crops on the Crow Creek Reservation; the Santees were confined by 1857 treaties to the Sisseton, Santee and Devil's Lake Reservations.

Wars in the Southwest

General James Carleton's choice of an officer to put a stop to nuisance raids by Mescalero Apaches and Navajos was an excellent one. Colonel Christopher (Kit) Carson was a plainsman, scout and ex-Rocky Mountain fur trader. An Indian agent from 1853 to 1861, he resigned in order to fight Confederates (and did so at the Battle of Valverde in February, 1862), not to combat Indians with whom he was likely to be in sympathy. But the illiterate colonel of New Mexico Volunteers was always in awe of successful, lettered, doers like John C Fremont and Carleton, and he allowed himself to be talked into heading a campaign against the Mescaleros.

Carleton wanted no talks with these Apaches. Women

Below: Carl L Boeckmann painted the 8th Minnesota Mounted Infantry at the **Battle of Kildeer Mountain**, North Dakota, 1864, when General Alfred Sully broke the back of Santee and Teton Sioux resistance subsequent to the Minnesota Uprising of 1862.

Below: A Charles Russell pen and ink sketch showing a **Pony Expressman** defending himself from pursuing Indians.

and children were to be taken prisoners, but all men were to be killed. The easy-going Carson discounted this showy ruthlessness of the General's.

Kit reoccupied Fort Stanton in southeast New Mexico and campaigned from there. After Lieutenant William Graydon outfought a war party, killing its two chiefs and nine warriors, the Mescalero Apaches began to sue for peace. They were pretty fair fighters. They carried in their left hands, or slung around their necks when not in action, shields which were of the size, shape and toughness of barrelheads. They were impervious to most pistol balls even at close range, beyond ten paces, and impenetrable at any real distance by glancing shots from muskets. But the Mes-

caleros did not have their hearts in the war. Soon, Carson was driving 400 of them to Bosque Redondo.

Bosque Redondo Reservation, a round grove of cottonwoods on the bank of the Pecos River under the guns of Fort Sumner, was called by the General's numerous critics, with tongues firmly in cheeks, 'Fair Carletonia'. It was a bleak and alkaline flat, dreary in the extreme.

Carson's campaign pretty well ended the Mescalero menace, though some young ones continued to raid from the safety of the Bosque Redondo Reservation. Kit tried to resign his colonelcy, to return to his family in Taos, but Carleton would not hear of it. He wanted him to repeat his success with the *Diné*, or Navajos.

Less truculent than their Apache kin, the Navajos, nevertheless, had lived a life of raiding livestock and enslaving women and children from both Mexicans and Pueblo Indians. (Naturally, both of the latter retaliated by enslaving Navajo youngsters.) General Alexander Doniphan had made peace with the Navajos during the Mexican War but expeditions into *Dinetah*, or Navajo Land, were necessary throughout the 1850s. At one point, the Navajos even besieged Fort Defiance itself.

Carleton thought that Bosque Redondo was just the place for the Navajos and that tough, patient, self-reliant Carson was just the man to put them there.

The tribal leadership was split into factions. Barboncito and Delgadito were, more or less, for peace. Manuelito was aloof, almost hostile. There was even a split-off group allied closely with the Army as scouts against their own people, called The Enemy Navajos by the *Diné*.

But all Navajos, from Manuelito to wee children, were possessed of a remarkably intense, even devout, love for their homeland. They refused to consider for even a moment the proposal that they migrate 300 miles from such sacred places as Cañón de Chelly to the barren Pecos flats, where the whites intended to turn them from semi-nomads into civilized, Christianized, self-sufficient farmers.

Any hope of cooperation by Navajos was ended in September 1861 when Lieutenant Colonel J F Chávez,

Above left: George Catlin met **Steep Wind**, a Sans Arc (No Bows) Sioux at Fort Pierre, SD, during his trip up the Missouri River in 1832. Catlin was noted for his accuracy in the depiction of costumes and war paint.

Left: Catlin painted **Black Dog** of the Santee Sioux circa 1835 when that tribe was still peaceable. It would later (1862) be responsible for the horrors of the Minnesota Uprising.

Above: Robert Lindneaux painted a version of what was, probably, the worst massacre in American history, that of **Sand Creek, Colorado**. On 29 November 1864, Colonel John M Chivington took his revenge for the murders of many miners and settlers by Southern Cheyennes and Arapahos emboldened by the absence of the Regular Army during the Civil War. Chivington was called the Fighting Parson because he was a minister who spurned a chaplaincy, saying that he wanted a fighting commission, not a praying one. He was the hero of the Battle of Glorieta Pass, New Mexico, in which the Confederate invasion of the Southwest was turned back. He led 700 Colorado Volunteers through the snow from Fort Lyon to fall on Black Kettle's sleeping camp of 500 Cheyennes and a few Arapahos on a bitter-cold dawn. Chivington ignored the white flag and Stars and Stripes that Black Kettle, thinking himself under the protection of Fort Lyon, quickly raised as a sign of peace. The Coloradans killed, and in many cases mutilated, 200 Indian men, women and children indiscriminately. The Chief escaped. Colorado was pleased by Chivington's brutal action but a Congressional committee denounced him. He resigned his commission but bore the stigma of the massacre for the rest of his life.

commanding Fort Fauntleroy (Fort Lyon), let a contested horse race between New Mexicans and Navajos deteriorate into a riot, and then a small massacre. *Anglo* soldiers were prevented by *Hispano* officers from protecting the Indians. Chávez even ordered his howitzers to open fire on the men, women and children as they fled the fort. Sergeant Nicholas Hodt pretended that he did not hear the order. Still, a dozen people were killed and, the Navajos said, 112 were enslaved. General Canby rebuked Chávez, but his announced court-martial never took place.

The publicly-unbending Carleton issued an ultimatum to the unyielding Navajos on 23 June 1863. The Indians had till 27 July to come in peacefully for transfer to Bosque Redondo. After that, said the General, 'Every Navajo that is seen will be considered as hostile and treated accordingly.'

Carson was given 736 men to tackle the Navajos, described as vexatious, insidious, perfidious folk, no more to be trusted than the wolves of the mountains. Besides infantry and cavalry, Kit had Apache and Ute scouts. He had a few good officers such as Captains Asa B Carey and Albert H Pfeiffer and a number of absolutely useless drunkards and worse.

Pfeiffer, a former Ute and Apache Indian agent, joined

the column late. Some New Mexicans considered him to be 'the most desperately courageous and successful Indian fighter in the West'. He was an Indian-hater after June 1863. Apaches caught him while bathing in a hot spring on the Jornada del Muerto, slaughtered his wife and her servant, and chased him, naked, back to Fort McRae. He was himself wounded in the side by an arrow.

Carson halted his tired animals at Ojo del Oso (Bear Spring), site of Fort Fauntleroy-Lyon, and began a scorched earth policy by turning his animals into the Navajos' wheat fields. He also lived off the land, taking corn and 75,000 pounds of wheat from the Navajo fields at Pueblo Colorado Wash, near Ganado. At abandoned Fort Defiance in Cañón Bonito south of Chinle Wash and mysterious Cañón de Chelly, he again turned Indian croplands into pasture for his mounts. Kit built Fort Canby near the ruins of old Fort Defiance.

By now, Carson was tired of his incompetent officers. He forced the resignation of an alcoholic major after that hero bragged of being the best pimp in all New Mexico. Next, he forced a lieutenant to resign after he was found drunk and in bed with an enlisted man, while officer of the day. One of Kit's surgeons was a drunk, too. A

less poetic Navajos called the bitter experience The Long Walk. Many people died on the long march even though the soldiers, taking their cues from Carson and Carey, pitied their charges more than they hated them. Some went on half-rations to share their food. The Navajos were disarmed for the march, but their guns were returned to them at Bosque Redondo. About 4000 Navajos under Manuelito held out in the West, but surrendered in 1866.

Kit allowed himself to be talked into supervising Bosque Redondo, but gave it up as hopeless after only a few months. The Navajos were not ill-treated at the agency, except by some Mescaleros, but it was a wretched place and they were desperately homesick and unhappy. Their headmen continued to beg to be returned to the New Mexico-Arizona country. General Sherman, shocked at the conditions at Bosque Redondo, approved the move *if* the Navajos promised to remain peaceful. Otherwise, he swore, they would be sent to Oklahoma Indian Territory. In 1868 the Indian Bureau relented and allowed the Navajos to return to their land. Carleton's experiment was a failure but the Navajos never went back on their word, expressed in the 1868 treaty. They never went on the warpath again.

By 1864 the Arapahos and Cheyennes of Colorado were almost as starved as the Navajos pinned atop Cañón de Chelly's Fortress Rock. Hunger sent them raiding the South Platte trails. But hunger was no excuse for the campaign of scalping and mutilating of victims and the burning of their homesteads. After supplies and mail were cut off from Denver and stages stopped running, authorities in that town inflamed public opinion by putting on exhibit the scalped and otherwise abused corpses of a settler, his wife and their two children.

The time was ripe for a hero to save Colorado from what its settlers, without blinking, called savagery. Major Jacob Downing surprised a Cheyenne encampment at Cedar Bluffs, a canyon 90 miles north of the South Platte. He gave the order, 'Commence killing!' and at the cost of one man dead and another wounded, wiped out 26 Indians and wounded perhaps 60 more, who got away. Downing boasted, 'I took no prisoners'. He said that only a shortage of ammunition prevented him from hunting down and killing more Cheyennes.

But Downing was not the man of the hour. That honor went to the hero of the Battle of Glorieta Pass, the man whose audacity turned the battle around and sent the Texans fleeing from the Far Southwest on 27 March 1862. Colonel John M Chivington was called 'The Fighting Parson' because he was a minister who had spurned a chaplaincy, a 'praying commission', in order to fight Rebels and Redskins.

In November of 1864 Chivington made it known that he was going to attack Black Kettle's Cheyennes. Brother

vindictive major who seized Navajos and tried to humiliate them into 'escaping', so that he could invoke the old Spanish *ley de fuga* and kill them, had to be relieved of duty, also. Another lieutenant was caught, 'beastly intoxicated' and in bed with a friend, but at least it was a woman and not an enlisted man. Another lieutenant filed a false report about imaginary Navajo casualties and was forced to resign.

The Navajos killed Major Joseph Cummings while he was on a scout, but there were few casualties on either side, even with Kit's relentless Navajo-haters, the Ute scouts. Only a few warriors were killed, though some women and children were captured and much property destroyed in Carson's search-and-destroy missions. He confiscated or killed all ponies he found, destroyed all corn and wheat fields and chopped down some of the Navajos' prized peach trees. But he was not severe with the Navajo *people*; he wanted them prisoners, not dead.

Delgadito gave up in this war of attrition in November 1863 but Carson had less than 200 Navajos to forward to Bosque Redondo. The turning point came with Carson's invasion in January 1864 of the tribe's inner sanctum, **Cañón de Chelly**. Army units had scouted it before, but it was still largely unknown territory to the Army. It was a sanctuary to the *Diné*, the site of their last-ditch stand.

Carson held the mouth of the Cañón and sent Pfeiffer to scour it from the eastern head. By mistake, he descended into the tributary Cañón del Muerto after a taxing march in the snow. Navajos dropped boulders on his men from the rims high above, but he flushed all warriors from the defile and followed it to its intersection with the main Cañón de Chelly. The Navajos, caught between Carson and Pfeiffer, began to give up. They were cold, hungry and afraid to build fires which would give their positions away.

By the summer of 1864, Carson accepted the largest Indian surrender in history. By year's end, 8000 people were marched from Forts Defiance and Wingate to exile at Bosque Redondo. Carey, not Carson, supervised this Southwestern version of the Cherokee Trail of Tears. The

Above: The Ruins of **White House**, a multi-storied cliff dwelling, is one of several that bear silent testimony to the level of culture attained by the pre-Columbian Anasasi people who populated Cañón de Chelly.

Right: **Cañón de Chelly**, with its high walls, was a natural fortress in the nineteenth century. Today it is populated only by a handful of Navajos and is accessible only by four-wheel-drive vehicles.

Below: The life-style of the **Navajos** in Cañón de Chelly today is little changed from that of their grandfathers, who encountered Kit Carson here.

officers argued that that particular band had surrendered already and was under the protection of Major Edward Wynkoop of Fort Lyon. But the ineffable 'man of God' just retorted that it was his belief that it was right and honorable to use any means under God's heaven to exterminate the people he characterized as 'women and children-killing savages'. And he added, 'Damn any man who is in sympathy with Indians!'

Black Kettle, camped on **Sand Creek**, an Arkansas River tributary, was probably an ambiguous fellow. He may have murdered settlers, but, at the moment, he was choosing the course of peace. A careful man, he had both a white flag and a Stars and Stripes to fly over his lodge to indicate his peaceable nature.

If Chivington actually saw the flags, he probably suspected treachery. Whatever the case, he fell on the unsuspecting village with 700 men and four howitzers. He separated the warriors from their pony herd as Black Kettle tried to reassure his people that they would not be killed. Soon, the chief had to flee with his wounded wife behind him on his horse. Perhaps remembering the grisly display in Denver, Chivington's men offered no quarter to anyone. The brutalized soldiers scalped and mutilated the dead. Chivington ran the Cheyennes for five miles, on a trail littered with corpses, giving up the chase only when darkness closed in.

Sand Creek was a battle, but it was a massacre also. The bloody parson had seven men killed outright and 47 wounded, of whom seven more died. But only two women and five children were taken prisoners. (Chivington wanted no prisoners.) And one report had a body count of the Indian dead totaling only 26 warriors of between 200 and 400 (estimates differed) dead on the field.

The 'Bloody 3rd' paraded in downtown Denver in triumph and a theater exhibited 100 Indian scalps on its stage. But the general public, to Chivington's surprise, was outraged by Sand Creek. After all, a witness had seen a three year-old shot by a soldier. Interpreter John Smith reported women ripped open with knives, children clubbed to death and then mutilated.

Above: In his painting *After the Skirmish* Frederick Remington depicts the cavalrymen relaxing in the dusty heat of the Southwest.

Opposite page: **Manuelito**, the last Indian chief to surrender (1866) in the Navajo War, held out with his 4000 followers long after Kit Carson moved most of his people to Bosque Redondo on the Pecos River in Texas. He was photographed when he was in Washington, DC, with a *Dineh* delegation.

A congressional invesigation issued 700 pages of testimony and condemned Chivington's actions. The embittered colonel was called to appear before a court-martial but was allowed to resign his commission without being punished. For years, the country was split into two camps by the shock of Sand Creek.

Chivington's opposite, Kit Carson, had one more campaign to carry out during the Civil War in the West. He rode out of Fort Bascom, New Mexico, in November with a force of New Mexican and Californian Volunteers and Ute auxiliaries. He was after hostile Kiowas, Cheyennes and Comanches. At **Adobe Walls**, the melting remnants of William Bent's old trading post in the Canadian River Valley of the Texas Panhandle, Carson fell on a combined force of Comanches and Kiowas which outnumbered him two to one. Victory was uncertain until Kit unlimbered his pair of 12-pound mountain howitzers. 'Throw a few shells into that crowd over there', was typical of his unmilitary commands. As fresh warriors sought to encircle him under the cover of smoke from a grass fire that they had set, Carson used a smokescreen of his own.

This First Battle of Adobe Walls was claimed by Kit as a victory, mainly because he was able to burn all 150 Kiowa lodges with all of their winter stores. But it was more like a draw, even with the artillery. Carson lost two killed and had ten wounded, and probably exaggerated a bit in guessing that his men killed 60 Kiowas and Comanches.

Carson's Battle of Adobe Walls took place on 25 November 1864. Just 19 weeks later, 9 April 1865, General Robert E Lee surrendered the Confederate Army to General Ulysses S Grant at Appomattox Court House. An era ended, but a new one would begin in the Indian Wars of the West.

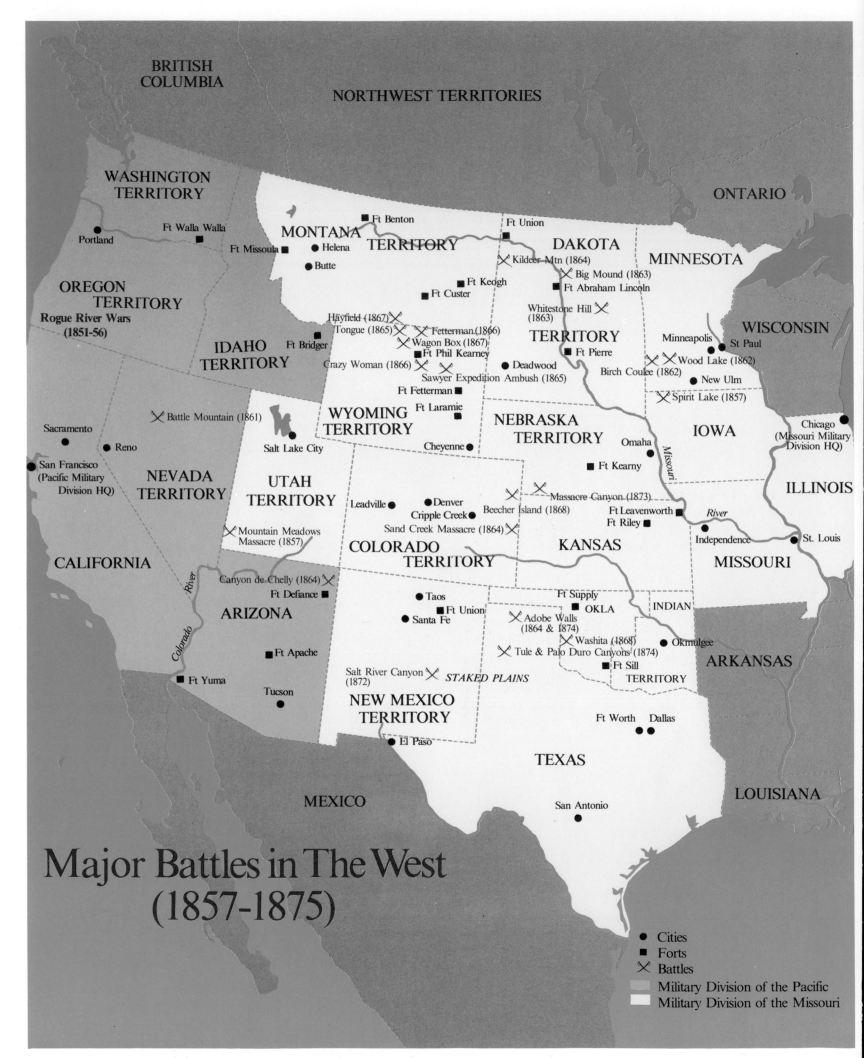

BRITISH COLUMBIA

NORTHWEST TERRITORIES

ONTARIO

WASHINGTON TERRITORY

- Portland
- Ft Walla Walla

MONTANA TERRITORY
- Ft Benton
- Ft Missoula
- Helena
- Butte

Ft Union

DAKOTA

MINNESOTA

Kildeer Mtn (1864)
Big Mound (1863)
Ft Abraham Lincoln

OREGON TERRITORY
Rogue River Wars (1851-56)

IDAHO TERRITORY
- Ft Bridger

Ft Keogh
Ft Custer

Whitestone Hill (1863)

TERRITORY

WISCONSIN

- Minneapolis
- St Paul

Hayfield (1867)
Tongue (1865) Fetterman (1866)
Wagon Box (1867)
Ft Phil Kearney
Crazy Woman (1866)
Sawyer Expedition Ambush (1865)
Ft Fetterman

Ft Pierre

- Deadwood

Wood Lake (1862)
Birch Coulee (1862)

- New Ulm

Battle Mountain (1861)

WYOMING TERRITORY
Ft Laramie

Spirit Lake (1857)

- Sacramento
- Reno

Salt Lake City

Cheyenne

NEBRASKA TERRITORY

Omaha

IOWA

Chicago (Missouri Military Division HQ)

- San Francisco (Pacific Military Division HQ)

NEVADA TERRITORY

UTAH TERRITORY

Ft Kearny

ILLINOIS

- Leadville
- Denver
- Cripple Creek

Massacre Canyon (1873)

Beecher Island (1868)
Sand Creek Massacre (1864)

Ft Leavenworth
Ft Riley

River

- Independence
- St. Louis

CALIFORNIA

Mountain Meadows Massacre (1857)

COLORADO TERRITORY

KANSAS

MISSOURI

Canyon de Chelly (1864)
Ft Defiance

ARIZONA

- Taos
- Ft Union
- Santa Fe

Ft Supply
OKLA

INDIAN

Adobe Walls (1864 & 1874)
Washita (1868)
Tule & Palo Duro Canyons (1874)

- Okmulgee

ARKANSAS

- Ft Apache

Salt River Canyon (1872) STAKED PLAINS

Ft Sill TERRITORY

- Ft Yuma

Colorado River

- Tucson

NEW MEXICO TERRITORY

- El Paso

- Ft Worth
- Dallas

TEXAS

MEXICO

- San Antonio

LOUISIANA

Major Battles in The West (1857-1875)

- • Cities
- ■ Forts
- ✕ Battles
- Military Division of the Pacific
- Military Division of the Missouri

THE PLAINS AND ROCKIES

1865-1875

The surrender of General Lee at Appomatox in April of 1865 signaled a new era in the Indian Wars. Old posts were re-garrisoned from back East and brought up to strength. New outposts were established and weaponry improved. Mobile cavalry troops replaced slower infantry companies. During this period were seen the opening skirmishes of two series of wars which were to dominate the West throughout all of the latter half of the nineteenth century. These were the Sioux wars of the North Plains and the Apache wars of the Southwest. There would be more than 200 fights in the West during the decade that followed the Civil War.

The post-Civil War era was ushered in by the departing Volunteers near Caspar, Wyoming. The town was named for Lieutenant Caspar W Collins, who was a transient officer unlucky enough to be stuck at Platte River Bridge Station at the wrong time. Some 200 miles west of Fort Laramie lay not just an improved river crossing, a ford, but a bona fide span where the California-Oregon Trail crossed the North Platte. Near the bridge a tiny village, of sorts, sprang up—a store, a stage station, and a stockaded fort sometimes called Camp Dodge.

Unknown to Collins or his commanding officer, Major Martin Anderson, 3000 Sioux, Arapaho and Cheyenne were hiding in the sandstone bluffs near the stockade, trying to make up their minds as to when and how to attack. They had been plotting a great campaign against the whites since May. It was now July 1865.

First, the lurking Indians tried to draw the soldiers out by sending a few decoys across the flat in front of the fort. But the Army, secure behind its log walls, would not budge, only responding with desultory howitzer fire. When reinforcements rode up, the Indians attacked them, but they got safely into the fort under covering fire from its walls.

On the morning of 26 July the besiegers tried to draw their noose tighter. They placed men both above and below the bridge to isolate it. They sent decoys even closer, to canter across the prairie in plain view of the sentries.

This time it appeared that the Army was swallowing the bait. The gates opened and a cavalry detachment trotted across the Platte Bridge. They were not chasing Indian decoys, but going out to escort an approaching supply train, spotted in the distance by a sentry on a wall. A round was fired from a howitzer to warn the train's escort of possible trouble.

Collins was in command of the 20 Kansas troopers only because none of their officers wanted to risk their lives so close to demobilization. The lieutenant was apprehensive. It is said that his fear of death lead him to wear his brand-new dress uniform on the mission.

Two long columns of Indians now made their moves. One rode out of a brushy draw and passed behind Collins, cutting him off from the bridge. The other moved in front of him, separating him from the five wagons guarded by Sergeant Amos J Custard and 25 men.

Collins spurred his unit forward to break the forming circle and, at the same time, to relieve the wagons. His men loosed a volley with their carbines, slid them back into their scabbards and broke out six-shooters. But the firing in his rear led Collins to order a retreat to the bridgehead. He led the way, slashing with his saber in head-to-head combat, troopers and Indians intermingled. The pistols took their toll at such close quarters, but when Collins turned back to pick up a wounded man, he was killed. Four of his men were also killed and eight more seriously wounded. All of the rest were hurt, too, but the wounded got back to the fort.

Custard, seeing his rescue party battered into a retreat, drew his wagons into the age-old circular posture of defense. It was the Sergeant's misfortune that he drew as an opponent a real fighter. Like Custard, he was only a warrior, not a chief. But he had many followers because of his fighting prowess. He was huge, 230-pound Roman Nose, a giant among Indians at six feet three inches in height. He thought himself well nigh invincible in battle, too, because of the strong medicine of his war bonnet.

The Cheyenne did not choose to have his men circle the trapped train on horseback, to be picked off by the concealed riflemen. He dismounted half of his braves and they crawled up on their bellies toward the wagonmen. The other half kept the fort busy. There would be no help for Custard from that quarter.

With astounding patience, Roman Nose settled down and took four hours to capture the wagons, killing and mutilating everybody and burning to death the last survivors, including the wounded sergeant. He might have taken the fort, too, but the Indians were unused to long sieges and had been badly hurt by Collins and Custard—suffering up to 60 dead and 130 wounded—so they broke off the attack and withdrew.

While the Indians were making scattered raids, such as that at Platte Bridge, the Army was concentrating on only one thing. The Californian, General Patrick Edward Connor, was trying to mount a major offensive, one worthy of the Civil War campaigns in the East. But the **Powder River Expedition** was slowed by muddy terrain, bad weather, mutinous troops, short rations and inadequate forage for the animals. Volunteers demanded their discharges. And some got them. Alarms from the Black Hills and Minnesota siphoned off Connor's manpower.

Finally, Connor moved out three columns to rendezvous at Rosebud Creek around 1 September 1865. Colonel Nelson Coe took the Right Column of 1400 men and Lieutenant Colonel Samuel Walker the Center Column of 600-plus men—but only after Connor faced the rebellious Kansans with his Californians and a loaded howitzer. Connor himself took the Left Column, about 600 men including Captain Frank North's Pawnee Scouts, with Jim Bridger as guide. It was the biggest Army operation in the West, except perhaps for the combined Sibley-Sully punitive raids of the Santee War.

Connor had several skirmishes, in one of which his Pawnees bested a Cheyenne war party. Near the Bozeman Trail crossing of Powder River he built Fort Connor, then fought a bloody draw with Black Bear's Arapahos. Red Cloud's Oglala Sioux and Dull Knife's Cheyennes were harassing his two other units, but he did not know it.

It was now 11 September and the only information on Cole and Walker that Connor had was the discovery by his Pawnees of hundreds of their horses, dead, and their saddles burned. Finally, with the Pawnees' help, the link-up was made on 24 September. But two of the three divisions of the Powder River Expedition were complete wrecks. Both Cole and Walker happened to cover ground which was without water or grass. Their horses died and their men were put on short rations. Cole's men escaped disaster by using their cannon, especially a rifled piece, and their Spencer repeaters effectively. But a sleeting norther crippled the now-combined force. Most horses were dead and most men starving when Connor rescued them.

Luckily for Connor, new orders arrived to break up the too-vast District of the Plains into four manageable districts. It was with relief that he terminated the expedition and headed for Salt Lake City.

The real reason for the Army's discontinuance of Connor's campaign was its excessive cost. The Army hurriedly cut back on large-scale operations. The Quartermaster General himself went west to investigate the expenditure in the District of ten millions for rations and forage and an equal sum for other supplies. The Indians were bankrupting the Army!

The great expedition of 1865 was a failure, though not the ignominious defeat that it has sometimes been painted. It was true that Cole and Walker barely avoided a disaster.

And while the former claimed to have killed or wounded from 200 to 500 Indians, the latter confessed that his men might not have killed a single warrior. But Connor fought the Arapahos to a bloody draw and his Pawnees won a skirmish. Connor was a good man, but the combination of hostiles, bad terrain and filthy weather beat his unwieldy army. Worst of all, his supposedly powerful expedition, instead of chastening the Indians, only emboldened them.

Before the Army replaced Volunteers with battle-hardened Civil War veterans from an Army reduced to only 25,000 enlisted men, the Government tried to duplicate Fitzpatrick's diplomacy of 1851. Another great Fort Laramie pow-wow was held on 13–16 June 1866 although General John Pope warned that the Indians meant to fight,

that they considered their treaties to be just white men's scraps of paper. In the chair was no less a personage than the Civil War hero, General William T ('War is Hell') Sherman, now commanding the District of the Plains which was being carved up into separate commands.

Sherman enticed Red Cloud, Dull Knife, Spotted Tail and other chiefs with goodwill gifts of powder, lead and food. Although they had turned back Connor, the Indians had been punished by the hard winter almost as much as the Expedition had suffered.

The Government asked permission for emigrants to cross the lands recently granted to the Sioux and Cheyenne, but the General also sought permission for three forts to be built on the Bozeman Trail connecting the Platte River with

Above: Winter campaigning, a trademark of the Indian-fighting Army, was hard on the troopers, but even harder on the Indians, who were often hungry and freezing in their *tipis*.

Montana's mines. Sherman knew that the chiefs were not Roman dictators; they could not guarantee, in advance, the conduct of their young warriors.

Red Cloud of the Oglalas spoke for both the Sioux and Cheyennes though he was, technically, not a chief. A born leader, he adamantly opposed any such concessions. He angrily broke off the talks when he saw Colonel Henry B Carrington's 700 men of the 18th Infantry marching through Fort Laramie on their way to build the forts in the Powder River country regardless of the council's outcome.

Below: The Amon Carter Museum's watercolor, *Indians Attacking*, by Charles M Russell is one of the most spirited paintings of Plains Indians combat by the artist in that Fort Worth institution.

When Carrington entered the peace tent, Red Cloud jumped to his feet and (correctly) accused the leaders in Washington of deceit, sending presents to buy a road while sending 'eagles'—he pointed to Carrington's symbols of rank—to steal it. He added, 'I prefer to die fighting rather than by starvation.'

All of the chiefs muttered their disgust at the Government's bald deception. Man Afraid of His Horses warned Sherman that his people would resist both road and forts. Almost all of the chiefs left in a huff, though three Brulés signed. Later, however, even they notified Sherman that their braves had repudiated their action. They warned all whites to look out for their scalps.

Colonel Carrington did not make policy, of course. He just carried out orders. But he was lumped by Chief Spotted Tail with the bureaucrats, all being liars in the chief's opinion. But Carrington was, at least, wise enough to resist a splendid example of penny-wise, pound-foolish Washington policy making. When orders came to fire his scout, mountain man Jim Bridger, to save his five dollars a day in pay, Carrington lied that the discharge was 'impossible to execute.'

As it was, the Government seemed hellbent on sending him into disaster with only a couple of howitzers and 700 men armed, mostly, with obsolete muzzle-loading Springfield rifled muskets. Only his bandsmen had seven-shot Spencer carbines.

After Sherman's pow-wow fell apart, Carrington proceeded west from Laramie with his long line of 226 wagons. They bore not only the usual lead, powder and rations, but also doors, window sills, locks, chains, butter churns, musical instruments, seeds for vegetable gardens, scythes and mowing machines, tools, blacksmith's forges, shingle and brick-making machines, even a steam-powered saw-mill. Apparently the Army meant to stay in the Powder River-Bighorn country; in the rear were ambulances or light wagons with Army wives and children.

At Fort Reno, old Fort Connor, 175 miles from Fort Laramie, Carrington on 28 June 1866 relieved Galvanized Yankee Confederates and Michigan Volunteers with his regulars. Some of his men he sent on reconnaissances, using the Volunteers' horses. He left a quarter of his men at Fort Reno and moved the balance to a grassy flat between the forks of (Big) Piney and Little Piney Creeks

near the Powder River. It was a superb site, with lots of grass, water and even nearby timber.

Carrington was a good man for the job of fort-building. A Yale graduate, he was both a draftsman and an engineer. But the Sioux slowed construction of his powerful 600-by-800 foot stockade of Fort Phil Kearny by picking off sentries on knolls and shooting up haying and woodcutting fatigue parties until frightened off by a few howitzer rounds. They then returned at night to snipe at sentries on the fort's rising walls. Worst of all was the gauntlet that had to be run by the wood wagons, seven miles from fort to timber.

It dawned on Carrington that he was being held a virtual prisoner in his new fort, so he appealed for more men and ammunition. He got 95 infantrymen and 65 cavalry recruits so green that the latter could hardly sit a horse. The position of the Government, which knew best, of course, was that the Powder River area was at peace.

All the while, Red Cloud and Dull Knife were being joined by allies: Black Bear of the Arapahos, Sitting Bull and Gall of the Hunkpapa Sioux, the bright young Oglala Sioux warrior, Crazy Horse, and the Miniconjou, Hump.

Opposite page: At a second great Fort Laramie peace-making pow-wow, held in 1868, the Army faced the Indian delegates with an impressive array of General officers including (together, right of center pole) **William S Harney and William T Sherman** and, behind the bush, **Alfred Terry**.

Above: A rather clumsy artist's version (with additions) of the Fort Laramie peace-treaty photograph, with **Chief Spotted Tail** standing. The officers present concluded Red Cloud's War – but strictly on that Sioux chief's terms. They abandoned the Bozeman Trail and its three forts, and the Powder River country, to the immense disgust of the Army's rank and file.

Even some of peaceful Spotted Tail's men joined the loose siege of the three forts, Carrington having added Fort C F Smith on the Bighorn River.

Jim Bridger arranged a talk between Carrington and Red Cloud. The former tried both to please the latter with band music and to scare him with demonstrations of howitzer fire. It did not work. The very next morning Red Cloud ran off 175 of the Colonel's horses and mules. When Army pursuers were well strung out, the Indians turned on them. So, casually, began the bloody Red Cloud's War.

Below: In 1919, Charles M Russell painted this oil on canvas, *The Buffalo Hunt*, now in the Amon Carter Museum. He showed the manner in which Plains Indians, mounted on nimble-footed ponies, circled a milling bison herd for close-range shots with bows and arrows and rifles they acquired from the whites.

Opposite page: Charles M Bell's 1880 photo is a portrait of **Red Cloud**, or **Scarlet Cloud (Makhpiya Luta)** c. 1822-1909, the Oglala Sioux who set back Army plans for the Bozeman Trail for years. The Pine Ridge Agency was originally Red Cloud Agency.

Right: The **Spotted Tail** Agency, later the Rosebud Agency, abutted the Oglalas on the west. The Brulé chief was more peaceful than Red Cloud and his agency more peaceable than the other until he was killed by Crow Dog in 1881. Out of anarchy emerged the Ghost Dance.

Red Cloud was serious, *deadly* serious. Old Gabe Bridger learned that he had even tried to get his deadly enemies, the Crows, to join the great war against the whites. In this he failed, but he got some modern weapons from the Sioux who lazed about Fort Laramie. This was important, for most of his braves still had only bows and arrows. Now Crazy Horse became an expert at decoying cavalrymen into traps.

Carrington made a brave show of formally celebrating the completion of the key fort of the three, Phil Kearny, by raising the Stars and Stripes on the last day of October, then hosting a feast and quadrille after a speech by himself. But there was really little cause for celebration. Morale was low, because he had not drilled or trained his troopers, but had used them as workmen. The strongly-built fort was understrength to act as the cutting edge of the frontier. Figuratively speaking, Fort Phil Kearny was cantilevered out over an abyss.

Jim Bridger continued to warn Carrington that Indian trouble, bad trouble, was brewing. Cocky younger officers, veterans of Sherman's fiery march to the sea in the Civil War, mocked him and derided Carrington's obsession with defense. Captain Frederick H Brown even delayed a transfer back East in order to get a crack at the Indians. He boasted that he would, personally, lift Red Cloud's scalp. He was outdone in braggadocio by Captain William J Fetterman, who bragged that he would march through the entire Sioux nation if given just 80 good troopers.

On 6 December Red Cloud baited Carrington and Fetterman with a fake raid on a wood train and stung them badly. By 21 December he was ready for the main event. He hid between 1500 and 2000 warriors behind Lodge Trail Ridge and laid an ambush on Peno Creek, only three miles from the fort. Crazy Horse and Hump led two small parties of decoys close to the fort as another band struck at the wood train. The pickets on the walls of Fort Phil Kearny, as usual, fired warning shots. Carrington promptly ordered out Captain James Powell to escort the woodcutters to safety.

But Fetterman wanted his taste of glory. He demanded the command on the basis of his brevet seniority, and he got it. Carrington gave him clear and strict orders. He was to go to the aid of the wood train only. He was not to pursue the raiders beyond Lodge Trail Ridge under any conditions.

Privately, of course, Fetterman considered Carrington much too cautious for his own good. He selected two firebrands, Brown and Lieutenant George W Grummond. The latter had almost been killed in a skirmish but had, seemingly, learned nothing. He left behind in the fort his bride of only a few months.

The overconfidence of these brash officers should have shocked the cautious Carrington into replacing them or revoking his orders. But he could not. His thoughts were on the safety of the trapped wood-cutting crew. As if it were a picnic, or a hunt, two civilians casually joined the detachment just to try out (on live targets) their new rapid-fire Henry repeating rifles.

Fetterman fancied himself a strategist as well as an Indian fighter. He did not head directly for the embattled woodsmen, but curved around to the rear of the marauders both to force a fight and to cut off their retreat. He was damned if he would let the redskins cheat him of his moment in the sun. The Indians countered in their usual fashion, Crazy Horse disengaging a few decoys. Fetterman fell for the trap, lock, stock and barrel. Either forgetting or, more likely, ignoring Carrington's orders, he galloped his force over Lodge Trail Ridge and out of sight of the fort.

On the far slope, quietly awaiting him, were Red Cloud and his main force, concealed in gullies. Once Crazy Horse gave the signal, the Sioux, Cheyenne and Arapahos fell on the 81-man force.

It was cold on the slope which came to be called Massacre Hill. Men and mounts slipped on ice and snow which soon became red with blood. Fetterman's trapdoor Springfields were dependable; they almost never jammed. And they were accurate. But, at such close range, the detachment

could not have survived had they all carried Henry or Spencer repeaters instead of the single-shot arm.

Grummond, in the lead, was shot early on. Within an hour, every man was either shot down or was a suicide. Both Fetterman and Brown apparently shot themselves so that they would not have to endure the tortures of the Indians. The latter hacked, butchered and disemboweled the bodies with devilish glee, enjoying their humiliation of the dead. They even killed a pet dog of one of the soldiers. The Army called it the **Fetterman Massacre** because the rash lieutenant lost every man of his command. The Indians called it the Battle of a Hundred Slain.

This was the Army's worst defeat, so far, in the West, and only the second engagement in its history in which there were no survivors. It is often forgotten that the foolish Fetterman fought well before being overwhelmed and blowing his own brains out. Some Indians even said that their total of dead and wounded was 200, but it is doubtful that Red Cloud lost the 60 dead claimed by the Army.

The men of the wood train, ignored by the Indians busy with their blood bath, made it safely into the fort. The sound of rifle fire beyond the ridge led Carrington to put together the strongest rescue force that he could. He took almost every able-bodied man. He left the fort and the women and children protected only by bandsmen, cooks, and prisoners he released from the guardhouse. It was a terrible risk, for Red Cloud could have destroyed Carrington's force and taken the post. But, inexplicably, he withdrew before Carrington's counter-attack.

When the Colonel pulled back, he expected the fort to be overrun. He planned to blow up the powder magazine and the women and children with it, to keep them out of the hands of the savages. But the weather saved Fort Phil Kearny. A blizzard dropped the temperature to 30 below. It was actually much colder outside the fort because of the wind chill factor. Even with fires, warm woolen clothing and blankets, Carrington had to change his guard details every half-hour to keep the sentinels from freezing. In their thin-skinned *tipis* the besieging Indians were not so flushed with victory that they did not huddle together, miserably, in shivering masses.

Trapped in the snowbound fort, Carrington asked the impossible. He wanted a volunteer to ride to Fort Laramie to get help. John (Portugee) Phillips, a veteran scout, stepped forward. The Colonel gave him his own horse to ride, a Kentucky bluegrass thoroughbred. He personally led the brave scout out through the gate and called into the swirling snowflakes behind him, 'May God help you!'

Portugee Phillips's desperate journey became a feat by which all horseback rides in the West have since been measured. Often, stiff and cold and frostbitten as he was under his layered clothing and buffalo robe, he had to dismount and lead—flounder—his horse through waist-high snow drifts. Wisely, he hid by day and traveled only by night.

Phillips reached tiny Fort Reno safely, but there was no aid to be spared there, not even a telegraph to alert Fort Laramie. So he rode on as a band of pursuers closed on

Left: Charles Russell painted a fine watercolor, **Smoke Signal**, now in the Amon Carter Museum in Fort Worth. It represented a party of scouts on an out-cropping of rock, their war ponies out of sight on the back slope of a bluff, as they exchanged signals with Indians on a distant butte.

Below: **Sitting Bull,** actually **Sitting Buffalo Bull (Tatankya Iyotake)**, was a medicine man of the Hunkpapa sub-tribe of Teton Dakotas (Sioux) who became a great warrior-politician. He unified the Sioux against the Army in 1876.

him. From the summit of a hill, he held them off till darkness came and he could give them the slip. At Horseshoe Station, he had the telegrapher wire Fort Laramie but, not trusting the wires, he rode on to deliver his message in person. It was lucky that he did; the telegraph message did not get through.

In classic dramatic fashion, the completely exhausted horse and rider staggered into the fort to interrupt a gala Christmas Eve ball. Phillips was hardly able to speak. He was nearly dead from exhaustion and exposure. But he got through, and Fort Laramie rushed the 1st Battalion of the 18th Infantry Regiment to Fort Phil Kearny before Red Cloud could mount his attack. The hostiles dispersed.

Naturally the Army had to save face. Not content with Fetterman, they made Carrington a scapegoat and relieved him of his command.

Much too late, the Army sent west the ammunition and supplies Carrington had requested. Single shot—but breech loading—Springfield rifles replaced the old muzzle-loaders. A few repeating carbines made their way to the forts. Red Cloud's strategy was to besiege the posts in the hope of stopping all traffic with them. It was his ill luck to have to do so in the face of improved Army weapons.

The Indians struck on 1 and 2 August at both Fort Phil Kearny and Fort C F Smith. Some 500 Cheyennes caught 30 civilian hay cutters and soldier-guards two miles from the latter post on 1 August. The soldiers, sheltered in a log corral, shot the first rush of men to pieces. Only one warrior made it to the barricade and he was shot dead. The Cheyennes set the grass afire, but the flames stopped 20 feet short of the logs, 'as though arrested by supernatural power', one of the defenders said. The smoke blew back on the Indians, who used it to retrieve their 20 dead or wounded warriors.

Guarding the ax-wielders at Fort Phil Kearny the day after the **Hayfield Fight** was a company of the 27th Infantry. They were struck by the elite of the Lakota nation— Red Cloud, Crazy Horse and American Horse. Crazy Horse first stampeded the mules and the horse herd, then

Above: The Hunkpapa Chief, **Gall**, who was to beat Reno and help crush Custer in 1876.

Below: **Fort Phil Kearny**, on a fork of Powder River, was the key Bozeman Trail post where Fetterman rode forth to annihilation in 1866.

Above: **Philip Sheridan** was General William T Sherman's lieutenant in the West and his disciple. He believed in total warfare and had no sympathy for the Indians he fought. After service in Texas, California and the Northwest, he won great fame in the Civil War as a daring cavalry commander. Sheridan was sent in 1867 to the Department of the Missouri and there began the Army's practice of winter campaigns against hostiles. Colonel George Custer's strike at Black Kettle, the Battle of the Washita of November 1868, was one result of this new kind of Plains warfare. Sheridan's grand design was to drive cavalry units deep into Kiowa, Comanche and Cheyenne country when the Indians least expected it. His drastic measures worked, gaining peace at least temporarily. Sheridan fought in summer, too, and the Battle of Summit springs (11 July 1869) was the culmination of his 1868-69 campaign. He sent Major E A Carr and five companies of 5th Cavalry from Fort McPherson, Nebraska, after Tall Bull and his elite (Cheyenne) Dog Soldiers. Carr was supported by the 150 Pawnee Scouts of Major Frank and Captain Luther North. William F (Buffalo Bill) Cody was Carr's scout. Carr killed 50 of the enemy, including Tall Bull, and captured 117 at a cost of only one soldier wounded. Sheridan dumped the idea of using civilian scouts in force after Forsyth's siege at Beecher's Island (1868), but gave Colonel Ranald Mackenzie his head so that he chased the Kiowas and Comanches out of their Palo Duro Canyon hideout. Sheridan then sent Mackenzie crashing across the heretofore sacrosanct Mexican border in search of hostiles. In 1869 'Little Phil' was promoted to lieutenant general and given the Department of the Missouri. He, among others, was credited with coining the phrase 'The only good Indian is a dead Indian.' In 1870 he went to Europe as a military observer in the Franco-Prussian War. On Sherman's retirement he took command of the Army. Sheridan always protected Custer and had him reinstated after his court-martial and suspension following the Hancock Campaign of 1867.

split the axemen from their escort. But the wood crew, dropping tools and picking up rifles, made it safely back to the fort. This was because the 1500 Indians were intent on another Fetterman butchery, with Captain Powell their chief victim this time.

But Powell was no Fetterman or Brown or Grummond. He had carefully forted up his men in a strongpoint prepared for just such a crisis. It was a miniature fort of 14 wagon beds out in the open with a good field of fire for his 31 soldiers and civilians. The wagon boxes had been left behind when the wood crew took their wheels and axles to haul logs. Powell filled the interstices between the boxes with logs and sandbags made of grain sacks. He even took the precaution of placing extra arms and ammunition inside the wagon bodies for emergencies.

The Indians had been stung badly in the six-hour Hayfield Fight, when a dozen civilians and 20 soldiers fought off odds of at least 20-to-one for six hours. **The Wagon Box Fight** was a replay of that engagement—and more.

Powell gave his best sharpshooters three repeating rifles each, probably. 50 caliber Spencers, with other soldiers at their sides to reload the guns. The rest of his men used their breech loading or trapdoor Springfields very well. He had his men hold their fire until the warwhooping 500 redmen were a scant 50 yards away. The sudden and unrelenting rain of fire split the Indian charge into bits. Never had the Sioux taken such losses and so quickly. At close range, some rifle-balls passed through one victim to kill or wound a second man behind him. There were none of the lulls in firing, the loading delays, on which the Indians counted.

The Sioux and their allies fled, leaving dead men and horses all around the improvised fort. Powell lost six dead and two wounded of his 32-man force. For once, white estimates of Indian losses were probably accurate—60 dead and 120 wounded. The Indians had rushed the defenders six separate times and Red Cloud's horse was shot from under him, perhaps by Powell himself.

The Hayfield and Wagon Box Fights were classic battles in which a few badly outnumbered men held off overwhelming odds.

While the Indians were virtually closing the Bozeman Trail to travelers, to the south another big Army push, like Connors's, was carried out by General W S Hancock and his right-hand man, the rising young star of the cavalry arm of the service, Colonel George A Custer. 'Hancock the Superb' of Civil War fame knew little of Indians and this 1867 campaign was Custer's first brush with redskins. So thinly spread were troops in so many far-flung posts on the plains that most had to remain strictly on the defensive, thereby intimidating hostile Indians not a whit. Ironically, Hayfield and Wagon Box battles gave the Indians more pause than **'Hancock's War'** of 1867. Its major accomplishment, Custer's destruction of Roman Nose's camp on Pawnee Fork, was 'disallowed' by the Government as illegal and Hancock was relieved.

In the fall of 1867 Sherman and other generals negotiated the Medicine Lodge Treaty in Kansas to create two large reservations in Indian Territory, one for Cheyennes and Arapahos and the other for Comanches, Kiowas and Kiowa-Apaches. Then in April 1868 the generals once more parleyed with Red Cloud and, to the consternation of the Army, virtually surrendered to him. They conceded all of his demands and abandoned the Bozeman

Trail and its three forts. A shock wave ran through the Army, which felt betrayed—after its bloody sacrifices—by higher-ups. Embittered troopers, marching out of the Powder River country, looked over their shoulders to see clouds of smoke as the Indians fired the forts. And what did Sherman get in exchange? Red Cloud's word to 'try' to keep his young men off the warpath.

The Bozeman Trail capitulation by the Army not only emboldened Red Cloud but also Tall Bull, the jingoist Cheyenne who opposed pro-peace Black Kettle. He was one of 500 Dog Soldiers, a Cheyenne guard of elite warriors. Roman Nose refused to sign the Medicine Lodge Treaty and the tall brave was not about to go on a reservation. Like Tall Bull, he would roam and hunt where he pleased.

When General Philip Sheridan, the Commanding Officer of the Army's Department of the West, made a tour of inspection in 1868, peace was firmly in the saddle. The Indians were to be persuaded, not forced, to go onto reservations. But Sheridan knew that a policy of weakness would never work. It was the 93 Army posts that kept the peace, such as it was, not appeasement.

The rank and file despised the Peace Commission's policies which, as they saw it, amounted to feeding the Indians in winter so that they could kill soldiers and civilians the next summer. Sheridan, at least, later got his old comrade, President Grant, to end the practice of making treaties with Indian 'nations' as if they were foreign governments. The tribesmen would be considered simply wards of the Government.

But Federal vacillation continued to plague soldiers and settlers alike. Guns and ammunition, promised to the Cheyennes by the Indian Bureau, did not arrive because Tall Bear raided the peaceful Kaw Indians. But when he threatened more trouble, the Government handed out arms on 9 August 1868 at Fort Larned, Kansas.

A separate party of Cheyennes, unaware of the deal, changed its mind and instead of raiding Pawnees, as planned, turned on whites along the Solomon and Saline Rivers, burning ranches, running off livestock, killing men and raping women. Peaceful Indians hurried south to safety as the Dog Soldiers and their ilk terrorized eastern Colorado and western Kansas.

Sheridan, Hancock's successor, thought that the cure for these hostilities would be a surprise winter campaign. But if he waited, all of western Kansas would be afire. So he adopted a plan of Major George A Forsyth for the fall. Forsyth had worked his way up from dragoon private to brevet brigadier general during the Civil War. He wanted the Army to operate Indian-style. He would use a strong scouting force to dog and harass war parties so that they could never rest. It was a brilliant idea, much too logical for the Army generals. He would split the hostiles into small and weak groups which would have to fight, and die, or surrender in a guerrilla war of attrition. He was sure that the Sioux and their allies, if kept hungry, off-balance and bloodied, would be able to besiege no forts, raid no stagecoaches.

Sheridan's approval brought the first 50 'first-class, hardy, frontiersmen' of hundreds of volunteers. Forsyth wanted real scouts, plainsmen, so he, deliberately, did not draw from the ranks but signed up tough civilians who were eager to fight Indians for a dollar a day. Because of Army

Above: No one left a greater impression on the post-Civil War Army in the West than **General William Tecumseh Sherman.** He graduated from West Point in 1840 but, after seeing little action in the Mexican War, resigned his commission in 1853 to become a California banker. He was in command of the California militia in 1856 but resigned when the Governor failed to back him up in the Vigilantes crisis. His march through Georgia, to Atlanta and the sea, in the Civil War and his 'War is hell' quote, won him immortality. From 1866 to 1869 he was commander of the Dept of the Missouri, covering the entire Plains. He skilfully used the Army, much reduced after the Civil War, to protect lines of travel and communication. He believed in total Indian warfare, even more than his loyal protégé, Sheridan, and was an outspoken opponent of the Bureau of Indian Affairs and his old friend President Grant's experiment with a 'Quaker' peace policy toward the redmen. He believed that Indians guilty of atrocities should be severely punished and all others placed on reservations. He wanted Indian affairs transferred to the War Department. In May of 1871, on an inspection of the Texas frontier, Sherman nearly lost his scalp to a raiding party of Kiowas led by Satanta. They passed up his ambulance to hit the wagon train behind him and kill six teamsters. The close call convinced the General that severe measures were not just desirable but absolutely necessary. He had no trouble getting Sheridan to loose Mackenzie and Nelson Miles, of course, in the Red River War of 1874-75. They broke the strength of the Kiowas and Comanches. (Mackenzie swept them from their Palo Duro Canyon hideout, killed 1,000 of their ponies and kept the rest.) However, Secretaries of War Rawlins and Belknap limited Sherman's authority though he was General of the Army, 1869-84. He felt humiliated and powerless, but he removed his headquarters (1874-76) from Washington to St Louis to get out from under their thumbs. Sherman retired in 1883, having dominated the Army's policies and strategy in the West for almost 20 years.

red tape, he had to enlist his fighting men in the Quarter-master Corps!

Forsyth's second-in-command, still limping from a severe Civil War wound, was Lieutenant Frederick H Beecher, the nephew of Reverend Henry Ward Beecher. The scouts brought their own horses, but the Army provided them with guns and ammunition. About a third of the men were Civil War veterans. One of them, First Sergeant W H H McCall, by rights, should have outranked both Forsyth and Beecher. He had been a brigadier general of Volunteers.

Early in September, Sheridan sent his new force into Colorado on patrol with a packtrain of four mules. Forsyth was on the heels of a large party of raiders, although he did not yet have enough men for the job. Those he did have, however, were tough and were very well armed with Colt revolvers and seven-shot Spencers. Few wore uniforms;

most were in buckskins or other civilian dress.

On 16 September 1868 Forsyth's men pitched camp on the west bank of the 'Arickaree', the Arikara Fork of the Republican River. The stream had just gone dry after a summer of drout in the area of the Colorado-Kansas line. Just as Forsyth made his inspection next morning, a sentry shouted 'Indians!'

A war party of 600–700 Sioux, Cheyennes and a few Arapahos charged on carefully-selected war ponies. They were led by Tall Bull of the Cheyennes and Pawnee Killer, the Sioux. They were outraged that the whites dared to invade their hunting grounds although they had themselves sworn not to cross the Arkansas into the area.

Forsyth ordered his men to dig slit trenches with their knives and tin cups in the sand and gravel of a small island in the middle of the stream bed. The isle measured barely 20

Left: Some cavalry officers never forgave the callous Custer for failing to search for **Major Joel Elliott's** missing 16-man command at the Washita in 1868. The detachment was intercepted by Indians and destroyed to a man, the brave Sergeant-Major Kennedy being the last one to fall in the bloody snow.

by 60 yards, but its tall grass and willows offered some cover. Once they ran off two of Forsyth's pack animals, which carried valuable medical supplies and even more precious ammunition, the Indians maintained a galling fire from both banks and from downstream.

Suddenly the main body of Indians dropped down the banks and charged up the stream bed like a troop of cavalry. They hoped to kill all of Forsyth's horses, then run over the island and kill the plainsmen at leisure. Tall Bull ordered his horsemen to charge through the low morning mist together, like white men (as Roman Nose had taught him), and not fight lone actions to count coups—and lose a battle.

As if in imitation of the Wagon Box fight, Forsyth had his men hold their rifle fire to the very last moment. When the Indians were almost upon the island, the company gave

them a fusillade that stunned them. The quick-firing Spencer rifles at only 50 yards cut the Indian force in two. But the Indians then surrounded the island and poured a heavy fire into it. For the moment, at least, Cheyenne medicine was good. Most of the whites' horses were killed. Wolf Belly made two passes along the fringe of willows without being hurt. Forsyth was down, hit in the right thigh, the left calf, and the scalp. As the first charge began to ebb, the wounded Major saw Beecher stagger and fall. As he died, the Indians regrouped and charged a second time and were again repulsed.

The Indians, now gun-shy, put off another charge even though they outnumbered the scouts about 14-to-one. They awaited the arrival of Roman Nose. The great Cheyenne warrior had violated a *taboo* by eating bread touched with metal (a fork) while visiting the Sioux. He had to make amends to the gods by purifying himself before his sacred and talismanic warbonnet would make him bullet-proof. He was a bit reluctant to join the fight, not sure that his 'medicine was good' again, meaning that he was not in the good graces of the great spirit. But, goaded by other Cheyennes, he painted his nose red, his chin black, his forehead yellow, and put on his magic 40-feather warbonnet.

Roman Nose led almost 500 pony soldiers in a third charge, planning to gallop right across the island, trampling the defenders into the sand. But the Spencers grew hot again and after the third and fourth volleys, ragged holes began to appear in the line of horsemen. Roman Nose was almost on the island, at the willow fringe, when a rifle ball smashed into his spine just above the hips. Someone later said that it was part of the sixth volley. The slug knocked him, mortally wounded, from his horse. He hid in the bushes until dark, then crawled to a bench of the stream that night and was carried to the top of a low hill on the right bank. There, where a historical marker is located today, he died in the night.

Forsyth took advantage of a breathing spell at nightfall to count his casualties. Of his original 51 men, seven lay dead, including Surgeon John H Mooers, or were dying. Seventeen more groaned with less serious wounds.

Next day, the Indians declined to attack. Roman Nose's death had taken away their desire to do battle. They settled down to starve Forsyth out. When he called for volunteers to go for help, every last ambulatory man came forward. He chose an ex-trapper, Trudeau, and 19-year-old Jack Stilwell to slip away in the darkness and get help from Fort Wallace, some hundred miles away.

On the third day, the Indians threw only a few rounds at the trapped men, letting the broiling sun do their work for them. The brave Forsyth, burning with fever, tended to his wounds. Carefully, he operated on himself—without any pain-killer—with his razor.

On the fourth day, the day that all rations gave out, the scouts saw the squaws break camp and leave. But the siege continued. By the fifth day of their entrapment, the survivors were so ravenously hungry that they cut hunks of flesh from the stinking, bloated, carcasses of their animals. One shot a coyote, another foraged some wild plums. The

Above: **James Butler (Wild Bill) Hickok,** 1837-1876, was a soldier and scout, but much more of a gambler, gunfighter and lawman. He was born in Illinois, but went to 'Bleeding Kansas' in 1855 where he was a teamster and stagecoach driver. He served in the Union Army during the Civil War but his activities remained cloaked in mystery. With his buckskins and long, Custer-like locks, Hickok soon became famous as a lawman. He was deputy US marshal at Fort Riley, Kansas, then he scouted for General Philip Sheridan for a time and even considered making a career as an Army scout. During this stint as a plainsman-scout, he was wounded in one arm (March 1868) during a skirmish with a Cheyenne war party. The injury was serious enough to require him to return to his boyhood home in Troy Grove, Illinois, to recuperate. When he returned to the Plains, it was not as a scout but as a guide for a hunting party of Easterners. He was next acting-sheriff of Ellis County and town marshal of Hays City, Kansas. By 1871, he was marshal of Abilene, Kansas, at the end of the Chisholm Trail, and his army scouting days were over. He later played himself in one of William F (Buffalo Bill) Cody's Wild West shows, 'Scouts of the Plains,' then worked his way up to the Black Hills of South Dakota via Cheyenne, Wyoming, mostly as a card sharp. He was murdered by Jack McCall as he sat in a Deadwood poker game. The cards that Wild Bill was holding have come to be called the 'Dead Man's Hand' – aces and eights.

men dug deeper in the sandbar and brought up muddy water. In an agonizing decision, Forsyth decided to send out two more messengers, though it weakened his defense. The first pair, he guessed, were lying dead on the plains somewhere.

Now, the Major felt his own strength ebbing. He ordered all able-bodied men to leave the island and fight their way to safety if they could. Sergeant McCall led a 'mutiny', speaking for all of the scouts in rejecting the order. 'We've fought together and, by God, if need be, we'll die together.'

But Trudeau and Stilwell did reach Fort Wallace safely, the young soldier helping the exhausted mountain man, but Trudeau died at the fort. A messenger was sent galloping after Captain Louis H Carpenter, already in the field with a unit of the 10th Cavalry. Forsyth's second pair of couriers also arrived safely.

Carpenter pushed his black troopers hard, covering 100 miles to the river in just two days. On 25 September the eighth day of siege, the Indians pulled out for their sanctuary south of the Arkansas, unwilling to give the black 'Buffalo Soldiers' a fight.

When Carpenter dismounted on the bloody island, he found his old comrade, Forsyth, calmly reading *Oliver Twist*, though with his Spencer across his knees, ready for action. Later, the Major confessed to his friend that his supposedly gallant gesture was really a cover-up, to keep himself from breaking down in desperation in front of his handful of totally exhausted men who, almost out of ammunition, looked to him for leadership.

Forsyth was dizzy with fever. As if his three gunshot wounds were not enough, he had given himself blood poisoning with his crude surgery on himself with an un-sterile razor. It took Forsyth two full years for his body to recover from the beating that it took on **Beecher's Island**.

The Indians called the battle the Fight Where Roman Nose Was Killed. Some of the surviving scouts thought that they had killed 'hundreds' of hostiles. Perhaps they wounded 100. The toll admitted to by the Indians, six dead, seems much too low and Forsyth's not all that high, at 35 dead warriors.

Sheridan now, unfairly, canceled Forsyth's plan. He returned to the use of regulars, especially cavalry patrols from permanent bases.

In 1868, four years after being treacherously attacked at Sand Creek, Black Kettle presided over a flourishing village of 51 friendly-Cheyenne lodges on the Washita River 40 miles east of Oklahoma's Antelope Hills. Unsure of the protection of the Medicine Lodge Treaty, he asked General William B Hazen at Fort Cobb, 100 miles away, for permission to move his people closer to the protection of the post. The General told him not to worry. His village would never be attacked by whites.

Was Hazen lying? Like Sheridan, he saw Black Kettle's refuge as a 'cancer'. Both generals knew that the chief proclaimed peace but, at the same time, welcomed young braves back from raids into Kansas. They brought scalps, white captives, even souvenirs in the form of dispatches captured from Army couriers. Custer, of course, followed his mentor, Sheridan. His orders were to destroy villages and ponies, kill or hang all warriors and take women and children prisoners.

The Rising Star of George Armstrong Custer

Custer, the Boy General of Civil War days, was the

natural choice to test Sheridan's new strategy of winter warfare, with poor Black Kettle his hapless first target. He would see to it that all Indians were given no rest during the worst season of the year when they were cold and hungry and their ponies worn out.

Sheridan fielded three columns to converge on the Canadian and Washita River valleys of Indian Territory. The main one was under his favorite. Custer led his 7th Cavalry out of Camp Supply, Indian Territory, after a last-minute conference with Sheridan. It was a below-zero morning but his spit-and-polish regimental band played the jolly air, 'The Girl I Left Behind Me'. Custer was young, handsome, dashing and brave. He was also politically as well as militarily ambitious, a sometimes-dangerous combination. And, like his brother Tom, with whom he shared many a similarity, he was rash to a fault, reckless. But Sheridan liked this side of Custer. He thought that boldness was a good trait in a cavalry officer. However, even Sheridan feared that Custer lacked common sense.

George Custer was determined to make a comeback after an interruption of his brilliant cavalry career. He had been court martialed and suspended from duty for a year for cruelty to his men in the Hancock Campaign of 1867. At that time, he drove his men hard on forced marches without even stopping for water. Desertions became frequent and when 15 men lit out at a noon break, Custer ordered them brought back—but not alive. Five were recaptured, and alive. Custer's subordinates had refused to obey what they saw as a clearly improper order—to murder. (One deserter-prisoner died of wounds, however.) The next day Custer hurried his regiment to Fort Wallace, then took 100 men to Fort Hays for supplies. He marched them 150 miles in 60 hours, giving them only six hours rest. Two stragglers were picked off by Indians. Finding no supplies, he pushed on to Fort Harker. Then, to compound his folly, he boarded a train to visit his wife!

Punishment was swift. In just ten days Custer was under arrest for leaving his regiment without orders, abandoning stragglers, shooting deserters and marching his men beyond endurance. The conceited and unrepentant colonel said that his actions were necessary for the safety of the 7th. As for his conjugal visit, he told the court that General Sherman had given him permission to go anywhere he liked: 'To Denver, or to Hell, if I wanted to.'

Thanks to his loyal friend Sheridan, who needed him to fight Indians, Custer was reinstated before his sentence even expired. Transferred to command of the 7th Cavalry from duty at Fort Hays, he made it into a crack outfit. His troopers were mounted on matched horses. He had a special unit of sharpshooters. Proficient trumpeters and a regimental band boosted morale. The musicians often played 'Garry Owen', the traditional West Point song which Custer adopted for his regiment. Most of Custer's men revered him; some despised him. Almost no one was neutral or indifferent toward the vainglorious officer.

For an elite outfit, the 7th Cavalry made a faltering start on Sheridan's winter war. Custer's Indian scouts got lost in a snowstorm. But the blond, long-haired colonel soon straightened them out with compass bearings. And his organizational gifts were apparent. Like Napoleon, he realized that an Army traveled on its stomach. Every night the supply train caught up with the column to give his men hot meals.

After a punishing three-day march over snow covered,

Above: In spite of the fact that he was Custer's favorite scout, **California Joe** remains a mysterious figure. He was probably not from California and his name was not Joe, though he was identified by some as Joe Milner (or Milmer) and Joseph Hawkins. California Joe's name was Moses Milner. He became Custer's chief of scouts in the Washita campaign of Sheridan's winter war. Joe headed a detachment of scouts and delegation of friendly Osages when Custer left Camp Supply to attack Black Kettle. When Custer sent word of victory to Sheridan, he chose Joe to carry the message. With another scout, Milner got through enemy country at night and in record time. Astride his conspicuous mule, he then led his scouts in the grand review of Custer's troops, just ahead of the dejected Cheyenne prisoners and the regimental band playing 'Garry Owen.' He was still chief of scouts in the Black Hills Expedition of the summer of 1874. This reconnaissance of the sacred mountains of the Sioux led to the gold rush of 1876. Custer sent a dispatch – 'I have on my table 40 or 50 small particles of gold, in size averaging a small pin head, and most of it obtained from one pan.' Joe, still an Army scout, was killed on 29 October 1876, shot in the back by Tom Newcomb at Fort Robinson, Nebraska. Newcomb did not have to stand trial; there were no lawmen and no courts in the Sioux country at the time.

frozen country, Custer slowed his advance and sent his second-in-command ahead on a scout, or reconnaissance. Major Joel H Elliott's squadron found tracks of a large number of Indians—automatically a war party in Custer's eyes. Guided by an Osage scout, Custer caught up with Elliott and reconnoitred Black Kettle's camp, near today's Cheyenne, Oklahoma.

Black Kettle, on his arrival home, had called a council to give his people Hazen's assurances that they would never be attacked. The chief awoke just before dawn the next morning, 27 November 1868, to hear a woman crying, 'Soldiers! Soldiers!' Sand Creek must have flashed through the chief's mind as he grabbed his rifle and fired a warning shot.

Black Kettle waited at the ford, hoping to stop the soldiers and talk peace. But they enveloped the village from four directions. So, under the fluttering Stars and Stripes and white flag of peace, Black Kettle got on his horse and took his wife (wounded at Sand Creek) up behind him. They were among the first to fall in a hail of bullets.

Black Kettle's 14-year-old son died in hand-to-hand combat with Captain Frederick W Benteen. Warriors who escaped from their tents made for the brush and ravines to fight back. But it took Custer barely ten minutes to secure the village.

Holding Black Kettle's village now proved to be a different matter from capturing it. Indians flocked from a chain of neighboring camps in the Washita Valley. They soon outnumbered the regiment. Because it resembled Sand Creek, the **Battle of the Washita** has been called a massacre. But it was not a clear victory for Custer. He suffered few casualties, but his ammunition supply was insufficient

Left: Custer hit a sleeping Cheyenne village on the **Washita River** of Oklahoma on 27 November 1868 in the major fight of Sheridan's winter war. Peaceful Black Kettle saw a repeat of Sand Creek, with the 7th Cavalry substituting for the Colorado Volunteers. As the battle wore on, Indian reinforcements joined the fray, forcing Custer to run and abandon Major Elliott's detachment.

Instead, he reformed his outnumbered column and marched it boldly up the Washita, guidons flying proudly in the wind and the band booming out 'Ain't I Glad To Get Out Of The Wilderness'. The astounded Indians gradually withdrew before him as he feinted an attack on the next village. The Indians pulled still further back under the cover of closing night, letting the puzzling Yellow Hair past.

When Custer briefly halted at the next camp, the Indians recovered their poise and set an ambush for him. But he smelled it out and fooled them again, making a right wheel in the direction of his planned withdrawal route and eluding the ambuscade.

The Washita campaign 'made' Custer, despite comparisons with Sand Creek. His unorthodox bluffing tactics worked beautifully. He lost only Major Elliott, Captain Louis M Hamilton (Alexander Hamilton's grandson) and 19 enlisted men killed, and three officers and 11 men wounded. He is said to have counted 103 dead Cheyennes on the field. (But there were whispers that only a dozen or so were really warriors.)

Later, a patrol found the mutilated remains of Elliott and his men. Arapahos coming to help the Cheyennes had intercepted the platoon of 20 men and killed everyone.

To welcome Custer back to Camp Supply, Sheridan turned out the entire garrison in a formal review. The men of the 7th waved scalps, including that of the pathetic Black Kettle. Sheridan congratulated him for his efficient and gallant service in wiping out 'savage bands of cruel marauders'. He termed Black Kettle's camp 'the winter seat of the hostiles.'

Sheridan shrugged off his critics, assuming them to be, largely, churchmen—'good and pious ecclesiastics'—who, in their misguided compassion, abetted the merciless red murderers of innocent men, women and children.

Sherman, of course, supported Sheridan and Custer. He paid no attention to Indian Agent Edward W Wynkoop, who resigned his post in protest of Sheridan's policies, crying out that Black Kettle had been betrayed by the whites whom he had trusted. The arguments of such so-called Indian lovers were weakened by the relics of Cheyenne raids found in the *tipis* of the 'friendlies', along with four white captives, two of whom were put to death by the Indians during the melee.

Sheridan promised to feed Cheyennes who surrendered unconditionally, and most survivors of the Washita gave themselves up at Fort Cobb. He sternly warned them, 'You cannot make peace now and commence killing whites again in the spring.'

When the first Comanches surrendered to him, Sheridan coined a phrase that has rivaled Sherman's 'War is hell'. When he asked a warrior for his name, the man answered, 'Tosawi, good Indian'. Sheridan shook his head and replied, 'The only good Indian I ever saw was dead'. This was shortly polished into 'The only good Indian is a dead Indian', the Plains Army's philosophy.

Custer erected Fort Sill as a watchdog over Comanches

for him to hold the site. In fact, he may have been saved from defeat by the opportune distraction of the Indians by the arrival of his seven supply wagons and mounted escort.

Custer reassembled the regiment to pull out. Elliott and his men were missing. The Colonel decided that he dared not look for them. (He would never be forgiven for this by some officers and men.) After burning the lodges as quickly as possible, with their 4000 arrows, 500 pounds of lead and an equal amount of powder, he shot to death most of the 875 captured ponies to hinder pursuit. He released his 53 women and children captives and left. It was becoming a difficult and dangerous situation.

Custer was erratic, perhaps half-fool and half-genius. With the valley crawling with hostiles, now thousands of them, he skillfully extricated his force from the jaws of a trap. He did not run like the wind, as the Indians expected.

Above: **George Custer** was controversial as a Civil War 'Boy General' and remained so to his dying day. Talented but reckless and self-centered, he was finally the victim, at Little Bighorn, of his overconfidence. *Above right:* There was often an element of social outing to Custer's campaigns, with ladies, relatives and civilians all mixed up with regimental officers, as when Custer took his ease under an awning at Fort Abraham Lincoln.

and Kiowas while the Cheyennes concentrated around Camp Supply. He planned more winter operations but was immobilized by insufficient supplies and much more than 'adequate' rain and mud. The bad winter also forced Major Eugene A Carr to take his column back to Fort Lyon, Colorado. But the Government deemed Sheridan's winter campaign a success, unlike Hancock's preliminary round, largely because of Custer's Washita victory and a Christmas present-surprise. On the holiday, Major Andrew W Evans beat the Comanches and Kiowas at Soldier Spring on the Red River's North Fork before winter forced him back to his base, Fort Bascom in New Mexico. The Indians, punished more by winter than by soldiers, now surrendered in droves at Fort Sill, where they were made to swear to keep the peace.

On 15 March 1869, Custer found two hold-out villages of Cheyennes on Sweetwater Creek below the Staked Plains. He seized four chiefs as hostages to trade for two white women captives and, by threatening to hang the four, persuaded all of the Indians to surrender.

Tall Bull still would not give up. He decided to join the Northern Cheyennes but struck at the Smoky Hill Trail on his way north. Major Frank North's Pawnee scouts found him and his followers on 11 July 1869 at Summit Springs. With North was a young scout, William (Buffalo Bill) Cody. The Pawnees alerted Major Eugene A Carr, who attacked Tall Bull's village from both east and west. He easily routed the villagers, most of whom escaped. But Tall Bull and 20 men fought on bravely from the cover of a ravine. The chief cut hand and foot holds in the wall of the ravine to climb up to a better firing position. He got off one shot, ducked down, popped up his head to take aim again—and a rifle slug slammed its way into his skull.

Carr's victory ran the Dog Soldiers out of Kansas, at last, and cleared the Smoky Hill, Platte and Arkansas Roads, and the Union Pacific and Kansas Pacific rights-of-way of all hostiles.

Firmness had worked, but President-Elect U S Grant, the old soldier, did not listen to his friends, Sherman and Sheridan, but, surprisingly, to the proponents of a Quaker Peace Policy in 1869. He wanted Indians christianized, fed, clothed and taught agriculture on reservations so that they should become self-supporting farmers.

Red River War

Most Westerners, especially Texans, scorned Grant's peace program. They saw Fort Sill and other posts and Indian agencies as just places of refuge for the 'bloody Quaker pets' who raided the Lone Star State and adjacent territories.

But the Comanches always insisted that the Army started the Red River War on the South Plains. As one chief said, 'It was you who sent out the first soldier, and we who sent out the second.'

The Comanches' allies, the Kiowas, were just as reluctant to trade a free life on the wide-open plains, chasing buffalo, for a confined existence on a reservation, perhaps herding sheep. Like the Comanches, they hid behind the proviso of the Medicine Lodge 'paper' which guaranteed them the right to continue hunting bison between the Arkansas and Red Rivers.

After Custer's victory on the Washita, Sheridan ordered all Kiowas, Comanches, Cheyennes and Arapahos to surrender at Fort Cobb. All but the Kiowas obeyed. Sheridan sent Custer to round up the delinquents.

Sheridan and Custer found Satanta's winter camp on Rainy Creek. Custer refused to take the hand offered in friendship. He was aware that Satanta was the murderer-kidnapper of the Box family in Texas in 1866, and that this was only one of several such crimes of which he was guilty. He curtly told all chiefs that they were under arrest. All but Satanta and Lone Wolf, though under close guard, managed to slip away from night camps on the march to Fort Sill. Sheridan swore that he would hang the pair if their people did not surrender themselves. They came in, and the General released the chiefs from custody.

Fort Sill kept a watchful eye on 2000 Kiowas and 2500 Comanches on the adjacent but spread-out reservation. War hero Ben Grierson's garrison was composed mostly of blacks who turned out to be pretty good cavalrymen. The

Indians called them Buffalo Soldiers because of their dark, curly hair. The Indian Agent was a kindly Quaker, Lawrie Tatum, 'Bald Head' to the Indians. He skillfully won the release of many captured Mexican boys from Kiowa slavery without paying ransom. He just cut off rations till his 'wards' came around.

Satanta swore for Sheridan's benefit that he would follow the white man's path, raise corn, and kill no more whites. Like all of his tribe, he really spurned agriculture even more than the Comanches did. He was content to trade buffalo robes and jerky to the Wichitas, who actually enjoyed growing maize, or Indian corn. What Satanta really wanted from Tatum were rifles and ammunition. He said that he wanted them only for hunting, but when General Hancock gave him a major general's uniform in

1867, he proudly wore it while running off the herd of stock at Fort Dodge.

The split between Kicking Bird's more peaceful Kiowas and Satanta widened after a great sun dance of 1870 on the North Fork of Red River. Many young men then rode off to kill Texans, especially buffalo hunters. Satanta, who had complained about the white man's waste in cutting timber, was aghast at the destruction of the buffalo. The commercial hunters were systematically wiping out the southern herd. He said, 'When I see that, my heart feels like bursting.'

Even Kicking Bird was driven to lead 100 braves on a raid into Texas with Lone Wolf, White Horse and old Satank. After goading Fort Richardson by capturing a mail coach, he gave a rescue force an all-day fight before letting it go. He then returned to the safety of the Fort Sill

Above: Photographer Illingworth captured Custer hunting during his Black Hills reconnoitering expedition. **Our First Grizzly** in 1874.

Left: Custer discovered the fate of **Lieutenant L S Kidder's** men, finding their bodies in July 1867 on Beaver Creek, Kansas.

agency. That winter, Satank, grieving for a son killed in Texas, brought his bones home to lie in state on a platform inside a special holy teepee. He placed offerings of food and water at the foot of the scaffold so that his 'sleeping' son would not get hungry or thirsty on his far travels.

Satanta wanted the Fort Sill officers to stop the Iron Horse from coming to ruin the buffalo hunts. Satank, old and wise, grunted that *talk* was foolish. Destroy the settlers, he advised. Big Tree wanted to burn the fort, then kill the soldiers as they should scurry out like ants from a mound. In any case, young 'buffalo hunters' evaded Grierson's guards at the main fords of the Red River and raided into Texas that spring and summer of 1871.

Satanta was told by a medicine man, Mamanti or The Owl, of a vision of his driving Texans into the ground. The shaman led him, along with Big Tree and Satank, on a raid penetrating all the way to the Butterfield Stage Road between Forts Richardson and Belknap in Texas.

Lying in wait by the roadside on Salt Creek Prairie just west of Fort Richardson on 18 May 1871, the Kiowas spotted a lone mule-drawn ambulance. Officers and, of course, wounded men traveled in these light Army wagons. It was escorted by only a handful of troopers. But Mamanti would not let his comrades attack it. The visionary predicted a richer haul if they would wait. He seemed to be a perfect prophet, for the single vehicle was shortly followed by a train of ten Army freight wagons. Satanta blew his bugle as dreams of rifles and ammunition danced before his eyes.

The teamsters knew that the wild tooting was the work of no Army bugler. They formed a quick defensive circle, but the Kiowas broke it and killed eight of the 12 defenders. The others escaped in the brush as the Indians excitedly plundered the wagons. To their disgust, there were no arms or munitions, only corn. So they took only the 41 mules when they started back to the asylum of their reservation. In the ambulance was General William Tecumseh Sherman, on a tour of inspection. Satanta could have easily brushed aside his small guard of honor.

Ranald Mackenzie and the Fourth; Quanah Parker and the Comanches

When the escaping teamsters reached Rock Creek, Sherman ordered units of Ranald Mackenzie's crack 4th Cavalry to the train's rescue, but they were much too late. Sherman was furious when Satanta bragged to Indian Agent Tatum that he—not the shaman—had personally led the raid. 'If any other Indian comes here and claims the honor of leading the party, he will be lying to you, for I did

Opposite page: Haughty **Satanta (White Bear),** decked out in an officer's coat and wearing a peace medal, was one of the most warlike of Kiowa chiefs. But he ended his days strangely; as an old man, he broke one of the strongest of all Indian taboos, committing suicide in 1878.

Right: **Colonel Ranald Mackenzie** was a dashing cavalry commander like Custer, but with more common sense. He smashed the Comanches in the Red River War of 1874-75 and hit at Kickapoo raiders, deep in Mexico, while under secret orders. Mackenzie went insane in 1883.

it myself'. He then insolently demanded ammunition and arms for future raids.

Tatum was now disillusioned and joined the General in a plot to snare Satanta. He did so because he refused to be a party to the Kiowas committing 'murder in the first degree' with impunity.

Rather than risk an open fight with Satanta, Sherman determined to use deceit. He invited him to a Fort Sill council. Satanta came alone, though Sherman ordered the other chiefs to come too. Satank then came in, but only by force. Big Tree, suspicious, tried to run. But he was herded to the pow-wow. Lone Wolf, true to his name, arrived alone and late.

Satanta saw no women and children when he entered the fort, but his suspicion was not aroused because there were hardly any soldiers about, either. He did not know that Sherman had hidden armed men in various buildings and 10th Cavalry troopers, saddled up, just inside closed stable doors.

Sherman and Colonel Benjamin H Grierson waited in chairs on the porch of the commanding officer's residence. Their visitors sat on the floor. Sherman was insensed when the braggart chief again boasted of killing the teamsters. The General told him that he and all others responsible for the atrocity would be arrested and taken to Texas for trial. Satanta's response was to extract a revolver that he had concealed under his blanket. He warned Sherman that he would rather be shot than imprisoned in Texas. At a signal, the shutters of Grierson's windows now flew back with a slam, to permit the black troopers inside, to cover the Indians with their carbines. At the same time, the mounted troops left the horse barns and formed a line in front of Gierson's whitewashed picket fence.

It was a standoff. Just then, Lone Wolf showed up. He carried two carbines and wore a pistol. He boldly gave one of the carbines to a chief and his pistol to another, saying in a loud stage voice, each time, 'Make it smoke if anything happens'. And when he sat down, he noisily cocked his own carbine.

Cooly, Sherman continued his pacing on the deck of the porch, arguing and reasoning. Stumbling Bear stealthily notched an arrow and began to bend his bow, with Sherman his target. But another Indian deliberately jostled him and the arrow sailed harmlessly into space. Grierson wrestled Lone Wolf for his carbine as the latter took aim at Sherman. They sprawled on the porch. One of Sherman's officers brought the line of cavalry carbines up, hammers back, but Satanta and Sherman both shouted 'No, no!', and the guns were lowered.

An outbluffed Satanta submitted to handcuffing, along with Lone Tree and Satank. They were taken from the Fort Sill guardhouse on 7 June 1871 and sent to Jacksboro, Texas for trial. Each of two wagons had three guards and a driver. Satanta and Lone Tree, resigned to their fate, were in one vehicle. Old Satank, in the other wagon, began to

wail his death song. The chant should have alerted his guards, but didn't.

As his wagon approached a tree by a stream, Satank called out to his comrades that he would not pass beyond it. Somehow, he slipped out of his manacles, pulled out a hidden penknife and stabbed one guard in the leg and pushed him off the wagon. He grabbed up a carbine but it jammed as he levered a shell into the chamber. While he was trying to clear the weapon, the lieutenant in charge of the guard detail shouted to his men to fire. Corporal John B Charlton, on the other wagon, shot Satank. But he did not fall and continued trying to fire his gun, so Charlton shot him a second time.

The lieutenant halted long enough for Satank to die, but neither buried him or hauled the corpse along. Instead, he callously had his men roll the body into a roadside ditch.

The murder trial began on 5 July 1871 in the Jacksboro courthouse before a jury of cattlemen. The jurors rendered a guilty verdict, to no one's surprise, and the judge sentenced the Kiowas to hang. But Governor Edmund J Davis, probably yielding to political pressure from the Indian Bureau, commuted the death sentences to life imprisonment in the State Penitentiary at Huntsville.

Sherman was, predictably, furious. He became even more angry later, in August 1873, when Lone Wolf persuaded the Governor to grant the pair their freedom in order to win the cooperation of the Kiowas in the Indian resettlement program. Even Indian Agent Tatum was so disgusted that he resigned.

Meanwhile, young Kiowas joined Quanah Parker's Kwahadi band of Comanches in the Palo Duro country of the Texas Panhandle. They struck in October 1871 and caught Rock Station asleep, rustling 10 horses in one night.

The raid embarrassed Fort Richardson's tireless commanding officer, 31-year-old Colonel Ranald Mackenzie. Before the Civil War (in which Mackenzie was wounded three times), U S Grant had called him the most promising officer in the Army. Mackenzie's 4th Regiment was all that Custer's 7th Cavalry tried to be. The 4th had almost no deserters. It was not because the privates loved 'the Old Man' so much, though they did respect him. No, it was

because the harsh disciplinarian's orders, like Custer's before his court-martial, were to bring in deserters dead or alive.

Mackenzie, 'Three Fingers' to the Indians because of a Civil War wound, was a first-rate Indian fighter, like Crook or Miles, but with a more dashing style. He was barred from invading the sanctuary of the reservations, but he learned how to handle another Indian refuge, the bone-dry Llano Estacado or Staked Plain. He took a Texas column to Fort Bascom, New Mexico, and back, working his way from waterhole to waterhole, just like an Indian. He also exposed, finally, the chief source of Kiowa and Comanche arms and ammunition, the Hispanic New Mexico traders called *Comancheros*.

On 29 September 1872 Ranald Mackenzie had his first revenge for his loss of face at Rock Station. From Fort Richardson he struck 262 Comanche lodges near McClellan Creek, a tributary of the North Fork of the Red. He killed between 30 and 60 men and took 124 women and children prisoners, burned the *tipis* and made off with a thousand ponies.

Even Mackenzie still had much to learn, however, and the Comanches in a counterattack on his first night camp recovered most of their horses and some of the troopers' mounts. But the Colonel got his hostages to Fort Sill, where he used them as leverage to get Mow-way's band back on the reservation. However, many of the latter's men stayed out with the rising star of Comanche fortunes, the half-blood, Quanah Parker.

Young Kiowas and Comanches who raided into Texas made the mistake of killing two Texans on their way home. Soldiers in a running fight near Fort Clark in December of 1873 killed nine of the Indians. One was a son of Lone Wolf, another casualty his nephew. The Chief swore revenge and emphasized this oath by burning his lodge, killing some of his favorite ponies, and cropping his hair in grief. Once that the grass was up in the spring of 1874, he took a party deep into Texas to recover the bodies of his young relatives. He skillfully avoided pursuits from Forts McKavett, Concho

and Clark, but a patrol finally forced him to rebury the remains before he got all the way back to his reservation.

That same spring of 1874, the Comanches invited their Kiowa friends to a sun dance. Cautious Kicking Bird did not attend, but Kiowas Satanta and Lone Wolf were there. At the ceremony, the Indians expressed their hatred of 'buffler' skinners of the Staked Plain. With the connivance of the Army, the buffalo hunters killed more than three and a half million bison between 1872 and 1874 alone, while the Indians' toll was perhaps 150,000 animals. Sheridan, asked by Texans how to stop such a wasteful slaughter of such a valuable Plains resource, answered that he did not want it stopped. He believed that the deliberate extinction of the species was the *only* final solution to the Indian problem, to bring peace to the West and to 'allow civilization to advance' among the Indians.

At the unusual sun dance, not a Comanche tradition, a young Kwahadi prophet, Isatai, seconded the motion of Quanah Parker that they and the Kiowas go to war to save their buffalo. He would help. Not only did he promise to vomit up, literally, whole wagonloads of ammunition, as needed, he guaranteed to stop the white men's bullets in mid-air with his medicine, or magic.

Down from reservations in the north came Cheyennes and Arapaho allies to swell Parker's force to 700 picked men. Just before sunrise of 27 June 1874, Quanah Parker closed a noose of warriors around the tiny buffalo hunters' settlement of Adobe Walls near the Canadian River in the top of the Texas Panhandle. They killed and scalped two men who tried to escape in a wagon, then charged the settlement.

A few ponies stepped in prairie dog holes and sent their riders sprawling, but most got so close that they could poke holes in the roof of one building to shoot at men inside. But the 28 buffalo hunters behind adobe walls or forted up in the buildings, would not be frightened and would not be decoyed. They refused to be intimidated by odds of more than 25-to-one and wasted no ammunition in panicky rapid firing. After all, they were all armed with heavy, long-barreled Sharps or Remington (rolling block) buffalo guns of powerful caliber and deadly accuracy.

They shot Quanah Parker's horse out from under him, then as he took cover in a wild plum thicket, another heavy slug creased his shoulder. Another Indian later remembered, 'One of our men was knocked off a horse by a spent bullet fired at a range of about a mile. It stunned him but did not kill him'. This was probably the miraculous long shot by Billy Dixon.

Adobe Walls was perhaps *the* classic defensive action of all the Indian Wars, even more so than Beecher's Island. The valiant buffalo men lost just three of their number, one of them lanced by Quanah Parker himself. They managed to kill at least 15 warriors and critically wounded many more.

Naturally the Indians were annoyed with the discredited Isatai. A Cheyenne lashed him with a quirt, but Quanah

Parker stopped the whipping. Lone Wolf and Satanta took their Kiowas back for the tribe's sun dance, inviting the Comanches to join them. One of the Comanches admitted, 'The buffalo hunters were too much for us.'

The bested Indians took out their anger by terrorizing routes of travel in Kansas, burning, raping and killing till even the Indian Bureau stopped apologizing for them and Sherman was able to give Sheridan carte blanche on 20 July 1874 to turn his troops loose in an all-out Red River War against 4000 Indians, perhaps 1200 of them warriors.

During that summer of drought and grasshoppers, probably half of Fort Sill's Comanches and Kiowas drifted away to join Quanah Parker's Kwahadi Comanches in the hidden chasm of Palo Duro Canyon, the Panhandle's equivalent of Cañón de Chelly. The deep gash in the plain was invisible till one was right on top of it. Called the Place of the Chinaberry Trees, it had been seen by few whites since Coronado's time. Late in that summer of 1874, the Comanches, Kiowas and Cheyennes made it into an inner sanctum where they laid in supplies for winter.

Sheridan revised his tactics, shifting from scattered small patrols to five powerful columns closing in on the Staked Plains. Among his field commanders were Colonels Nelson 'Bear Coat' Miles and John W 'Black Jack' Davidson. The latter was sometimes eccentric because of an old sunstroke

Left: **Satank** did not wait seven years, like Satanta, to die after being arrested. Satank's 'suicide' was condoned by Indians. En route to prison in Texas, he sang his death song, stabbed a soldier with a pen knife that he had hidden, and got his gun. He was shot dead before he could escape.

attack. And, of course, Sheridan employed Mackenzie.

There were skirmishes, one involving Billy Dixon of Adobe Walls fame. Because it involved a siege in a mud hole, it was called the **Buffalo Wallow Fight**. The 110-degree heat of August turned to September rain and mud. Surprisingly, Satanta and Big Tree surrendered.

As Mackenzie closed the ring on the Indians, he was the victim of a night attack on 26 September 1874. He beat it off and, this time, kept the marauders from stampeding his horse herd. In the morning, he took up the pursuit and his Tonkawa scouts found the Palo Duro Canyon hideout. One of the first to see it was Satank's old nemesis, John B Charlton, now a sergeant. He fetched Mackenzie.

The Colonel brought his whole column to the lip of the long defile at daybreak of the 28th. He could find no trail down to Prairie Dog Town Fork in the bottom, so he simply plunged down the steep slope at the head of his men.

Mackenzie's men swept the canyon, hitting Lone Wolf's Kiowas first. They were dismayed to find interlopers in their haven and fled like antelopes. Troopers pursued them and the other Indians for five miles. They caught only a few and killed only three braves—but only because the battle was such a complete rout.

Stealing a page from Carson's Cañón de Chelly campaign, Mackenzie did a masterful job of scorching the earth. He burned all lodges and precious winter rations, then drove 1424 ponies into the head of Tule Canyon. He picked out the very best animals for his men, then slaughtered the balance, more than 1000 horses. This action virtually dismounted both tribes. Destitute, many Kiowas and Comanches were back on the reservation by October. At Christmas, most of Mackenzie's troops were in warm, snug, quarters.

Lone Wolf and about 250 Kiowas did not stop running till 25 February 1875, then surrendered at Fort Sill. On 2 June 1875, even Quanah Parker, who had scorned all treaties, was disheartened. He had to give up, ending the Red River War.

Sheridan made sure that it stayed ended. He sent 74 Indian leaders to the stone dungeons of ancient Castillo de San Marcos, Fort Marion, in St Augustine, Florida. He forced Kicking Bird to select Kiowas for exile, among them Lone Wolf and the shaman, Mamanti. The latter put a curse on Kicking Bird, who died mysteriously after drinking a cup of coffee. In just three months, the medicine man was, himself, dead in Florida, supposedly having willed himself to death in remorse for having killed his chief.

Satanta had violated his parole in joining in the war. After he surrendered at the Cheyenne Agency, 24 October 1874, he was put in the guardhouse in irons, then returned

Below: One of the finest of all frontier photographers was also a painter, William Henry Jackson. He crossed the continent to California in 1866 and accompanied the Hayden Survey to Yellowstone in 1871, the year that he took this picture of **Pawnee lodges** on Loup (Wolf) Fork, Nebraska.

Above: The San Carlos Reservation agent **John P Clum** posed in buckskins with the Apaches **Diablo** and **Eskiminzin** in 1875 at the Agency. Eskiminzin was the victim of Arizona vengeance in the Camp Grant Massacre of 1871 when Mexican, American and Papago vigilantes destroyed his village, killing most of his people and forcing the remainder into the cruel bonds of slavery.

to Huntsville. In 1878 he succumbed to despair and committed suicide by throwing himself out of an upper-story window of the prison hospital.

About the same time, a malaria-stricken Lone Wolf was allowed to return to the West from Florida. He died within a year, ending the reign of the Kiowa and Comanche horsemen as Lords of the Southern Plains.

In the spring of 1873 the energetic Mackenzie was transferred to the Rio Grande to put an end to raids into Texas from Mexico. The marauders were a few Lipans, many Mescalero Apaches, and a large group of Kickapoos. The last were emigrés from Kansas.

Mackenzie asked Sheridan for permission to cross the line and invade the Mexican sanctuary. Sheridan ordered him to do so, secretly (no records were kept), and when Mackenzie asked for explicit instructions, the general pounded his fist on a table and erupted, 'Damn the orders! You must assume the risk. *We* will assume the final responsibility.'

The Americans crossed the Rio Grande into Coahuila and attacked a Kickapoo village near Remolino, 40 miles west of Piedras Negras. Mackenzie's men swept through the camp, dismounted and fought their way back in again on foot. They killed 19 and took 40 prisoners, but mostly women, children and old men, since many of the warriors were away at the time of the attack. The Colonel had one man killed and two wounded. Before a collision could occur with Mexican troops, Mackenzie bolted for the border.

Mexico protested, of course, but Mackenzie was quietly praised by his government for a job well done. The Kickapoo lesson was not lost on the marauders. They lost some of their faith in the middle of the Rio Bravo stream bed. For three years, West Texas enjoyed a respite from Coahuilan raiders. When the attacks started up again, veteran General E O C Ord used Lieutenant Colonel William R Shafter and Mackenzie to repeat the lesson. In 1880, however, Mexican protests, dwindling raids and the removal of Ord ended the strictly illegal policy.

The Apache Wars

Early in 1871, civilians re-ignited the smouldering Apache War in Arizona. Indian attacks led the Tucson *Citizen* and its readers to suspect Chief Eskiminzin's small band of San Carlos or Western Apaches of being guilty, even though these Aravaipa Apaches were seemingly peaceful and sedentary people, camping on Aravaipa Creek and the San Pedro River. The Chief had established a rapprochement with an enlightened commandant of nearby Camp Grant, Lieutenant Royal E Whitman. A lowly lieutenant could not make treaties, but he let the Indians stay rather than going to the White Mountain reservation of the Coyotero Apaches.

Whitman wrote to General George Stoneman for instructions, but his letter was returned. It was not in the proper form; he had neglected to summarize its contents on the outside of the envelope. The disgusted subaltern let the Indians stay where they were.

The Aravaipas turned in their guns, even their bows and arrows, settled down to planting corn and cooking mescal. Whitman paid them to cut hay for the post so that they could buy supplies. Nearby ranchers began to hire some of the men as cowhands. In the middle of March about 100 Pinal Apaches joined the Aravaipa experiment.

An old Indian fighter, William Sanders Oury, teamed with prominent Tucsonians to form a Tucson Committee of Public Safety. These Vigilantes, six Anglos and 46 Mexicans, then recruited almost 100 Papago mercenaries. On 28 April they set out to teach Eskiminzin a lesson.

An Army unit in Tucson warned Whitman of the danger to his neighbors and he sent messengers to the Chief to bring everyone inside the fort. He was too late. He recalled, 'My messengers returned in about an hour with intelligence that they could find no living Indians.'

The posse descended on the sleeping village about 4:30 am, raking the wickiups with fire and shooting down their occupants as they fled. It took the Vigilantes only half an hour to 'clean up' the village. The Committee held 27 captives, all children, who were handed over to the Papagos to sell as servants (that is, slaves) in Mexico.

Whitman found the burning village littered with stripped and mutilated corpses, bristling with Papago arrows and often with the heads smashed. Reports disagreed on the number of bodies—86, 115, 125, 145 and 150. Almost all of the dead were women and children. Some of the women had been raped before being shot. Children, even infants, had been shockingly hacked with knives as well as shot. A horrified Fort Lowell surgeon corroborated Whitman's description of the sickening scene. The lieutenant buried the dead, hoping that the Aravaipas would not blame him.

The Camp Grant Massacre was termed 'pure murder' by President Grant, who threatened to place Arizona Terri-

Below: In a pen and ink sketch, Charles Russell pictured mounted Indians watching the engine of their destruction, the **Iron Horse**, and a construction train, circa 1869.

tory under martial law. It even shocked some Westerners, used to such atrocities. But Tucson was not ashamed. Instead of punishing Oury and Elías, his right-hand man, the townspeople called for the removal of Whitman for giving asylum to the Indians. And they nearly got it. He survived three trumped-up court-martial proceedings which were ultimately dropped. But after serving for years without promotion, he resigned his commission.

Elías considered the massacre of the innocent women and children as swift punishment of red-handed butchers, 'a memorable and glorious morning'. So strong was the outcry in the East, however, by a press and public still mindful of Sand Creek, that the Vigilantes were brought to trial in December 1871. The trial lasted five days but the verdict, for aquittal of course, was brought in by the jury in just 19 minutes. This was so although the Camp Grant guide, sutler, beef contractor and mail carrier all backed Whitman's protests that the defendants' claim—that a trail of Apache raiders led directly to Aravaipa Creek—was false.

Grant relieved Stoneman and replaced him with Lieutenant Colonel George Crook, jumping him over 40 angry full colonels. The President also sent out peacemakers Vincent Colyer and General O O Howard, the humanitarian soldier who had lost his right arm in the Civil War. They chose four Apache reservations in Arizona and one in New Mexico. The locals derided Colyer as 'Vincent the Good', but it was Howard who dumfounded Crook, when he said that God meant him (Howard) to be the Moses of the American Indians.

The unkempt Crook, dressed in mufti or an enlisted man's uniform, was such a tough man that his appointment as Stoneman's successor to command the Department was applauded by most Arizonans. But since the eccentric behind the muttonchop whiskers tried to be fair, in his way, some critics were shortly calling him an Indian lover. Certainly his first words did not endear him to Arizonans, 'I think the Apache is painted in darker colors than he deserves.'

Crook added, however, that the Apaches had but two simple choices. They could settle down and cultivate the soil, like Pimas and Papagos, or they could continue stealing and raiding—and be killed. The General saw his government's vacillating policy, misinterpreted as fear by the Apaches, to be fueling the fires of war. To put a stop to the tribe's traditional depredating, Crook meant to go after the Apaches in a 'sharp, active campaign' as soon as he could, to save millions of dollars and many, many lives, both white and red.

Crook was the perfect choice to bring the Apaches to heel. Of all the Army commanders, he was most like his foes. He thought like an Indian. In serving his apprenticeship in California, Oregon, Washington and Idaho, he had learned to fight Indians. He could also live off the land as they did. Like them, he knew the weaknesses of the army and frontiersmen—their politicking, drunkenness, revenge.

Soon, many Apaches turned themselves in. By the fall of 1873, 6000 were at least on reservation rolls. But Crook had to send cavalry into the Chiricahua Mountains to flush out one of their chiefs, Cochise. The Chief's old friend, Indian

Below: Even the **Sheepeaters** renegade Bannocks of Idaho, had a war (1878) with the Army.

Opposite page: Timothy O'Sullivan photographed a Wheeler Survey **Coyotero Apache scout** in the 1870s, proud of his repeating rifle. The Winchester '73 succeeded the Henry, which replaced the 7-shot Spencer lever-action rifle and carbine of Civil War days.

Right: **General George Crook** was the Army's worst-dressed officer, but its best Indian-fighter, even if the Sioux beat him on the Rosebud. Crook was very effective against the Apaches, fighting them as nearly as possible on their own guerrilla terms.

agent Tom Jeffords, got the Apache and Howard together and they came to an agreement. Cochise got the reservation that he wanted and the agent that he wanted—Jeffords. Cochise kept his word and kept the peace, but he fell ill and died in 1874, as Jeffords hurried to Fort Bowie for an Army surgeon to treat the chief.

Crook hired Apache scouts in 1872 to track their hostile brothers that winter. He accepted no excuses for losing a trail. He replaced wagons with pack trains, and horses with mules trained to carry overloads—320 pounds, up from 175. And they had to march an extra 20 miles a day for him. The General wanted to be as mobile as his enemies. Unlike most officers, he was just as happy with infantry as horse soldiers, since the Apaches most often moved and fought on foot in their mountain territory.

On 15 November 1872 Crook invaded the Tonto Basin under the Mogollon Rim, hoping to catch his prey immobilized in winter camps. His orders were to find a trail and follow it to its end. If horses or mules played out, his men were to follow a foe on foot. Nine units scoured the basin and killed perhaps 200 Apaches in 20 separate actions.

Crook's ceaseless campaigning soon began to sap the Apaches' will. They were unable to sleep, to rest, to cook their mescal—for the smoke would surely bring Grey Wolf, as they called Crook. They could not hunt, except with bow and arrow, since gunshots brought troopers and Apache scouts even through the snow.

After Christmas, Crook's Apaches found a stronghold of Yavapais in a canyon of the Mazatzal Mountains, perhaps the band which, long before, kidnapped Olive Oatman in a classic Southwestern captivity. The scouts led Captain William H Brown's squadron of the 5th Cavalry, dismounted, through a cold night to a mesa commanding the canyon. A Lieutenant Ross and a dozen sharp-shooters went ahead with the Apache scouts, posting themselves in the canyon to support a dawn attack.

But the wan light of daybreak showed Brown that he had miscalculated. The enemy was not camped on the valley floor, but in a cave on a slope and on a rock shelf outside the opening. And the campsite was protected by huge boulders.

There was no time to change plans. Ross's marksmen opened fire, killing a half-dozen warriors with their first rounds. The major advanced 40 men to the lieutenant's position, then followed to bottle the Yavapais (called Apaches by the soldiers) in what would later be dubbed Skull Cave.

The Indians refused to heed Brown's call to surrender or his offer of safe conduct of women and children. Again he had his men fire at the angled roof of the cave where it was exposed so that the rifle balls would ricochet into the cavern's defenders. The soldiers heard cries of pain. Again Brown asked for a surrender, but he received no reply, only a strange chant. His Apache scouts told him that it was the Indians' death song. He prepared for a charge.

As the Indians swarmed from the cave the soldiers opened fire from the shelter of the boulders. A few warriors retreated into the cavern, but most hid behind rocks on the ledge. Now Captain James Burns joined the fray from the canyon's rim, his men taking pot shots at the Yavapais below, even rolling boulders down on top of them like the Navajos fighting Pfeiffer in Cañón del Muerto.

After the great rocks tumbled in clouds of dust, Brown signaled Burns to stop. He then sent skirmishers scrambling up the slope. They hardly had to fire a shot. The silence was eerie. They found 75 'Apaches' dead or dying. Another 18, bruised and dizzied by the artificial avalanche, were taken prisoner.

Crook continued to send his officers on such expeditions even when epizootic fever took a heavy toll of his horses and mules. His foot soldiers simply carried everything on their aching backs.

At Turret Peak, south of Camp Verde, Captain George M Randall and a battalion of the 23d Regiment cornered Apaches on 27 March 1873 much as Brown had brought the Yavapais to bay. He had no artillery to blast them loose, so he sent his footsoldiers scurrying up cliffs—at midnight —to charge the enemy at dawn. Surprise was complete and the only escape for the Apaches was either surrender or hurling themselves to their deaths. Most preferred to become prisoners. Turret Peak broke the back of Apache and Yavapai resistance.

By the spring of 1875, Arizona Territory was peaceful. Crook was the hero of the hour. He took advantage of the hiatus in the fighting to improve roads and forts and to stretch 700 miles of telegraph wire over the Territory. Promoted to brigadier general, he was sent to command the Department of the Platte in 1875, to keep the Sioux from rebelling.

Red Cloud, after winning his personal war with the United States, had, surprisingly, accepted agency life and was, by 1873, the leader of the reservation Sioux on the upper White River of Nebraska. But he and Spotted Tail had trouble restraining their rambunctious young men, even with the presence of nearby Forts Robinson and Sheridan.

A much greater source of worry for the Army than malcontents on the Red Cloud and Spotted Tail Agencies

Below: Between 1867-74 Will Soule of Fort Sill, Oklahoma, took a picture of the lodge of a chief, **Little Big Mouth**, perhaps a Cheyenne, to show details of construction. It was made of buffalo hide (hair-side inside) sewed with thongs on travois poles, its doorway closed by a flap held in place by wooden pegs. At its apex the conical tent was ventilated by a hole with smoke flaps that could be shifted according to the wind.

was the roaming about of Crazy Horse, hero of the victory over Fetterman, and 40-year-old Sitting Bull. The ex-warrior still limped from a Crow bullet in one foot, but he was now an Indian politician, even a statesman. His influence extended beyond the ranks of his Hunkpapas and the Oglalas to all of the Teton Sioux and even to Cheyennes and Arapahos. He called reservation Indians fools for making slaves of themselves in exchange for fat bacon, hardtack and sugared coffee. Thanks to the likes of Sitting Bull and Crazy Horse, the Sioux were bound to explode into war again; the only question was when and where.

The Modoc War

During Crook's Apache War, a conflict erupted in the most unexpected place, California. A booming state since 1850, it was the most tamed part of the West, a place with the only metropolis, San Francisco, beyond Chicago, St Louis and New Orleans. The war proved to be a short one, but it seized the public's imagination, like the Seminole Wars.

The Modoc War was fought in the Modoc Lava Beds. This *malpais* or badland was an absolutely worthless volcanic highland on the south shore of Tule Lake in Cali-

Above: In the 1870-80s desert **Apaches** posed for a photographer.
Below: **Mojave braves** posed for O'Sullivan (1871) in western Arizona.

fornia's northeast corner. The Modocs turned ancient gas vents into trenches, breastworks and communication tunnels. Their leader, Captain Jack, never had more than 60 to 75 men, and perhaps more like 51 effectives in all. The soldiers who fought him adopted his name for the area, The Land of Burnt-Out Fires, but changed it to 'Hell With the Fires Out.'

The 300-odd Modocs, remnants of a once-warlike tribe that had raided Gold Rush wagon trains until it was put down with great severity, spoke broken English and dressed in hand-me-down white men's clothes. Jack once said, 'I have always lived like a white man and wanted to live so'. He saw no reason in the world why Modocs and whites could not live happily, side by side. The men worked as ranch hands from time to time, and shopped with their wives in Yreka's stores, just like the white people. The only strife between these neighbors of differing races was caused by the infrequent killing and butchering of cows by hungry Modocs who saw livestock as no different than deer, put there by the Great Spirit for their use.

The Modocs were known by disparaging nicknames— Captain Jack (Kientpoos), Boston Charley, Curly Headed Doctor, Bogus Charley, Shacknasty Jim, Steamboat Frank, and Ellen's Man George.

Captain Jack did not reckon on the land lust of the whites. He was ready to live on a reservation at Lost River, but the ranchers and farmers were pre-empting that farmland just north of Tule Lake in Oregon. They pressured the Government to herd the Modocs onto the Klamath Reser-

Above: The Modoc War temporarily brought a 'town' – of muslin and sailcloth – to the south shore of **Tule Lake** early in 1873. Lines of tents, panoramically photographed from the signal station on a height above the lakeshore, included a hospital (left), the quarters of Colonel Alvan Gillem and other officers to the right, the camp of peacemakers Jeff Riddle and his Modoc wife, Toby (or Winema) in the center, and the restaurant of Charley La Booth and Pat McMann's general store.

vation, just as it had mixed Mescalero Apaches and Navajos at Bosque Redondo. Although distantly related, Klamaths and Modocs were foes in a long-standing feud.

Naturally, the more numerous Klamaths bullied the Modocs. So Captain Jack withdrew his homesick people in 1865 and returned to Lost River. In 1869 he was persuaded to return to the reservation by his friend, Superintendent of Indian Affairs for Oregon Alfred B Meacham. But the Klamaths continued their hazing of his people. The last straw, which led to the bloody Modoc War, was their stealing of the fence rails which the Modocs had cut for themselves.

In 1870 Jack and his followers left the Klamath Reservation forever. He made no trouble; he still favored peaceful relations with whites. He traded again in Yreka, where he had many white friends. But the settlers petitioned the Government to order him back to 'where he belonged.'

Meacham had been replaced by Thomas B Odeneal. He got Fort Klamath to send Captain James Jackson and 43 men of the 1st Cavalry to oust Jack from Lost River and to escort his band to the reservation.

When Jackson surrounded Captain Jack's camp, the

Above: Eadweard Muybridge was rivaled only by Carleton Watkins as California's pre-eminent early photographer. In 1873 he hurried to the **Modoc Lava Beds** in the northeasternmost corner of California. There he found the US Army encampment on the south shore of Tule Lake. Among the photographs that he took to make stereoptican slides was this view of Warm Springs Indians, scouts for the Army, sprawled about their stacked Springfields as they took a break in the sun.

latter said, 'I will go'. But he scolded the officer for sneaking up in the dark on his sleeping people. (He explained that they no longer trusted white men.) For his own part, Jackson tried to mollify the annoyed and now derisive Modocs. He told Jack that he had not come to make trouble.

But when Jackson asked him to surrender his rifle, the Chief balked. He pointedly reminded the Captain 'I have never fought white people yet, and I don't want to'. But he grudgingly dropped his gun on the ground, and his men followed suit.

Scarfaced Charley, a fierce and evil-looking fellow because of a great gash disfiguring his face, was the last to lay his rifle on the pile and he kept his holstered pistol. Jackson ordered Lieutenant Frazier Boutelle to disarm him.

'Give me that pistol, damn you! Quick!' This was the way that Boutelle handled the delicate situation.

Scarfaced Charley laughed to relieve the tension. But he was deadly serious when he reminded the lieutenant that he was not a dog to be cursed that way.

Boutelle drew his service revolver. 'You son of a bitch! I'll show you how to talk back to me!'

As he brought up the muzzle of his gun, Charley quickly drew his own pistol and snapped off a quick shot. His slug tore through Boutelle's coat without hurting him. The two gunshots merged into one as the lieutenant's pistol shot missed Charley entirely.

The Modoc grabbed his rifle from the top of the pile and the other Indians followed his lead. Captain Jack did not want war and he ordered his people to leave. But, before they could do so, they had to fight their way out. In a hot exchange of fire, a sergeant lay dead and seven privates were badly wounded. Jack and his people lost one person killed and had another wounded. He led the families into the cover of the dense tules, or tall bulrushes, which ringed Tule Lake, and got them safely into the Lava Beds.

A posse of civilians tried to arrest another Modoc band, led by Hooker Jim. The attempt failed, and the whites opened fire, killing an old woman and a babe in arms before they retreated and holed up in a cabin.

Hooker Jim now sealed the tribe's doom by retaliating with the murder of 14 or more innocent people in isolated ranch houses before he joined Jack in the Lava Beds.

For weeks, the Hot Creek band and Hooker Jim's followers argued for war while Captain Jack held out for peace. He thought his Modocs would be safe in his stronghold, with its perfect defenses. It was so hostile and utterly useless a country that (he thought) only a lunatic white man would risk his life to seize it. But he sadly asked Hooker Jim, 'What did you kill those people for? I never wanted you to kill my friends.'

After a reconnaissance, Lieutenant Colonel Frank Wheaton attacked Captain Jack's Stronghold on 16 January 1873. He had two columns of mixed regulars and California and Oregon volunteers converge from east and west to pinch off any escape by the Modocs. Bugle calls echoed through the dense tule ground fog, and were followed by the sounds of cannon fire. But only a few rounds were lobbed into the lava. The fog was so thick that the gunners could not see the muzzles of their own howitzers. They were afraid that a rolling barrage would drop on the advancing infantry and not the enemy. The guns were silenced.

Even this late in the bloody game, Jack was willing to surrender. But Hooker Jim and other militants forced him to call a council where he was democratically outvoted, 37 to 14.

Progress by the troops was painfully slow. In the blinding fog, the fatiguing advance over sharp-edged lava rocks and boulders was accompanied by many falls, resulting in sprains, cuts and bruises. The Modocs took perfect advantage of the hellish terrain, hiding in nooks and crannies and wearing camouflage, wisps of sagebrush in their headbands. They moved from point to point as they fired, to render ineffective all countering fire. This maneuver fooled the now-frightened soldiers into believing that they were facing 150 rather than 51 Modocs.

The two columns never linked up, their way being blocked by chasms. The soldiers were pinned down and Wheaton was able to extract them only after dark and a last-light charge led by Captain Jack and Ellen's Man George. Estimates of casualties varied from 11 to 16 dead and 26 to 53 wounded on the Army's side. Even the unhurt men were exhausted and demoralized by their ordeal. Many were terrified by the uncanny accuracy of the Modoc marksmen, all of whom were deer hunters. Even when the fog lifted, no soldier ever saw an enemy! Captain Jack did not lose anyone killed or wounded.

Most, if not all, of the Army dead were left on the field to be plundered by the needy Modocs. They found nine very welcome modern carbines and six belts of cartridges, to

Below: Muybridge titled this ***A Modoc on the Warpath*** to promote sales, but his subject was actually a Warm Springs Indian scout from Oregon, aiming his Army-supplied Springfield carbine at a non-existent enemy.

Opposite page: The photographer is unknown, but this portrait of **Scarfaced Charley** was taken c. 1876 on the Quapaw Reservation of Indian Territory. The scar belied Charley's nature; he was the noblest Modoc.

SCAR FACED CHARLEY   008   MODOC.

keep up the fight. That night, the Modocs celebrated their victory with a big, blazing bonfire. Inexplicably, Army gunners did not even throw a few shells onto the inviting nighttime target.

Colonel Wheaton asked for 300 infantry reinforcements immediately. He estimated that it would take 1000 men, supported by mortars and mountain howitzers to storm Captain Jack's Stronghold. The California and Oregon volunteers rejected the idea, disbanded and went home.

Wheaton was removed after his disaster and General E R S Canby took over personally. He hoped to end the sorry affair by peaceful means. He worked with Captain Jack's friends, Mrs Toby Riddle (Winema), actually Jack's cousin, and her husband, Frank, as well as rancher John Fairchild and ex-Superintendent Meacham. Jack was now ready to yield on his Lost River reservation idea; he only asked for the worthless Lava Beds now for a *ranchería*, or reservation.

The very day that the whites made their first peace feelers the Modoc's unity splintered. Hooker Jim and his men

Above: Muybridge caught the Army's Chief Scout, **Donald McKay**, in the Modoc War as he leaned against a boulder near some of his men. A half-breed, he was Chief of the Warm Springs Indians. The Oregon Indians reconnoitered the volcanic *malpáis* or badlands well enough and joined Gillem's attack on Captain Jack's Stronghold in April 1873 in the Lava Beds. McKay capitalized on his brief fame by taking a wild west show to Europe in 1874. He was also the subject of a dime novel-like book, *Daring Donald McKay*, that was really a pitch for the quack medicine of its publisher.

appeared at an Army base to surrender. They thought better of it when they learned that the governor of Oregon meant to hang them for murder. Captain Jack then complained to the whites about 'civilized man's' double standards of justice. They insisted that he surrender Hooker Jim and his cohorts to the hangman. He said, 'I have a bad heart about these murderers, [but] I have got but few men, and I don't see how I can give them up. Will they [the authorities] give up their people who murdered my people while they were asleep? I never asked for the people who murdered my people.'

Canby headed a Peace Commission and had a peace tent

Above: Cavalry troopers stood at ease for the photographer, ready for inspection in the Army camp at the base of **Gillem's Bluff.** They would soon advance into the Modoc Lava Beds, a lunar landscape of jumbled volcanic boulders that the Modocs aptly called The Land of Burnt-out Fires. Some of the men would die; many would be wounded; some would panic and run for camp, battered and cut from falls on the sharp-edged rocks of the badlands. They were no match for the Indians, fighting from defensive positions in their own familiar terrain.

erected in no-man's land between the Indian and Army lines. He and his fellow-commissioners, Meacham and the Reverend Eleazar Thomas, with the Riddles and Indian Agent L S Dyar, met Captain Jack on 11 April 1873. It was Good Friday.

Toby Riddle warned the whites that the meeting was a trap of Hooker Jim's to kill them all. But Canby scoffed at the idea. While negotiating with Jack, he had reinforced his army to 1000 men and encircled the Lava Beds tighter and tighter as he waged peace. He was sure that the Modocs would not dare try any treachery.

What the General did not know was that the Modocs had had a showdown during an angry council on the night of

7 April. The warmongers had shouted down Captain Jack's peace talk and had taunted him. 'You're a woman! A fish-hearted woman! You are not a Modoc! We disown you.' They threw a shawl over his shoulders, clapped a woman's bonnet on his head and tripped him and threw him to the ground.

Hooker Jim told Jack that he *must* kill Canby; if he did not, his own braves would kill him. Jack protested that it would be a cowardly act but, finally, burning with shame, he blurted, 'I will kill Canby.'

The Peace Commission was escorted to the peace tent by Bogus Charley and Boston Charley, who were armed with rifles. No one else had a rifle except men hidden by Captain Jack in ambush in rocks near the tent. But all of the Modocs were armed with concealed pistols. Some of the whites had taken the precaution to arm themselves secretly, too. Meacham and Dyar had small derringers in their pockets.

Canby first opened a box of cigars and handed them out to Captain Jack and the five Modocs accompanying him, also to his two-man 'escort.' Then the General began to talk. He had come to make peace, he said, and whatever promises

Below: The Army captured the Stronghold because Captain Jack chose to abandon it. Officers, enlisted men and civilians posed in the natural fortress of trenches and shelters formed by volcanic action as Colonel Gillem crowed, 'I have dislodged the Modocs from their Stronghold,' but added, 'The country is exceedingly difficult.'

Right: **Captain Jack, Chief of the Modocs**, was really named Kientpoos or Kintpuash, meaning 'Having the Waterbrash' (ie, pyrosis, or heartburn). He was as nervous as his name suggests and melancholy. He was used to wearing white men's clothes, he knew some English, he worked on ranches, he shopped in town (Yreka, California). Jack was a man of peace who was forced into war by both whites and 'hawks' of his own tribe and bullied into the murder of General Canby by the same braves – who turned against him and hunted him down for the Army. He was hanged at Fort Klamath, Oregon, on 3 October 1873, along with three of his warriors. The picture was taken while he was a prisoner at the fort.

he made would come true.

Then Hooker Jim took Meacham's overcoat and put it on. He strutted about, saying to no one in particular, 'You think I look like Meacham?' The latter, jokingly, offered his hat, but Jim spurned it, saying, ominously, 'You keep a while. Hat will be mine, by-and-by.

Captain Jack interrupted Canby's oration by suddenly jumping to his feet and shouting a signal in Modoc to the men in ambush, 'All ready!' He drew a concealed pistol and pointed it at Canby's face, only three feet away. It misfired. He cocked it again and at point-blank range shot the General in one eye. The veteran officer refused to fall, even after Jack drew a knife and stabbed him several times, and broke into a shambling run though more dead than alive. Ellen's Man George finally killed him.

Boston Charley killed the preacher, Thomas, but Toby Riddle knocked Schonchin's gun aside and saved Meacham's life. He was partially scalped as he lay on the lava, presumably dying, but he survived. Dyar and Riddle ran for their lives and made it safely to the Army lines. Troopers who tried to come to Canby's aid were turned back by fire and a lieutenant was killed.

The betrayal and murder of the popular Canby under a flag of truce ended all idea of Modoc negotiations. It was almost a death blow for Grant's Peace Policy, finally killed three years later at Little Bighorn.

There was no turning back now. Jack had murdered the only general to be killed in the Indian Wars. (Brevet major general George Custer was only a lieutenant colonel in permanent grade.) When Captain Jack stripped off Canby's uniform and put it on to symbolize his role of war chief, the action meant battle to the death.

The entire nation was outraged by Captain Jack's treachery. Sherman wired General Schofield that he would sustain 'any measure of severity to the savages.'

Colonel Alvan Gillem led 1000 men into the Lava Beds, 15–17 April 1873, in an advance duplicating Wheaton's. But he cut the Modocs off from their water supply, Tule Lake. Gillem even managed to kill three Modoc men, as well as eight women, before the remainder slipped away into hiding. (Actually, two of the braves died accidentally. A shell from a Coehorn mortar failed to explode. A curious brave hammered at the dud till it exploded and blew him up, along with a companion.)

On 26 April, Scarfaced Charley caught 65 of Captain Evan Thomas's 4th Infantry and Warm Springs, or Tenino, Indian scouts in a trap worthy of guerrilla textbooks. He sneaked up on the soldiers as they ate a pleasant lunch in a rocky depression. When a relief column got through, it found all five officers and 20 men dead and another 16 wounded. Charley could have killed everyone, but he grew tired of the slaughter; he was not a killer by instinct. He called out as he let the survivors withdraw, 'All you fellows that ain't dead had better go home. We don't want to kill you all in one day.' In this defeat, as usual, the Modocs did not lose a man.

General Jeff C Davis took over from Gillem and finally won a battle for the Army when a counterattack scattered Modocs hitting a camp at Dry Lake, originally called Sore Ass Lake by the cavalry. Davis also seized the stronghold 14 May, now abandoned by Jack.

Before the Modocs could beat the Army again, the bloodiest of them, Hooker Jim, turned on his own people. He and his followers deserted to the Army, offering to run their chief to earth. To its eternal shame, the Army struck a bargain with them. Davis welcomed the renegades with open arms, though he correctly described Jim as 'an unmitigated cutthroat.' In exchange for their betrayal of Captain Jack, he promised to forgive them for their sins and crimes.

The renegades easily led the Army to Jack's trail. Shortly, after 65 holdouts surrendered, they scouted ahead of the troopers and actually entered his hiding place. Jack scornfully tongue-lashed them. 'You intend to beg your liberty and freedom by running me to earth. You, who forced me to promise that I would kill that man, Canby.'

All the Army now had to do was to follow Hooker Jim and corner Jack and his few loyal friends. By the end of May, General Davis was remarking that it was now 'more of a chase after wild beasts than a war.'

Jack gave up early in June. Only two braves still stuck by him. His uniform, Canby's, was filthy and tattered. His only excuse for quitting was that his legs gave out.

Left: Some of the most prominent officers of the Modoc campaign gathered together for a group portrait by Eadweard Muybridge, although not one of them really distinguished himself fighting the handful of Indians who, regularly, beat the Army before falling back to new defensive positions. From left to right in the front-row chairs were **Major Edwin C Mason, Colonel James A Hardie, Colonel Jefferson C Davis** (with muttonchops), and 1st Cavalry CO **Colonel Alvan Gillem.**

The War Department wanted Canby's assassination avenged. Sherman particularly wanted retribution. He said that Davis should have killed every Modoc. The US Attorney General ruled that a military commission could try only those responsible for the murders of Canby and Thomas. Hooker Jim and friends were freed. In fact, they did the military equivalent of turning state's evidence in the July trial at Fort Klamath and performed as star witnesses for the prosecution.

Captain Jack and five of his lieutenants were sentenced to die, but President Grant commuted two sentences to life imprisonment on Alcatraz Island in San Francisco Bay. The betrayed but unrepentent Captain Jack, tricked into murdering Canby, was hanged along with the old plotter, Schonchin John, Black Jim and Bogus Charley, at Fort Klamath on 3 October 1873.

The next night, the corpses were secretly dug up by 'resurrectionists' for display in Yreka. Later, they were decapitated and the skulls sent to the Army Medical Museum (and later to the Smithsonian Institution) for anatomical study.

Captain Jack's 155 Modocs were sent to the Quapaw Reservation in Indian Territory. There, Hooker Jim died six years later. Scarfaced Charley took over as tribal leader.

Left: The true hero of the Modoc War was a heroine, **Winema** or **Toby Riddle**. Captain Jack's cousin, she fought as hard to avoid war and to restore peace as any soldier or warrior fought to defeat his enemy. *Top:* **The Peace Tent**, where General E R S Canby was murdered. *Above:* The Army camp in the Lava Beds. *Opposite page:* **Donald McKay** of the Warm Springs Scouts posed for the photographer with his favorite weapon, apparently an old Sharps carbine.

In 1909 the last 51 Modocs, ironically the exact number of braves in the stronghold in 1872–73, were allowed to return to the Oregon–California border.

Jack's 51 men had stood off 1000 soldiers in the Army's most costly war, in terms of enemies involved. They killed at least eight officers and 39 enlisted men, 16 civilians and two Indian scouts, and wounded 67 more whites. Hooker Jim murdered 14–18 settlers. The Modocs lost five men in battle and a few women and children.

The seven-month long conflict cost the American taxpayers a half million dollars, plus the cost of exiling the Modocs to Indian Territory and the usual payment of war claims, honest or fraudulent, by citizens. The war was so remarkable that Sherman was doomed to disappointment when he said, after the exile was begun, that 'the name of Modoc shall cease.' Instead, Captain Jack and his brave band have never been forgotten in the history of California.

Shoshoni. 1.

Below: In 1870 William Henry Jackson recorded **Chief Washakie's encampment** of skin lodges or *tipis.* Always friendly toward the white man, Washakie and his Shoshone braves even scouted and fought against the Sioux for the Army.

BRITISH COLUMBIA

NORTHWEST TERRITORIES

ONTARIO

WASHINGTON TERRITORY

Bear Paw Mtn (1877) ✕

Ft Benton

Ft Union

DAKOTA

MINNESOTA

Ft Walla Walla ■

Portland ●

Willow Springs (1878) ✕

MONTANA TERRITORY

Ft Missoula ■

Helena ●

Butte ●

OREGON TERRITORY

Whitebird Creek (1877) ✕

Big Hole (1877) ✕

Ft Keogh ■

Ft Abraham Lincoln ■

Sioux Wars (1854-90)

WISCONSIN

Canyon Creek (1877) ✕

Ft Custer ■

Little Bighorn (1876) ✕

Rosebud (1876) ✕

TERRITORY

Minneapolis ●

St Paul ●

Ft Bridger ■

IDAHO TERRITORY

Ft Phil Kearney ■

Ft Pierre ■

Deadwood ●

New Ulm ●

Lava Beds (1873) ✕

Modoc Wars (1872-73)

Dull Knife (1876) ✕

Ft Fetterman ■

Wounded Knee (1890) ✕

IOWA

Sacramento ●

Reno ●

San Francisco (Pacific Military Division HQ) ●

NEVADA TERRITORY

WYOMING TERRITORY

Salt Lake City ●

Ft Laramie ■

Cheyenne ●

NEBRASKA TERRITORY

Omaha ●

Ft Kearny ■

Missouri

Chicago (Missouri Military Division HQ) ●

ILLINOIS

Thornburg Massacre (1879) ✕

Meeker Massacre (1879)

UTAH TERRITORY

Leadville ●

Denver ●

Cripple Creek ●

KANSAS

Ft Leavenworth ■

Ft Riley ■

River

Independence ●

St. Louis ●

MISSOURI

CALIFORNIA

COLORADO TERRITORY

River

Colorado

Ft Defiance ■

ARIZONA

Apache Wars (1881-1900)

Ft Apache ■

Taos ●

Ft Union ■

Santa Fe ●

Ft Supply ■

OKLA ●

INDIAN

Okmulgee ●

ARKANSAS

Ft Yuma ■

Tucson ●

Geronimo Surrenders (1886) ✕

NEW MEXICO TERRITORY

STAKED PLAINS

Ft Sill ■

TERRITORY

El Paso ●

Ft Worth ● Dallas ●

MEXICO

TEXAS

LOUISIANA

San Antonio ●

Major Battles in The West
(1876-1890)

● Cities
■ Forts
✕ Battles
Military Division of the Pacific
Military Division of the Missouri

CUSTER AND THEREAFTER
1876-1891

The Sioux Campaign

The battles and wars in the Plains and Rockies in the ten years that followed the Civil War set the stage for what was to be the climactic chapter in the conflict between the Indians and the white man. General Sheridan's campaign in the summer of 1876, which led up to the Battle of the Little Bighorn, was the turning point. George Custer's defeat at the Little Bighorn was the most spectacular victory achieved by the Indians in the wars on the Plains and it was also the last major victory. The defeat of Chief Joseph and the Nez Percé a year later in the summer of 1877 at the hands of that determined fighter, Nelson 'Bearcat' Miles, was to pave the way for breaking the back of all Indian resistance in the West. After Joseph, the only major holdouts were Geronimo and the Apaches in Arizona. The Apache wars were the principal area of conflict during the 1880s, a time when most of the West had been pacified. War in the Southwest generally came to an end when Geronimo surrendered to General George Crook in 1889. The period of Indian Wars that had gripped the North American continent almost since the first white man set foot on it finally ended in 1890 at the Battle of Wounded Knee.

Once the Modoc War was over, the Army shifted its attention back to the Sioux, the one tribe—aside from the Apaches—which seemed to pose a continuing, perhaps permanent, threat to Western settlement.

In 40-year old Sitting Bull, the Sioux now had a master politician as well as a war chief. In 25-year old Crazy Horse they found a natural military genius. And since he was married to a Cheyenne, ties between Sioux and Cheyennes grew stronger as war approached.

In 1873 Sitting Bull blocked surveys of a Yellowstone River route for the Northern Pacific Railroad. Twice, Lieutenant Colonel George Custer had to fight off Sioux assailants in tenacious encounters.

The next year, 1874, Custer explored the Black Hills, a sacred area to the Sioux. The hills had been ceded to them in 1868 as their land 'forever,' part of the Great Sioux Reservation. But some of Custer's men found gold in the Black Hills and miners began to prospect its streams by the

Above: **Black Hills** (Deadwood, SD) miners angered the Sioux in 1876.

summer of 1875. The Army removed the pioneer party of miners from Gordon's Stockade, near modern Custer, but others only followed. So many men slipped past patrols that a gold rush occurred as public pressure to open the hills to legal white settlement increased. The Army was soon swept aside and, to the anger of the Sioux, Custer City and Deadwood became boomtowns reminiscent of California's Mother Lode of 1849.

That same year, George Custer's brash young brother, Tom, captured a rising Hunkpapa, Rain In The Face. The warrior later made his escape, swearing that he would eat Tom Custer's heart.

The Government offered to pay the Sioux six million

dollars for their holy mountains. Some Indian leaders were amenable to selling the Black Hills, in any case lost to them already, but they wanted five times that paltry sum. Others would not hear of selling the sacred place for any price. So, between the railroad building and the Black Hills gold rush, the Sioux drifted back onto the warpath, ignoring the Government's orders to return to the reservation.

By the time that the proud Centennial Year of 1876 rolled around, to be celebrated with a great world's fair in Philadelphia, the Sioux and Cheyennes were preparing a celebration of their own. It would show their independence of the Great White Father in the East and his Long Knives on the Western Frontier. By 1876, 50,000 Indians were in rebellion. Only 15,000 were bona fide warriors, and probably no more than 4000 took the field against the bluecoats.

The 1876 Campaign on the North Plains

The War Department sent its very best man, Crook, to put down the Sioux and their Northern Cheyenne allies. He had ten companies of cavalry and two of infantry. His field commanders were polar opposites—the reckless Custer and the timid Alfred H Terry. Crook was supposedly only an observer in the field, but usurped command from his nominal expedition head, Colonel Joseph J Reynolds. He did not want to be slowed down, so he left his 80-odd wagons behind (also his pack-mule train) as he hurried out of Fort Fetterman on a clear 1 March.

On the **Bozeman Trail** the Bighorn Expedition found a more formidable foe than even the Sioux. A series of northers roared down the trail, freezing the troopers

Left: The artist titled this picture **Desperate Charge of General Crook's Cavalry at Battle of Rosebud.** Crook had little chance to charge the enemy there, because he was preoccupied with organizing a retreat to avoid being overwhelmed by the Indians. He was hours on the defensive when the Sioux, tired or bored – but certainly not beaten – pulled out. Crook tried to call it a victory, but retreated and stayed put for eight weeks, bandaging wounded and begging for reinforcements. The Sioux, free of restraint, helped crush Custer at the Little Bighorn.

although they were bundled up in long underwear, blanket-lined overcoats, fur caps and buffalo robes.

Reynolds, on the point of Crook's column, halted his advance when his scouts reported a Cheyenne and Sioux encampment in a cottonwood grove under the bluffs of Powder River. He tried to surprise the Indians, but a young herder gave the alarm. The Colonel's squadrons drove into the village only to meet a punishing rifle fire which turned them back. Reynolds dismounted his men in the village and had them dig in as the advantage shifted to the attacked. The Colonel had the Indians' food supplies and pony herd, but warriors on the bluffs pinned down the soldiers with a steady fire.

Reynolds lost his nerve and ordered a retreat back to the main force. He let the Indians retake their ponies and he

moved his men out so fast that he left behind either two dead men or one dead trooper and one wounded man—the latter to be tortured to death by the Sioux. (His total losses were two dead and six wounded.)

Crook was furious with Reynolds. He abandoned the advance in order to return to base and prefer charges against him.

Crook's Sioux campaign of 1876 had begun poorly. His Crow scouts reported that the humiliation of Reynolds on Powder River had greatly increased the recruiting of warriors by Crazy Horse. Unknown to the Army, it would face in the Rosebud-Bighorn country the greatest concentration of warriors in the entire history of America's Indian wars.

After refitting, Crook left Fort Fetterman again at the end of May with more than 1000 cavalrymen and infantrymen and almost 50 officers. He had many teamsters and packers, too, and he carefully armed them as auxiliaries. In the field, he added Crow and Shoshone scouts, 262 of them. His column was one of three comprising Sheridan's pincers movement in imitation of the successful Red River campaign of 1874 and 1875.

The General wanted to split the rumored large force of Indians into several smaller bands, then deal with them separately. So he had Colonel John Gibbon move eastward from Montana to make contact with General Alfred Terry (and Colonel Custer), moving westward from Fort Abraham Lincoln. As the columns converged, Crook, moving northward, would roll back the Sioux on the Terry–Custer column.

Crook leapfrogged his strung-out column along the dusty Bozeman Trail, sending his infantry ahead, but soon to be passed by the horse soldiers. Both reached bivouacs ahead of the supply train and rearguard. When he entered hostile territory in mid-June, Crook halted his wagon train under a strong guard of 100 infantrymen, then made 200 of their companions into mounted infantry or quasi-cavalry, to take along. At Tongue River a courier from Sitting Bull and Crazy Horse warned him not to cross a symbolic line scratched in the dirt. If he did cross, he would have to fight. This suited Crook perfectly.

General Crook knew the Apaches much better than he did the Sioux. He was surprised—his troops enjoying a coffee break—on the morning of 17 June on the Rosebud. Only the splendid fighting of his Shoshones and Crows prevented a disaster. Never was conflict fiercer than in the broken terrain, terrible for cavalry or even any kind of concerted battle plan. Several troops were roughly mauled and gave way. Crook sent Anson Mills to seize Crazy Horse's village (which he mistakenly thought lay just to the north). With his main force so battered, Crook wisely called off Captain Mills. The latter swung around behind the hostiles and forced them to abandon the battlefield. This led Crook to claim a victory in the Battle of the Rosebud, since he was left in possession of the battle site.

Actually, Crook was humbled by Crazy Horse. Though

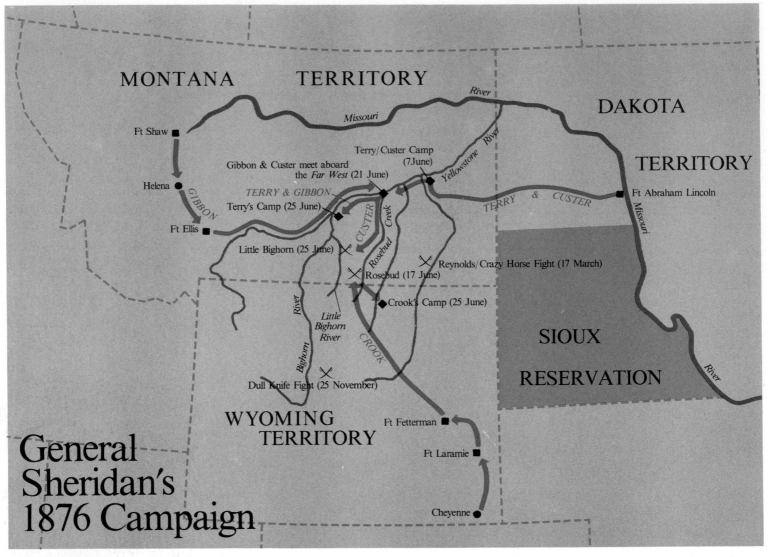

MONTANA   TERRITORY

DAKOTA

TERRITORY

Missouri *River*

Ft Shaw ■

Terry/Custer Camp
(7 June)

Gibbon & Custer meet aboard
the *Far West* (21 June)

Helena ●

TERRY & GIBBON

Terry's Camp (25 June)

Ft Ellis ■

Yellowstone *River*

TERRY & CUSTER

Ft Abraham Lincoln ■

Missouri *River*

Little Bighorn (25 June) ✕

✕ Reynolds/Crazy Horse Fight (17 March)

Rosebud *Creek*

✕ Rosebud (17 June)

◆ Crook's Camp (25 June)

*Little
Bighorn
River*

SIOUX

Bighorn *River*

CROOK

RESERVATION

✕ Dull Knife Fight (25 November)

WYOMING
TERRITORY

Ft Fetterman ■

Ft Laramie ■

River

General
Sheridan's
1876 Campaign

Cheyenne ●

he admitted to only ten dead and 21 wounded, many believed the casualty count of Chief Scout Frank Grouard, instead—28 killed and 56 wounded. The neutralizing of Crook by Crazy Horse, who lost no less then 36 dead and 63 wounded in the fray, guaranteed Custer's utter defeat at Little Bighorn. Gibbon and Terry would eventually meet, but it would be too late to save the 7th Cavalry.

The Battle of the Little Bighorn

The heart of Terry's force was Custer's 7th Regiment. Some of the Colonel's officers were real fighters—Captains Frederick Benteen, Myles Keough and Tom Custer. (George's brother, Tom, had won not one but two Medals of Honor in the Civil War.) But Colonel Custer's second-in-command, Major Marcus A Reno, though a Civil War veteran, was untried in Indian warfare. While Gibbon camped on the Yellowstone at the mouth of the Rosebud, Reno scouted the Powder and Tongue River valleys. Terry's base was the mouth of Powder River.

Terry called a pow-wow in the cabin of the steamer *Far West* on 21 June to outline his strategy to Gibbon and Custer. He was worried that he could not catch the enemy in order to defeat him. He wanted Custer to time his cavalry attack so that Gibbon's slow-moving infantrymen would be in position in the north to block any flight of the Sioux. Terry issued written orders so that there would be no misunderstanding his plan. This was to bottle up the hostiles in the Little Bighorn Valley between Custer and Gibbon.

Custer, in buckskins, led between 600 and 700 horse soldiers. His Arikara scouts did not know the country, so he borrowed six of Gibbon's Crows. But he declined Terry's offer of four troops of the Second Cavalry and a Gatling gun platoon. He did not want to be slowed down by the horse-drawn artillery and he certainly did not want his beloved 7th Cavalry to share victory honors with the Second Regiment.

The stage was set for the debacle when Crazy Horse engaged Crook at Powder River, forcing him to pull back. And the ambitious Custer was much more overconfident than the plodding realist of Apache campaigns.

Custer was later accused of direct disobedience of orders. There is no doubt that he bent them badly, ignoring Terry's instructions to ascend the Rosebud to its head before turning west after the Indians, whose trail had been found by Reno's scout. (This delay would give Gibbon's foot soldiers time to get into position to support the cavalry in the Little Bighorn Valley.) Instead, when the hostiles' trail left the Rosebud for the Little Bighorn drainage, he followed it. This rashness compounded his initial mistake of underestimating terribly the number of his foes. A tragedy of errors was thus set in motion.

To be fair to Custer, not even his Indian scouts dreamed that he was opposed by such enormous numbers of warriors. He had chosen the single moment in history when 3000 braves, at the very least, were gathered to fight together. Many were armed with Winchester repeating rifles against the troopers' single-shot Springfield carbines. And, for once, the Indians' strategy was to stand, and not fall back

Above: **Sitting Bull (Tatonka-I-Yatanka)**, the Hunkpapa Sioux leader, was photographed in feathered headdress by David Barry in 1885.

Above: A freckled Colonel (and Brevet General) **George Armstrong Custer** posed for the great Civil War photographer, Mathew Brady.

into one of their usual running fights. Finally, the warriors were led by such men as Sitting Bull, Crazy Horse, Gall and Rain In The Face.

Custer knew that the Indians had spotted him and were, probably, aware of his strength. For his part, he was completely unaware of the fact that he was outnumbered five to one. He had not even been able to see the Indian village from a high point he called **Crow's Nest**. (Actually, the Indians occupied a series of populous villages in the valley of the Greasy Grass.) But, once more, ego and ambition overruled prudence, even common sense.

If Custer ever considered a withdrawal, which is unlikely, it was probably too late to effect it now, in any case. So he decided to smash straight through the enemy, but this time, incredibly, he guaranteed disaster for himself by fragmenting his regiment. Leaving one troop (company) to guard the pack train, he kept only five for himself. Suicidally, he split off three troops under Benteen in a scout to the south and three more with Reno. The latter was to chase a party of 40 Sioux into the upper end of the village. He promised to support the Major with 'the whole outfit.'

Custer, however, hesitated after his promise to Reno, then apparently changed his mind. Rather than riding to his support, he veered off to the north to strike the lower end of the village.

Everything went wrong. Reno charged as ordered, but could not make a dent in Chief Gall's huge force. There was no sign of Benteen, supposedly ahead of him, or of Custer supporting him from the rear.

Reno did the best that he could with just 112 men. He re-

trieved his men from the outskirts of the village, where Sioux swarmed like angered ants from a nest. He dismounted his troops in a patch of timber, but Indians infiltrated his line. Seeing a trap closing on him, he ordered his men to remount and fell back across the stream to dig in on a bluff above the river.

Reno's withdrawal, sane enough, was held against him in the later court-martial in which he was used as a scapegoat for Custer's disaster. He had lost only a couple of men, so far, and may have panicked. Some say that he led the retreat instead of covering it from the rear. Worse, some of his troopers were left behind, trapped in the cottonwoods. A lieutenant wanted to go back for them, but Reno forbade it, as Indians counted coup by dragging soldiers from their mounts as they splashed through the shallow Little Bighorn. Quickly the toll began to rise. In just 45 minutes on 25 June 1876, Reno lost half of his command in dead, wounded and missing.

Meanwhile, Custer came in sight of the first village and found it to be an armed camp. He rushed a courier to Benteen, ordering him to join him and to bring extra ammunition. 'Bring packs! Bring packs!' he scribbled on the note that he gave to his orderly. Custer then charged, but soon hauled up in the face of overwhelming odds and led a withdrawal to a high grassy ridge. It was Gall who pushed him back, but now Crazy Horse struck from the north while another force left Reno's shattered command to be in on the kill.

Benteen topped a rise and saw soldiers surrounded on a bluff. He took them to be Custer's men, so he galloped to

their aid. So it was that the captain kept Reno from being overrun. When both officers heard shooting from downstream, they knew that Custer was also engaged.

Reno did not know what to do. Should he risk going to Custer's aid, as some of his officers insisted, now that he was reinforced? Or should he stay put in his defenses? After all, Custer was supposed to come to the support of his second-in-command, not vice versa. But Custer had ordered Benteen to reinforce *him*, not Reno. And the latter, at least on paper, had a stronger force, six companies, than his commanding officer.

Finally, a captain who was either very brave or foolhardy, Thomas B Weir, could no longer tolerate Reno's inaction. Against the latter's orders, he began to ease his way back down the bluff to the Little Bighorn. Benteen followed Weir's troop and, grudgingly, Reno gave the command to follow suit. But progress was very slow, since Indian rifle fire continued. Also, the wounded had to be carried in blankets for want of stretchers.

Helping Custer was a forlorn hope at best. Reno's force

Above left; David F Barry photographed **Gall,** the Hunkpapa Sioux warrior, holding a bow and arrow at Fort Buford, ND, in 1881. *Above:* **Rain in the Face** (1835-1905), photographed by F Jay Haynes, was the Hunkpapa who bragged that he would kill Captain Tom Custer and eat his heart – and presumably did so at Little Bighorn. *Opposite page:* The artist's *Heroic Death of Custer*, showing Custer surrounded by downed men and horses on his hill above the Little Bighorn River, was based on conjecture since there were no survivors of the battle.

was too battered. It was too late, anyway. Crazy Horse, apparently employing more Cheyennes than his own Sioux, had already surrounded and destroyed Custer's entire command. It took him only an hour. Crazy Horse was helped by Gall after he split his force, but easily kept Reno and Benteen pinned down while assaulting Custer at the same time.

'Custer's Luck' was over, forever. Every man of his command was killed and most were mutilated by the victors. Rain in the Face, as he had promised, cut out Tom Custer's heart and ate of it.

Crazy Horse and Gall turned to destroy Reno and Ben-

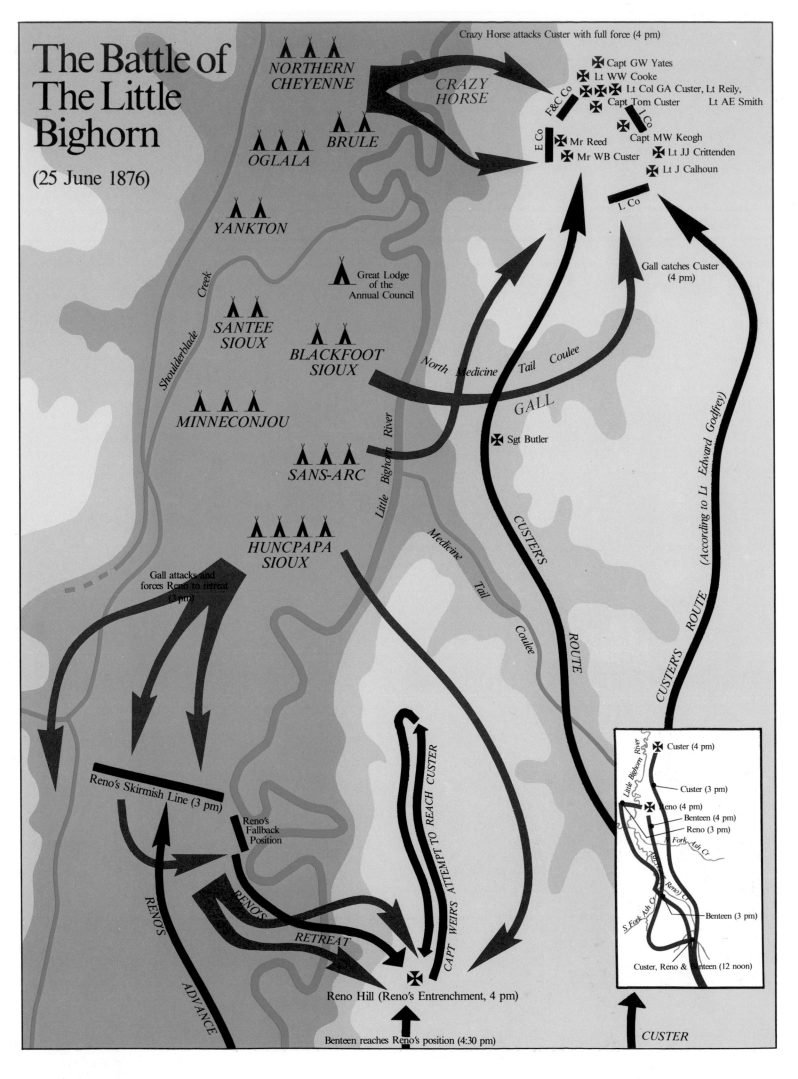

The Battle of The Little Bighorn

(25 June 1876)

Crazy Horse attacks Custer with full force (4 pm)

NORTHERN CHEYENNE

CRAZY HORSE

Capt GW Yates
Lt WW Cooke
Lt Col GA Custer, Lt Reily,
Capt Tom Custer
Lt AE Smith

F&C Co

BRULE

E Co
Mr Reed
Mr WB Custer

I Co
Capt MW Keogh
Lt JJ Crittenden
Lt J Calhoun

OGLALA

YANKTON

L Co

Shoulderblade Creek

Great Lodge of the
Annual Council

Gall catches Custer
(4 pm)

SANTEE SIOUX

BLACKFOOT SIOUX

North Medicine Tail Coulee

GALL

MINNECONJOU

Little Bighorn River

Sgt Butler

SANS-ARC

Medicine Tail Coulee

CUSTER'S ROUTE

CUSTER'S ROUTE   (According to Lt Edward Godfrey)

HUNCPAPA SIOUX

Gall attacks and
forces Reno to retreat
(3 pm)

Reno's Skirmish Line (3 pm)

Reno's
Fallback
Position

RENO'S

RETREAT

RENO'S ADVANCE

CAPT WEIR'S ATTEMPT TO REACH CUSTER

Reno Hill (Reno's Entrenchment, 4 pm)

Benteen reaches Reno's position (4:30 pm)

CUSTER

Little Bighorn River

Custer (4 pm)

Custer (3 pm)

Reno (4 pm)
Benteen (4 pm)
Reno (3 pm)

N Fork Ash Cr

Benteen (3 pm)

Custer, Reno & Benteen (12 noon)

211

Above: At the Cheyenne River Agency in 1881, **Red Horse** drew a pictograph of Miniconjou Sioux warriors advancing against whites (out of sight) at the Battle of the Little Bighorn in 1876. *Below:* Horse skulls, ribs and other bones made the **Little Bighorn Battlefield** an ossuary. The photographer's view was westward down the slope of Custer's Hill to the river, the site of a Cheyenne camp on 25 June 1876 (see map, *left*). *Below right:* A detail of **Red Horse's** pictograph that recorded how warriors closed in on Custer's doomed command, with some of his men already decapitated or otherwise mutilated by the blood-lusting braves.

Above: In an 1877 photograph of the heart of **Custer's Battlefield** at the Greasy Grass, the Indians name for the Little Bighorn Battle site, two cavalrymen view the recently implanted grave marker of the Irish adventurer, Captain (Brevet Colonel) Myles Keough.

teen. They easily chased them back to their bluff. The troopers fought well to save their lives but, even in rifle pits, they suffered 18 more deaths and had 43 wounded. Enemy fire did not slacken until nightfall, when the besieged soldiers watched a wild scalp dance below them, illuminated by the glare of campfires. In the darkness the officer and 16 men trapped in the copse of cottonwoods slipped safely through Reno's lines.

With the first light of dawn, the siege was tightened. Benteen and Reno had to throw back two assaults. Bravely, Benteen led a few counterattacks to keep the Sioux and Cheyennes at a respectable distance.

That evening the Indians withdrew, setting a grass fire to screen their movements. Their scouts had spied the approaching relief column of Terry and Gibbon. The puzzle is why they did not swamp Reno and Benteen, or harass Terry. For the only time in history, they had sufficient warriors to do the trick.

Terry had been alerted by his scouts to the disaster. Ironically, Reno and Benteen as yet did not realize that Custer's force had been destroyed to the last man of the original 215. The Army buried the dead, took 52 wounded men in wagons, and fell back to Fort Abraham Lincoln. Reno's casualties were 47 killed and 53 wounded. Estimates of Indian losses ran all the way from 30 to 300.

The shock waves of the Custer calamity rippled across the entire country from the grassy plains of Montana and Dakota to New York, New Orleans, San Francisco. The Army looked for a live scapegoat since the real blunderer, Custer, was now a dead hero and martyr. Reno seemed to be a good bet because of his vacillating. He was censured and a court of inquiry found that he had done less for the

safety of his men than certain subordinates. This was true enough. But the decision of the court was that there was nothing in his conduct, otherwise, deserving reproach. Nevertheless, a humiliated Reno took to drinking, was court-martialed in 1880 and dishonorably discharged.

Grant blamed Custer for the needless sacrifice of so many men. Sherman agreed, stating that Custer should never have broken his regiment into three pieces in the face of overwhelming numbers of Indians—even in such unconventional warfare as that practiced on the Western plains. Sherman also correctly laid some of the blame on Crook's mismanaged pincers move and retreat a week before Custer's Last Stand.

The Aftermath of the Custer Defeat

One of the many myths surrounding Custer's calamitous last campaign is that the Army was momentarily paralyzed by the destruction of its crack cavalry regiment and most brilliant commander. True, Terry and Gibbon patiently waited for reinforcements. But Crook, also in the field, was joined by a new man, young Colonel Wesley Merritt, commanding the Fifth Regiment of Cavalry. Before meeting Crook, Merritt intercepted one of the many bands of Indians joining Crazy Horse because of his great triumph over Custer. It was 17 July, barely three weeks after the Battle of the Little Bighorn, when Merritt took on 800 Cheyennes who had just taken off from the reservation.

Merritt fooled the Cheyennes by setting up an ambush on Nebraska's Warbonnet Creek, sometimes mundanely called Hat Creek. He did so by posting snipers in the draws and cramming 200 hidden soldiers inside his apparently unescorted wagons. The Indians charged right into the young Colonel's trap. The skirmish, however, amounted to pretty much of a duel between Merritt's scout, Buffalo Bill Cody, and Chief Yellow Hand, sometimes identified (like Custer) as Yellow Hair. In a knife fight which has become legend, Cody killed his opponent. Lone Wolf's warriors broke so fast for the safety of the reservation that Yellow Hand was the only fatality. (There were a few Indians wounded.) So the skirmish has come to be called the 'First Scalp For Custer.'

Crook was more annoyed with Merritt for his tardiness than pleased at his success at **Warbonnet Creek**. With him, he now had 2000 men and when he joined Terry, their combined strength was almost 4000. Naturally, Sitting Bull and his followers were not about to tackle such a formidable force. The chiefs spurned another open fight and broke up their temporary army into the usual small bands.

Crook did not repeat Custer's mistake of breaking his force into parts. But Terry tired of the chase and shortly disbanded his expedition. Crook persevered, though his men, exhausted by cold and muddy going, were almost out of rations. His campaign was now being called the Horsemeat March.

Crook's loyal aide, Lieutenant John G Bourke, described the command as 'a brigade of drowned rats.' Lieutenant Colonel Eugene Carr called Crook and Terry 'two fools' who did not know their business. The Shoshones apparently agreed. Chief Washakie took them home. Cody left, too.

The first real opportunity to revenge Custer, if Warbonnet Creek did not count, came by accident. Crook sent Captain Anson Mills and scout Frank Grouard, with four officers and 150 men on the soundest horses, to bring back

Below: **Low Dog,** veteran of Little Bighorn, was never without his tomahawk.

Below: Charlie Russell's 1917 painting of **Buffalo Bill's** classic duel with **Yellow Hand** at War Bonnet Creek, 1876. Cody pulled his Winchester before the Cheyenne could reach him and took the 'First Scalp for Custer.'

Opposite page: Two major figures of the Indian Wars, Northern Cheyennes **Little Wolf** (left) and **Dull Knife**, posed in full – if confusing – regalia. Dull Knife's fine peace pipe of Minnesota catlinite contrasted sharply with Little Wolf's incongruous and enormous pectoral cross with pendant, Navajo-like *najas*. The two chiefs led the pathetic homeward flight from Indian Territory toward Montana in 1878. *Right:* Braves like **Short Bull** were proud of their fancy breastplates.

61 pack-mule loads of food from Deadwood. Near **Slim Buttes** in the northeast corner of South Dakota, they stumbled on a Sioux village of 37 lodges. Mills sent a messenger back to Crook and waited in a drenching rain until daylight.

The villagers were completely unprepared for Mills's attack. Most scattered madly to the hills, though a few, led by Chief American Horse, fled to a box canyon and dug in. American Horse shouted warnings that Crazy Horse would soon come to rescue him. Mills appropriated the Indian food in the village and penned up the hold-outs in the dead-end gully till Crook should come to his assistance.

Crook arrived before the regrouping Sioux could counterattack against the game Mills. He posted vedettes on the hills to keep a sharp watch for Crazy Horse as rifle fire raked the ravine. Finally, American Horse gave up. He was shot, and was holding in his intestines with his hands. He died in the lodge that Mills turned into a makeshift hospital tent.

Even with Crook's mounted pickets, the Sioux suddenly exploded out of a pine woods as the soldiers relaxed over their first decent meal in days. But the Indians would fight only from a distance, and they withdrew after a day of long-range fire against the rear guard. Because of the aborting of Mills's supply mission, Crook was in no shape to pursue them. Again he sent Mills to Deadwood. This time the Captain returned with a herd of cattle and wagonloads of flour, bacon, coffee and hardtack, just as the column staggered up to the edge of the Black Hills.

Slim Buttes was hardly an answer to Little Bighorn. It was no smashing, decisive, victory. But it improved morale by ending the Army's string of reverses.

Guards at the reservations were reinforced and Colonel Ranald Mackenzie skillfully disarmed and dismounted the followers of Red Cloud, allowing Crook to replace him with the more peaceable Spotted Tail as chief of all of the Sioux. The Government then forced the tribe back to the Black Hills.

In October, Colonel Nelson Miles met with Sitting Bull. The talks broke down after Sitting Bull told the Colonel that God had made him an Indian, but not an *Agency* Indian. Miles then beat the Chief with his 'walk-a-heaps' (infantry) in a running battle that began in a grass-fire set by Sitting Bull. It progressed to a hasty hollow square defense, as the Sioux turned savagely on their pursuers, and extended over two days and 40-odd miles to the Yellowstone. Shortly, Miles took some chiefs hostage and forced 40 lodges to surrender, then chased Sitting Bull until December.

Crook, seemingly rendered almost as timid as Terry himself by Custer's debacle, put together a large army—too large for effective work—and marched up the Bozeman Trail into the teeth of a mid-November blizzard. He was after Crazy Horse, but when a scout reported a Cheyenne encampment, he sent Mackenzie for a look.

The doughty Scotsman led a thousand horse soldiers across the snow-covered Wyoming plains to arrive in

position on a fork of Powder River on the bitter cold eve of Thanksgiving Day. The Cheyennes of Dull Knife and Little Wolf were having a celebration of their own, a victory dance after striking the Shoshones.

As usual, Mackenzie waited for dawn before attacking. He surprised his adversaries completely, driving all 400 warriors from the village. He killed off most of their ponies and fired the skin lodges after he found grim mementoes of Custer's defeat in them. In stubborn—savage—fighting, the Indians battled back from river bottom, valley, slope and rim and almost won the day. But the superb fighting of Mackenzie's Indian scouts, and another of Crook's remarkable marches of reinforcements (26 miles in 12 hours) gave the victory to Mackenzie.

Some Cheyenne survivors were sheltered in Crazy Horse's Sioux camp, but most who did not freeze to death in the 30-below weather, without food, blankets, horses or shelter, chose to surrender. No one knows how many died of exposure, but Dull Knife lost 40 men in the battle itself, and had many others wounded. Mackenzie had one officer and five enlisted men killed and another 26 men wounded.

So severe was the weather at year's end that Crook had to call off the winter campaign of 1876 in late December. But 'Bear's Coat' Miles was not ready to quit. He almost got the surrender of Crazy Horse's huge village (600 lodges, 3500 people), over the Chief's objections on 16 December. But the Colonel's Crow scouts attacked the Sioux peace delegation. A furious Miles punished the Crows by dismounting them, and sent the Sioux the Crow ponies as an apology and payment for the five emissaries killed.

Proof that Miles's peace overture had misfired was a Sioux attempt to draw soldiers into ambushes. Miles was ready to play the game, even with his tired infantry. He followed the decoys after disguising two of his cannon

Below: A detail of the painting, *Jumped,* in which the Montana artist Charles Russell suggested how mounted Plains Indians made **hit-and-run surprise attacks** on prairie schooners out in the open grasslands.

as supply wagons. He was lucky. He captured some Cheyenne women and children, including a few relatives of Crazy Horse. That evening, 200 of the would-be ambushers tried to recapture the prisoners, but the colonel was ready for them. He prepared carefully for a battle on the next day and his hunch was right.

Shortly after daybreak of 7 January 1877, Crazy Horse himself led 500 Sioux and Cheyennes in an attack across country covered with several feet of snow. Miles heard Crazy Horse shouting in English, 'You have had your last breakfast!'

Because of the snowy and steep terrain, Miles could flush the Indians from positions atop steep bluffs only by a frontal assault. The overconfident Sioux and Cheyennes let the sweating, freezing, soldiers struggle up the slope in their burdensome buffalo coats. But before the Indians could wipe them out at close range, Miles unlimbered his disguised artillery. The Indians did not run, but were taken aback by this lively cannon fire. The leader of the assault, Major James S Casey, got a foothold atop the bluff. The battle seesawed back and forth till Chief Big Crow fell. The Indian defenses began to collapse.

A blizzard kept casualties low on both sides, but the Indian allies withdrew from the Battle of Wolf Mountain. Miles, short on supplies, turned back to the Tongue River Cantonment. From there he boasted to General Sherman, and to all who would listen, of his prowess. He compared his success with Crook's so-so showing. He suggested that Generals Pope and Terry be sent packing. He wanted an Army department all for himself; he was not content with his new District of the Yellowstone.

Miles bragged to Sherman that if given departmental command, and only half the troops there, he would end the Sioux War in four months, and 'once and forever.'

Sheridan and Sherman were annoyed by Mile's boasting. But they recognized his achievement by enlarging his District of the Yellowstone to include Crook's Powder River country, and by giving him more units to command.

As the new year opened, Sitting Bull said that he was calling off the war. He invited the Sioux to accompany him to the land of the Great Mother (Queen Victoria). Those Sioux and Cheyennes who did not follow him decided to scatter. Some went back to the reservations. Spotted Tail

Above: The camera caught **General Nelson 'Bearcoat' Miles**, fourth from left, spurning a fur cap, as he and scout **L S 'Yellowstone' Kelly**, mounted, prepared a winter pursuit of Crazy Horse in Montana.
Opposite page: Handsome – if scarred – **Plenty Coups**, with earrings, shell bead necklaces and pipe tomahawk with studded handle, typified the Army's Crow allies who fought their hereditary Sioux enemies.

persuaded virtually all of his people to opt for peace, not war, by April of 1877. On 6 May, even Crazy Horse came in, throwing his three Winchesters on the ground, in sign of surrender, at the Red Cloud Agency. Most of the Indians surrendered to Crook, thanks to Spotted Tail. This angered the jealous Miles. But revenge would be his. He would go after the last hostile band, that of Lame Deer, the Chief who had vowed never to surrender.

Miles took as scouts such recently-surrendered Sioux and Cheyennes as Hump, White Bull and Brave Wolf. They found 50 lodges on Muddy Creek, a tributary of the Rosebud. A dawn charge on 7 May 1877 scattered the Miniconjous. Miles slaughtered half of their pony herd of 450 head, keeping the others to mount four companies of infantry. The Colonel counted 14 Sioux dead on the field. He lost four men killed and had one officer and six men wounded. But he nearly lost his own life in the battle's aftermath.

Hump, a Miniconjou Sioux himself, persuaded Chief Lame Deer and his head warrior, Iron Star, to surrender. They laid their rifles down and were grasping the hands of the colonel and his adjutant when a scout rode up and covered them with his rifle. Thinking that he intended to shoot them, the two 'renegades' grabbed up their own weapons. Lame Deer fired at Miles, at almost point-blank range. The Colonel dodged, in time, but the shot killed a cavalryman behind him. The warriors ran up a hill, but both were shot down.

Fugitives drifted in that summer and fall as Miles built two strong posts in the very heart of the Sioux nation to prevent any repetition of Little Bighorn. General Sherman visited Fort Carter (the other was Fort Keogh) and prophesied that the Dakotas would never regain their country. He was right, but he was premature in assuming that the Sioux War was over. The shrewd Sitting Bull had fled to Canada, but Crazy Horse was perceived as only biding his time before going on the warpath again.

Right: A detail of Frederick Remington's narrative painting, ***Through the Smoke Sprang the Daring Soldier***, depicted cavalrymen in a snowy line of defense as a brave fellow went 'over the top' in a one-man charge.

Crazy Horse was angered by rumors of a forced move of his people to a Missouri River reservation and offended by the Army's use of Sioux scouts against the Nez Percés. Crook, fearful that Crazy Horse's temper was nearing the flash point, ordered him arrested. He was taken into custody, but when both soldiers and Indians tried to disarm him, 7 September 1877, he fought them. Crazy Horse received a stab wound that proved mortal. To this day, it is not known for certain whether a soldier's bayonet or an Indian's scalping knife killed him.

Red Cloud and Spotted Tail, with Crook's support, talked President Hayes into granting them reservations west of the Missouri. Some of Crazy Horse's followers fled into Canadian exile with Sitting Bull. But most of the Sioux settled down in 1878 on the Rosebud and Pine Ridge Agencies. These were the old Spotted Tail and Red Cloud Agencies.

Homesick Northern Cheyennes on the Indian Territory reservation that they shared with the Arapahos bolted on 7 September 1878. Troops converged on Dull Knife and Little Wolf as they headed north. After hot-headed warriors killed civilians in direct disobedience of the chiefs' orders, Dull Knife and Little Wolf split. The former led his people to Camp Robinson to surrender; the latter kept on toward the Yellowstone.

In a sad affair foreshadowing Wounded Knee, the Army ordered the surrendered Cheyennes back to Indian Territory. When they refused, offering to go to Pine Ridge only, the commander of Camp Robinson tried to starve and freeze them into submission. He cut off all food, water and firewood. After a week of suffering, the Cheyennes made their break. With a handful of arms concealed by the women, they shot their barracks guards and fled into the January snow of 1878. The garrison soon overtook the weakened Indians and killed almost half of them—men, women and children. The Government, shamed by the stupidity and brutality of the enforcement of a bureaucratic decision, now yielded. Dull Knife was allowed to take his survivors to the Pine Ridge Agency.

Little Wolf remained at large till 27 March 1879, when he surrendered. Miles signed his warriors on as Army scouts and after service at Fort Keogh, the Northern Cheyennes were allowed to drift back to the Tongue and Rosebud. In 1884 they were finally given a reservation of their own, the Lame Deer Agency near the Muddy Creek battleground.

Sitting Bull was still a source of serious worry to the Army. He and Gall and other chiefs built up a colony, just across the Canadian border, of 4000 Sioux and Nez Percés. The North-west Mounted Police kept an eye on them from Fort Walsh, but had no trouble, thanks to firm but fair dealings with the Indians. When the strain of feeding so many exiles taxed the Canadian buffalo herds, an attempt was made to return the Sioux to the US. But the Army's choice of General Terry as a commissioner doomed the initiative. The Sioux embraced the Mounties, but would not even shake the hand of their enemy. Sitting Bull accused Terry of coming only to tell lies and shouted, 'We don't want to hear them!'

Miles, scornful of Terry and as vain and ambitious as

Above: Cheyenne **Little Wolf** with his peace pipe and his goateed captor, **Captain Clark** of the Second Cavalry, became friends before the latter's death. Little Wolf finally surrendered to the troops when his weakened forces were brutally overtaken. Many of his Northern Cheyennes became Army Scouts, and the tribe was eventually given a reservation of its own.

ever, was apparently ready to risk an international incident by invading Canada to grab Sitting Bull. Sheridan and Sherman tried to keep him away from the border, but failed when the Sioux, unwisely, moved across the line to hunt buffalo. Miles hurried to collar them on Milk River. An indecisive fight between his scouts and Sitting Bull's own hunting party was ended by Miles's arrival with new Hotchkiss rapid-fire cannon. The colonel pursued Sitting Bull and expelled a few hundred *métis* or 'Red River half-breeds' who supplied him with ammunition. But, to the immense relief of Sherman, he halted at the border, then pulled back to the Missouri to end his expedition. This act of sanity led Sheridan and Sherman to join Terry in showering praise on the bellicose Miles.

As the buffalo herds dwindled, hunger forced most of the Sioux to return to the US in 1879 and 1880. The last to surrender was, predictably, Sitting Bull. It was 19 July 1881. The Army would not let him live freely with his people, but kept him under house arrest at Fort Randall for two years. Sitting Bull's surrender symbolized the end of the Sioux Wars, except for the aberration of Wounded Knee, almost a decade later.

Miles was rewarded for his success by being given a brigadier general's rank and command of the Department of the Columbia at the end of 1880. A first-rate regimental commander and a dogged, able, field campaigner, he had easily out-performed Crook, of whom the Army expected so much. His use of infantrymen to wear down Sioux and Cheyennes led to a Congressional debate over the merits of cavalry versus footsoldiers. But, actually, the innovative Miles used a mix of cavalry and footsoldiers and often turned the latter, at least temporarily, into mounted infantry. Like Crook, he used Indian scouts skillfully, too. The Sioux had finally met their match not in the flamboyant Custer but in the indomitable Miles.

The Nez Percé Campaign of 1877

The saddest and most unnecessary of all Indian wars, surpassing even the Modoc and Seminole affairs, was the Nez Percé War. It was absolutely uncalled for. For 70 years after the Nez Percés took the hand of Meriwether Lewis in friendship (1805), the tribe remained at peace. It was its proud boast that it had never drawn the blood of whites.

In 1863 Washington had planned to move two bands of these staunch friends from their ancestral homes on Idaho's Salmon River and Oregon's Wallowa Valley to a Lapwai Reservation in northwest Idaho. Old Chief Joseph fought back—without violence. His people came to be called 'non-treaty Nez Percés,' but he pointed out that Governor Isaac Stevens's 1855 treaty extended the reservation to include the Wallowa Mountains. He had refused to sign only the outrageous pact of 1863 which would have stripped away those lands on which gold had been found.

In a Presidential order, Grant in 1873 conceded that Chief Joseph (who died in 1871) had been correct. But the executive order was revoked only two years later because of the outcry of land-hungry Oregonians. The Wallowa Valley was designated a part of the public domain and thrown open to settlement. The younger Chief Joseph continued his father's work, but negotiations stalemated in late 1876.

One-armed General O O Howard was a humanitarian who sympathized with Joseph. But his hard-line Christianity led him to confuse Joseph's spirituality with a forerunner of the Ghost Dance, the Dreamer cult of Smohalla—who called for extermination of all whites. Reluctantly, Howard advised that force be used if persuasion should fail.

The Army tried to avoid being the scapegoat of the Indian Bureau, but was ordered to occupy the Wallowa Valley and did so. Chief Joseph gave in and began to move his people to the reservation. But drunkenness had debauched some of his young men and they went on a whiskey-fueled spree in which about 20 settlers were killed. Joseph wanted to explain to Howard and to continue to the reservation, but his people persuaded him to join White Bird's people on the Salmon River.

Howard sent Captain David Perry, a Modoc War veteran, with three officers and 90 cavalrymen to prevent further attacks. He made a grueling night march in the mountains to cut off the Nez Percés before they could cross the Salmon River. Perry started his tired men down the steep canyon of White Bird Creek on 17 June 1877. At the mouth of the 3000-feet deep gorge lay Chief Joseph's lodges. The Chief meant to gather his stock there and, avoiding war, to move east to the buffalo plains as his people had done, seasonally, for centuries.

Joseph decided to talk peace with Perry, but to prepare for a fight, should it become necessary. He sent away his women and children, even his horse herd. Chief Joseph had only between 60 and 70 effectives. An equal number of warriors were sleeping off the huge drunk.

Captain Perry's men were preceded by a force of volunteers which opened fire on Joseph's truce party in spite of its white flag. The Nez Percés returned the fire with such deadly marksmanship that Perry's charge never got rolling. Instead, the volunteers fled and exposed his flank. Soon the Nez Percés were chasing the 1st Cavalry up the canyon. At the top of White Bird Hill, Perry attempted a stand, but had to fight his way back to the settlement of Mount Idaho

Above left: In 1877 F Jay Haynes made an excellent photographic portrait of *Chief Joseph* (1832-1904) of the Nez Percés, probably the most distinguished – and humane – of all Western warriors. *Above:* One-armed Civil War vet **General O O Howard**, who pursued Chief Joseph in the Nez Percé War, was a Christian warrior who sympathized with the Indians he fought.

on Camas Prairie. In killed alone, the Captain lost an officer and 33 soldiers. Joseph had no warriors dead and only three wounded.

General Howard now took personal command of the pursuit of Chief Joseph, but sent Captain Stephen Whipple to capture Chief Looking Glass, who was (so far) neutral. Whipple planned to parley but, like Perry, let his volunteers determine the action. They shot up the village, captured 600 ponies, scattered the unprepared Nez Percés—and drove Looking Glass into Chief Joseph's arms.

Chief Joseph skirmished with Whipple and volunteer units, then joined Looking Glass on the Clearwater. There Howard found them with their 800 followers, including 300 fighting men. It was 10 July 1877 and the Nez Percés were besieging a force of civilians. General Howard attacked, but soon found himself on the defensive as warriors swarmed up ravines and bluffs to force him back from the valley rim to an open prairie. **The Battle of the Clearwater** was a desperate one, but Joseph made the mistake of fighting it on the Army's terms instead of in his hit-and-run style. In a pitched battle of seven hours' duration. Nez Percé sharpshooters were no match for howitzer bursts and raking Gatling gun fire, even though the Indians captured Howard's pack train and, temporarily, some of his artillery.

Howard later said that the Nez Percés fought as well as any troops that he ever saw, but they were finally outflanked and driven from the field. They crossed the Clearwater and fled northward. Howard was too bloodied to pursue. He had 15 men dead and 25 wounded, to Joseph's four dead and six wounded.

While the Nez Percés took Looking Glass's advice and marched, via Lewis and Clark's old Lolo Trail, across the rugged Bitterroot Mountains, Howard built up the strength of his force for the pursuit. The Nez Percés planned to hunt buffalo on Montana's plains and perhaps join the Crows. If necessary, they were ready to trek to Canada to join Sitting Bull. Howard finally moved out after them on 30 July with 560 cavalry and infantry, 25 Bannock scouts, and 150 packers and other citizens with his 350-mule pack train. As Joseph struggled over the Lolo Trail, described by General Sherman as one of the worst routes for men or beasts on the entire continent, Howard telegraphed ahead for forces to intercept Chief Joseph in his flight.

A mixed bag of 150 regulars and quasi-militiamen fortified the pass by which Chief Joseph would exit from the mountains. His scouts sniffed out the whites, of course, and Joseph asked for permission to pass, promising that no harm would be done to settlers. When his request was refused, he tied up the strongpoint with desultory rifle fire and slipped his main force around it on secret Indian trails. Once he bypassed the defensive position, derisively called Fort Fizzle by Bitterroot Valley people who traded with the Nez Percés, he picked up speed in more open country.

But, still unaware of Howard's use of the 'talking wire,' Chief Joseph gave in to Looking Glass's demand that they

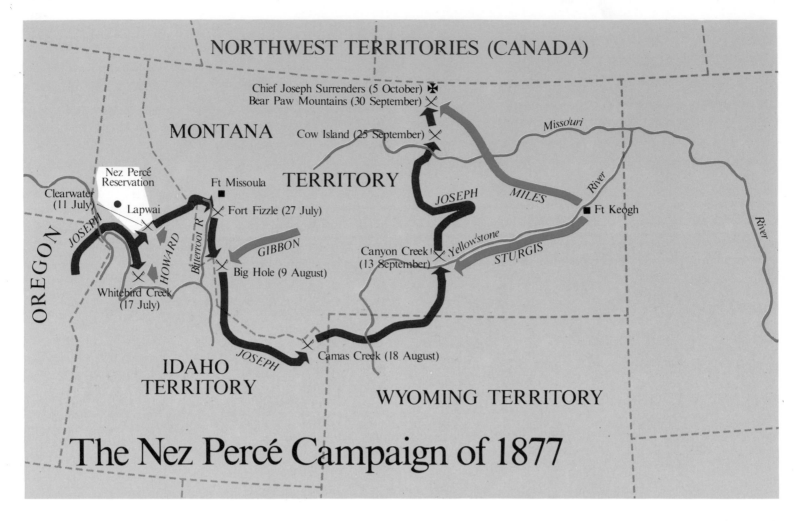

The Nez Percé Campaign of 1877

rest in Montana's Big Hole Basin. Their people were tired and wanted to cut lodge poles. They had had no shelter since the Clearwater fight.

Colonel John Gibbon, the Sioux War veteran, heeded Howard's telegraphic appeals and brought 15 officers and 146 infantry in wagons, plus 45 volunteers, and caught the native military genius napping. Joseph felt so secure on 9 August on the Big Hole River, because of the lead that he had built up over Howard, that he neglected to post sentries.

The dawn attack took Chief Joseph completely by surprise. He lost his campsite in just 20 minutes. He and Looking Glass regrouped their marksmen in riverside thickets, however, and brought Gibbon's attack to a standstill. The Nez Percés outfought the whites in hand-to-hand assaults and the colonel wisely retreated from such a ferocious foe. The tide of battle changed so completely that soon Gibbon was pinned in a patch of timber, from which he sent a messenger to Howard for help.

Next morning, while troopers 'feasted' on raw horse meat in the woods, Joseph seized the Army's laggard supply caravan, disabled the Colonel's howitzer, and captured 200 very welcome rounds of ammunition. Sergeant Milton K Wilson bravely recovered the ration wagons, but the fighting dragged on all day, with Gibbon, himself, being wounded. Joseph exploited a wind to light a grass fire to cover his advance, but the wind shifted and burned itself out. Before the Chief could attack again, his scouts alerted him to Howard's approach and he pulled his men out of action.

Howard broke Joseph's siege of Gibbon, but it was an expensive victory for the Army, costing 32 dead and 37 wounded. But the **Battle of the Big Hole** was much costlier

to Joseph. Gibbon had nothing to be ashamed of. Joseph lost 87 people, some of them women and children, but mostly warriors he could not spare.

Gibbon's force was too shattered to follow Chief Joseph as he re-crossed the Continental Divide into the Lemhi Valley of Idaho, where the formation of militia companies led the Nez Percés to kill some civilians. But Howard took up the chase immediately and soon was less than a day behind his quarry.

When Joseph turned on Howard on 19 August, he pulled off one of the most astonishing strategems of the war. He personally led 45 of his 200 men straight—and noisily—at Howard's camp at Camas Meadows. He imitated a cavalry column of fours. Sure enough, the sentries mistook his party for Lieutenant George R Bacon's force, returning from Targhee Pass. They let the horsemen pass. When a guard finally gave the alarm, Joseph was driving off 150 of Howard's pack mules and some of his picketed cavalry horses.

Three troops galloped out at first light, just as Joseph hoped, and rode into his trap. He had regrouped his four columns into three, drawn up in an ambuscade. Two troops got out, but Howard had to rescue the third with a loss of one man killed and seven wounded.

Almost leisurely now, Chief Joseph withdrew through Targhee Pass, abandoned too soon by Howard, and into Yellowstone National Park on 22 August. That volcanic wonderland had already seized the public's imagination and, alas, the Nez Percés terrified tourists in the Park and killed two of them.

Howard, halted at Targhee Pass, was temporarily demoralized. He was unable to catch Joseph with his ragged and discouraged soldiers, many of whom were ill

as well as exhausted. The general rode to Virginia City, Montana, for provisions, then telegraphed Sherman that he thought he ought to stay where he was. Sherman told him to pursue the Nez Percés to the death, 'lead where they may.' So Howard resumed his pursuit.

From the Little Bighorn country of bloody memory came Colonel Samuel D Sturgis with six troops of Custer's rebuilt 7th Cavalry. He was followed by Colonel Wesley Merritt with units of the Fifth Regiment. Joseph simply feinted toward the Stinking Water, or Shoshone River, to draw Sturgis there, then nipped along Clark's Fork to reach the open plains, making the Colonel look like a fool.

A mistake of Joseph's scouts now hurt him. Receiving incorrect reports that his direct route was blocked, the Chief led his people in a long, roundabout and time-wasting detour. The delay gave Sturgis, now joined by Howard, the opportunity to catch up with him at Canyon Creek, near Billings, on 13 September 1877.

But Joseph held off Sturgis so successfully that the latter's critics, in their frustration, later accused him of timidity and even cowardice, although he lost three men killed and had 11 more wounded. The Nez Percés were tiring, but they slipped away from the battered Sturgis and headed for Bear Paw Mountain, only 40 miles from the safety of the Canadian border. On the northern slope, Joseph unwisely paused again to rest his exhausted people at the urging of Looking Glass.

Once more, their scouts failed the chiefs. Not all army units were behind them. The nemesis of the Sioux, Colonel Nelson Miles, had been alerted by couriers from Sturgis. Now he moved a strong unit to cut off the Nez Percé withdrawal. Miles had almost 400 men, mostly cavalry and infantrymen mounted on Indian ponies. He quickly moved

Above: Chief Joseph, in his masterful 1877 retreat toward Canada, and a possible link-up with Sitting Bull's exiled Sioux, had to penetrate the Blackfoot country of north-central Montana. Luckily, he did not run afoul of any war parties of **Plegans**. *Below:* The 1877 Battle of Big Hole was one of four major Nez Percé War battles. Colonel John Gibbon took the village there in only 20 minutes, but the Nez Percés rallied and counterattacked, pinning the Army down in **rifle pits** *(below)* in a siege that lasted until General Howard came to the rescue. Neither side won, but the Army could better afford its losses of 32 dead and 37 wounded than the Nez Percés their 87 dead, including many women and children.

northwestward, ferrying the Yellowstone and Missouri Rivers in a race with the Nez Percés for the Canadian line.

The Colonel's Sioux and Cheyenne scouts found the Nez Percé camp in the Bear Paw ravine of Snake Creek early on 30 September 1877. Miles attacked by mid-morning and found that, unaccountably, the Indians had again failed to post guards. The Nez Percés fled to the ridges, leaving teepees and ponies to the soldiers. Still, when units of the 7th charged Indians on the heights above a cutbank, they were rebuffed with heavy losses. Like Modocs, the Nez Percés concentrated their fire on officers and non-commissioned officers. True, Miles had 22 enlisted men killed and 38 wounded, but a captain and a lieutenant were dead, two more captains and three lieutenants wounded. Seven sergeants were killed, including all three of the 7th's first sergeants. Three sergeants and a corporal were wounded. Such a casualty list was enough for Miles to give up his assault and to settle down to a siege.

The Nez Percés dug trenches with knives, tomahawks, even frying pans, as their sharpshooters dodged shells from the howitzer and the up-ended 'Napoleon' fieldpiece and exchanged fire with Miles's marksmen. Joseph sent a messenger to Sitting Bull, only a day distant, asking him to come to his aid. But the old chief did not come, or even answer the message.

Uncharacteristically, Miles seized Chief Joseph under a flag of truce, but had to release him in exchange for one of his lieutenants who strayed into the Nez Percé lines. General Howard arrived, but let Miles retain his command until he could accept the Nez Percé surrender.

Finally, after five days of siege, Chief Joseph decided that he had done all that he could for his surrounded people. He sent a message to Miles, asking him to tell Howard 'I am tired of fighting.' He then met with the two officers.

Above: Major Lee Moorhouse took a photograph of mounted, war-bonneted **Nez Percés**, long after the Indian Wars on 4 July 1906.

The handsome chief who rode into Miles's camp on 5 October wore buckskin leggings and, oddly, a gray woollen shawl—pierced with several bullet holes. His scalplock was tied with otter fur in part, the rest of it plaited in pigtails. His head and one wrist were slightly bloodied by bullet wounds. Ceremoniously, he gave his rifle to Miles, then smiled and shook Howard's hand. He surrendered 400 tribesmen, less than 100 of them warriors. About 100 of his men had joined Sitting Bull, along with 200 women and children.

Of his 800 people, Joseph lost 120 dead during his epic, three-month, 1700-mile retreat, more than half of them braves. The Nez Percés killed about 180 whites, mostly soldiers, and wounded about 150 more. They won some battles, accepted a draw or a defeat in one or two more, but consistently outmarched and outfought the Army. The whole country was impressed by the Nez Percés. Miles described them as 'the boldest men and best marksmen of any Indians I ever encountered.' Sherman praised them for their fighting skill and courage, but especially for their humanity. 'They abstained from scalping, let captive women go free, did not commit indiscriminate murder of peaceful families.'

Chief Joseph was not the only Nez Percé chief, of course. There was Looking Glass, and White Bird, also Toohool-hoolzote and the half-blood guide, Poker Joe. But it was Chief Joseph who most impressed the whites. Miles said of him that he was 'the highest type of Indian I have ever known; very handsome, brave, and kind . . . a man of more sagacity and intelligence than any Indian I have ever met. He counseled against the war and against the usual cruelties

Above: Spike-helmeted officers and men in dress uniforms and white gloves stood at ease for the camera at **Nevada's Fort McDermitt**.

practiced by the Indians, and is far more humane than such Indians as Crazy Horse and Sitting Bull.'

Chief Joseph was one of the most eloquent of Indian orators. His moving words of surrender have been much quoted, by whites and Indians alike. 'I am tired of fighting. Our chiefs are killed. Looking Glass is dead . . . It is cold and we have no blankets. The little children are freezing to death . . .' The much-wronged Nez Percé closed his pathetic message—'I want to have time to look for my children and see how many of them I can find. Maybe I shall find them among the dead. Hear me, my chiefs, my heart is sick and sad. From where the sun now stands, I will fight no more, forever.'

After their heart-breaking ordeal, the Nez Percés were not allowed to go to Lapwai, as Miles had promised. He was overruled by Sheridan and Sherman. Over his protests, Joseph's people were exiled to distant Kansas and the Indian Territory. There, many sickened and died. Chief Joseph remained the tribe's leader. But even with the support of Generals Miles and Howard, he could not get the Government to return his people to the Northwest until 1885. His people were allowed to settle on Washington Territory's Colville Reservation, the followers of Looking Glass and White Bird on the Lapwai Reservation. But Oregonians refused to let Chief Joseph return to his beloved Wallowas, and he died at Colville in 1904.

As Howard, Gibbon and even Terry quarreled with the aggressive and arrogant Miles over the spoils of Nez Percé War glory, peace began to spread over the West. It was helped along by the Indian Bureau reforms of Interior Secretary Carl Schurz.

Above: **Sergeant John Nihill**, 5th Artillery, modeled a German-style helmet, in vogue in the US after the Franco-Prussian War.

The Bannocks

But peace was interrupted in a region supposedly pacified by Crook in the 1860s. The desert-ranging Bannocks and Western Shoshones of the Idaho-Oregon-Nevada border country became rebellious. Asked why, Crook answered, 'Hunger; nothing but hunger.'

But a stupid clerical error of 1868 helped bring about war a decade later. The clerk who was transcribing the terms of the treaty by mistake guaranteed a non-existent 'Kansas Prairie' to the Bannocks rather than their Camas Prairie. Naturally, whites settled the latter. Several hundred of the Bannocks' kin, the Malheur Paiutes, joined them and when the Bannock chief, Buffalo Horn, was killed, the Paiute, Egan, succeeded him.

It was O O Howard's job to pacify the Bannocks and he did a better job than with the Nez Percés, thanks largely to Captain Reuben F Bernard. Winnemucca, chief of most of the Paiutes, did not want to fight and Bernard, through the chief's daughter, Sarah Winnemucca, arranged his defection and escape. Howard appointed the girl his interpreter.

It took Bernard just two skirmishes, plus one by Captain Evan Miles, to scatter the Bannocks, though the last did not surrender until September.

The Bannocks infected the tiny tribe of Sheepeaters, renegade Shoshones and Bannocks, with rebellion, too. These people lived by hunting mountain sheep in the rugged Salmon River Mountains of Idaho. They probably numbered about 50 fighting men in all, but their haunts were so inaccessible than even Bernard could not find them. They found Lieutenant Henry Catley, however, and ran him off so fast that he was courtmartialed. But dogged pursuit by small Army detachments wore them down and the 'mass' of the Sheepeater nation, 51 men, women and children, surrendered in October of 1878.

The Ute War

The Utes of Colorado, Kit Carson's old friends, were auxiliaries of the Army against Navajos and Plains Indians. Their main chief was a peaceful statesman, Ouray. Yet they went to war in 1879 after their country was overrun by silver-seeking whites.

The direct cause of the conflict was the utopianism of White River Indian Agent Nathan Meeker. He was determined to make instant farmers of the Utes. They resisted; he asked Army help. Major Thomas T Thornburgh was sent with a force of 153 men. Misunderstandings between him and the Ute leader, Jack, led to a fire-fight. Thornburgh was killed and his command, now under Captain J Scott Payne, badly mauled. He had lost ten dead and 42 wounded by the time a rescue party of black cavalrymen joined him, only to be pinned down also. Most of the horses and mules were dead, too. Escape was impossible, but Colonel Wesley Meritt, making one of his remarkable forced marches, broke the siege by driving the Utes away.

Ouray and Schurz tried to make peace but the Agency massacre and mistreatment of the women enraged the country. Army reinforcements poured into Colorado but Interior Department Special Agent Charles Adams released

Right: Charles Russell documented the awe of the Plains Indians who spied the first **fireboats** ascending the Missouri River.

tensions and negotiated the release of the captives. The Ute War was ended by diplomacy. A commission decided that only a dozen Utes were guilty of the **Meeker Massacre**. They were tried for murder. The rest of the Utes were transferred to the Uintah Reservation in Utah.

Geronimo and the Apache Wars

Custer's disaster, and its aftermath, drew the public's attention away from the Mexican border. But it simmered in lawlessness and violence during the last half of the decade of the 1870s. However, General E O C Ord's raids from Texas into the former sanctuary of Mexico, actually carried out by Colonels Ranald Mackenzie and William Shafter and, especially by the black Seminole scouts of Lieutenant John Bullis, shifted frontier incursions westward into New Mexico and Arizona.

The two territories were ripe for trouble. Cochise, the peacemaker, had died in 1874 and Crook had been transferred away the following year. The best efforts of able Indian agents John P Clum and Tom Jeffords were frustrated by Apache truculence on the one hand and, on the other, by the Tucson Ring. This was a cabal of Army contractors and other sharp businessmen, politicians, whiskey peddlers and gun runners.

Concentrating different bands of Apaches on the San Carlos reservation was a monumental, disastrous, bureaucratic error. It ensured the rise of cruel and cunning

Geronimo as leader of the Chiricahuas who refused to go to the agency. Clum bravely arrested him and dragged him and his people to San Carlos, but the Warm Springs chief, Victorio, led a mass exodus of both bands in 1877.

The Apaches marauded more into Mexico than in the American Southwest, which did not particularly disturb the US Army. But there were enough atrocities north of the line for cavalry companies, joined by cowboy volunteers and Texas Rangers, to chase Victorio's Warm Springs Chiricahuas and Mescaleros through Arizona, New Mexico, Texas and Mexico in 1877–79.

Victorio ambushed two Mexican parties in 1879 and

slipped out of a trap set for him by Colonel Edward Hatch in April 1880. It was almost impossible to run him down, though he was bested—and wounded—by a company of Indian Army scouts in May of 1880. He would stop to fight only when he could choose the ground. He and his followers rode their horses to death, then ate them and stole new mounts. Cavalry horses became so utterly exhausted that it can be said that Victorio dismounted the 9th Regiment. Colonel Hatch complained of Victorio's secret ally—the terrain. Compared to the San Mateo Mountains or the Black Range, he said, the Modoc Lava Beds country was a lawn!

When Victorio switched his border raiding back to the east again, he ran afoul of an almost-forgotten Civil War hero, Colonel Benjamin Grierson of Grierson's Raid. The Colonel surfaced from obscurity quickly by posting his tough black cavalrymen as guards on the critically-few desert waterholes. Twice in July and August 1880 he turned Victorio back, at Tinaja de las Palmas in Quitman Canyon, and again at Rattlesnake Spring, and forced him to retire into Mexico.

At last, in 1880, diplomacy—and common sense—triumphed over suspicion and nationalistic jealousies.

Below: During the **Apache campaign** against Geronimo in 1885, men of A Troop, 6th US Cavalry, took a coffee break around shady trees of the desert mountains of the Arizona-Mexico border.

234

Below: Frederick Remington was Charles Russell's major rival as the foremost artist depicting the nineteenth century West. Both men were accurate interpreters of Indians, and of cowboys as well, but Remington excelled in his pictures of Army life. His camp scene was painted late in the Indian Wars; **the cavalry troopers wore new web belts** for their 45/70 Springfield carbines.

FREDERIC REMINGTON-

236

Above: In 1883 a 6th Cavalry unit en route to Fort Apache, Arizona, from Mexico made camp just outside of **Zuñi Pueblo, New Mexico.**

Mexico and the United States cooperated against their common menace, Apache raiders. They encircled Victorio in the Tres Castillos Mountains of Mexico. There, Colonel Joaquín Terrazas sent the Americans home, however, ostensibly because he did not trust the Apache scouts of Captain George Buell. Probably he just did not want to share any glory with them. Terrazas trapped and killed Victorio on 15 October 1880, along with 60 of his fighting men and about 18 women and children.

The old chief, Nana, succeeded Victorio, although he was 70, rheumatic, and had only about 15 warrior-followers. He led the Army on another exhausting chase through New Mexico in the summer of 1881, fighting in more than a half-dozen skirmishes and murdering ranchers and miners before heading westward into Arizona and Sonora to join Geronimo as his lieutenant.

There were many chiefs still active in Arizona during the 1880s, including Nana, Chato, and Nachez, Cochise's son, but it was a merciless non-chief, Geronimo, who took over the leadership of Apache resistance to the increasing white settlement of the territory.

Boredom, liquor (*tizwin*) and the natural inter-band antipathies made the restless San Carlos Reservation into a training ground for 'renegades,' warlike Warm Springs and Chiricahua Apaches. Crook termed them the 'tigers of the human race.' If they needed an excuse to strike out on the war trail again, it came in 1881.

Not only the White Mountain Apaches but even some of the Army's own Apache Scouts at that time fell under the spell of a shaman who anticipated the Ghost Dance. Nakaidoklini claimed to have the proper medicine to raise dead warriors to life and to rid Arizona of its troublesome whites.

Indian Bureau pressure brought Colonel Eugene Carr on the run. Nakaidoklini submitted to arrest but, that evening, his followers attacked Carr at Cibicú Creek. It was 30 August. At the same time, Carr's White Mountain Scouts mutinied. They shot Captain Edmund Hentig in the back, killing him, then killed six soldiers and wounded two more. The shaman tried to escape by crawling off into the brush but Sergeant John MacDonald, though wounded in one leg, shot him three times in the head. (Some say that he survived the gunshots and had to be finished off with an axe.)

The shaman's converts and the treacherous scouts got Carr's horses, but the colonel led a night withdrawal which probably saved Fort Apache. Rarely, indeed, did Indians ever try an assault on a garrisoned post but, after cutting the telegraph wires, the Apaches surrounded and attacked Fort Apache, and actually overran some of the post's outbuildings before they were driven off.

Reinforcements rushed in and most of the culprits surrendered. Some of the mutinous Apache Scouts were hanged and some were imprisoned on Alcatraz Island in San Francisco Bay. Carr was accused of incompetence by his superior, General Orlando B Willcox, but a court of inquiry largely vindicated him. His major error—surely a human one—was in trusting his heretofore loyal Apache Scouts too much.

While Army officers wrangled over responsibility for the Cibicú fight and mutiny, the Chiricahuas decamped from the reservation and ran for Mexico. From there, Geronimo, Nachez, Chato and Juh were soon raiding the Gila Valley, killing between 30 and 50 whites in April of 1882. Lieutenant Colonel George A Forsyth soon engaged the enemy in a desperate fight, but they got away and turned back another unit which followed them into Mexico. Forsyth then chased them even deeper into that country, stopping only when ordered out by a colonel of Mexican infantry who had just

ambushed the fleeing, unwary Apaches. At a cost of 22 dead and 16 wounded, his men killed 78 Indians and captured 33 more. But most of them were women or children, not fighters.

In July 1882 White Mountain 'renegades' took to the field and tried to trap Captain Adna Chaffee's troop on the Mogollón Rim's Crook Trail between Camp Verde and Fort Apache. But scout Al Sieber discovered the trap and Chaffee attacked the ambushers. He enjoyed that rare luxury, a conventional pitched battle with his opponents, and thrashed them. He killed 20-odd warriors and probably wounded all the rest before they fled the scene. The Army misnamed the fight, calling it the **Battle of Big Dry Wash** when it actually took place at East Clark Creek.

Sherman now replaced the controversial Willcox by recalling Crook, who took over on 4 September 1882 and set about correcting a sorry situation. He saw three tasks as being necessary: to re-establish control over the reservation Indians; to crush hostiles operating from Mexico's Sierra Madre and, the result of these two measures, to protect the lives and properties of Arizona's citizens.

Crook personally visited the reservations with only a small escort. He threw squatters off Indian land. He put together a cadre of officers who knew the Apaches, like Captain Emmet Crawford and Lieutenant Charles Gatewood. They recruited trustworthy Apache Scouts who patrolled the border.

Not until 1883 were the so-called renegades able to mount a raid into Arizona again. But Chato looted and murdered his way from the Fort Huachuca area to New Mexico and back to Chihuahua, making fools of the military and volunteers who tried to chase and intercept him.

A furious Sherman ordered Crook to destroy the Apache hostiles and to ignore the international boundary. Crook took the precaution of conferring with the authorities in Sonora and Chihuahua first, then penetrated the rugged

Above: Camillus S Fly happened on **two Apache men at their family ranchería** with all the comforts of home – *olla* and basket, remains of a cookfire, brush *wickiups*, and trusty Springfield rifles. *Below:* **Peaches**, looking delicate and timid for an Apache Scout who favored the gunman's cross-draw, posed for Ben Wittick in the natural surroundings of a studio's prop yuccas and junipers.

Below: Charles Russell's 1908 painting, **The Medicine Man**, portrayed a shaman taking the lead in breaking up and moving a village by travois to a new location near the shallow ruts of the Overland Trail on the open grasslands of the High Plains country.

Above: Ben Wittick made this classic picture of grim **Geronimo (Goyathlay)** kneeling with his Springfield at the ready. The Chiracahua obligingly posed in a studio setting of yucca and *biznaga*, barrel cactus.
Below: **Geronimo and his Chiracahua Apaches** lined up, ominously, on a grassy ridge dotted with clumps of Spanish bayonet, or yucca.

Sierra Madre. His force was a small efficient one—almost 200 Apache Scouts under Crawford and Gatewood, plus Chaffee's 45 6th Cavalry troopers. They were supported by 350 pack mules and guided by a crack Apache 'friendly' nicknamed Peaches by his Army buddies.

Crook's patience, thoroughness and doggedness paid off. Crawford stormed and destroyed an Apache village on 15 May. Crook was able to persuade all of the chiefs but Juh to give up. Chato, Benito, Loco, Nachez, Nana and even Geronimo came in, though the last-named was laggardly and appeared to be reneging on his agreement to surrender. He did not join the others on the San Carlos Reservation until March of 1884.

By a tenacious pusuit rather than rounding up his enemy, Crook won his Sierra Madre campaign of 1883 in spectacular fashion, silencing his jeering critics and proving his theories of Indian-style warfare. He kept a watchful eye on his charges at San Carlos, now completely under Army, not Indian Bureau, control. He used Apache spies as intelligence agents and when young Kaytennae challenged his authority, sent the Apache to Alcatraz prison.

But, after a big *tizwin* binge, all of the chiefs except Chato bolted for Mexico, some of them raiding while en route. Crook, from his new headquarters, Fort Bowie in Apache Pass, first locked up the border with 3000 soldiers, mostly cavalry, patrolling and guarding every watering place between the Santa Cruz River, south of Tucson, to the Rio Grande. Behind them he placed a second line of defense, a reserve force scattered along the Southern Pacific track. Then he sent Crawford and Lieutenant Wirt Davis deep into Mexico with mixed units of cavalry and scouts. (The reciprocal border-crossing agreement with Mexico had been renewed.)

Four times in the summer of 1885 the punitive parties hit the Apaches but, each time, they evaporated from view in the hot desert air, their losses very small. Two bands even counterattacked, one giving Crook's heavy border patrols the slip and stealing horses in southeast Arizona Territory. Worse, a little-known warrior, Josanie, led a month-long raid with another war party that covered 1200 miles of both territories. He killed almost 40 people without an Army patrol even sighting him, much less cutting him off.

By now, Crook so trusted his Apache Scouts that he sometimes sent them, without any regulars along, to track and fight their own kin. In January of 1886, Crawford hit the enemy again and secured a truce for a parley. But Mexican militiamen attacked Geronimo's camp. When Crawford tried to stop the shooting, the Mexicans shot him dead. Still, Geronimo and other chiefs talked with his lieutenant and agreed to meet Crook in two months.

Crook demanded unconditional surrender at a meeting, 25–27 March, a dozen miles below the border. He swore, 'If you stay out, I'll keep after you and kill the last one [of

Above: **General George Crook** was the Army's least by-the-book soldier. He bested the Apaches of Arizona and New Mexico in developing a style of warfare to counter their hit-and-run guerrilla tactics. He used Apache Scouts like Dutchy (left) and Alchiso (Alchisay) skilfully against their hostile kin. He preferred mules, like his faithful *Apache*, over horses because they withstood the heat and fatigue of Southwest desert campaigning better than any breed of horse.

Over: J McDonald in 1886 photographed **Geronimo** (first row, third from right) and **Chiricahua prisoners** as the Apaches rested on an Arizona railroad embankment below well-guarded passenger coaches that would carry them off into exile in Florida. By 1894, however, Geronimo was back in the West at Fort Sill, Oklahoma.

Above: **Apache prisoners,** Fort Bowie, Arizona, 1884.

you], if it takes 50 years.' Shortly however, he relented and offered terms. He then wired news of Geronimo's surrender to Sheridan—too soon. Nana and Geronimo got drunk on *tizwin* again and fled to the mountains.

Sheridan, who distrusted Crook's Apache Scouts, was angry at him for letting Geronimo slip through his fingers. Now he demanded unconditional surrender or the complete destruction of the Apaches—including those who had already surrendered to Crook on his terms. Crook's honor was at stake. On 1 April 1886 he asked to be relieved of his command. Sheridan hurriedly replaced him with Miles.

Sheridan ordered Miles to depend on his regulars, not Indian scouts. He did so. He also added heliograph stations to the telegraph lines to improve communications between mobile columns. But he sent Captain Henry Lawton into Mexico in May to harass and wear out the Apaches, with Apache Scouts as guides. At the same time, his defensive forces chased a raiding party out of the Santa Cruz Valley and back into Mexico.

Lawton's march was a grueling one, mostly on foot, as the horses gave out in the desert sun during the first week. The Captain lost 40 pounds of weight and his surgeon, Dr Leonard Wood, lost 30. Enlisted men had to be replaced with new rankers as they wilted and dropped during the 2000-mile march. Only once did Lawton catch up with the Apaches, on 14 July, and they got away, unscathed.

In the meantime, Miles made sure that there would be no reinforcements for the hostiles from the San Carlos Reservation. He rounded up the agency's Chiricahuas and exiled them to Fort Marion, Florida, by train. Then he persuaded the brave Gatewood, though ill, to risk his life by 'talking in' Geronimo as Crawford had almost done. He was the only officer left in the Department of Arizona who had Geronimo's trust.

Geronimo finally agreed to give up, but only to Miles. The General took his surrender at Skeleton Canyon, 65 miles south of Apache Pass, on 4 September 1886, after Miles guaranteed that the renegades' lives would be spared and that they would not be separated from their families. The prisoners entrained for Florida.

Now President Cleveland ordered that the Apaches be held at Fort Bowie for criminal trials. But when Miles protested, like Crook, that he had given his word, the President came around on this point of Army honor. However, the men were separated from their families in Florida. In any case, they all sickened and died equally in the humid climate, including the loyal Apache Scouts. Crook now joined the Indian Rights Association to seek justice for his old enemies. To his discredit, Miles did not.

Crook died in 1890 but, four years later, the dwindling Apache survivors were allowed to migrate to Fort Sill, Oklahoma, over Miles's opposition. (There Geronimo died in 1909.) In 1913 some were allowed to move to New Mexico's Mescalero Reservation.

Partisans of Crook and Miles squared off to claim credit for the termination of the Apache Wars. The pro-Crook war correspondent, Charles Lummis, wrote of 'the mongrel pack which has barked at the heels of this patient commander.' The careers of the former's protégés, Lawton and Wood, advanced, but Crook's brave subordinate, Gatewood, was forgotten. He died, only a first lieutenant, in 1896.

The self-centered Miles closed out the Apache Wars because he was an excellent officer. But students of these bloody and difficult campaigns realize that he could do so only because of the groundwork done by Crook. And it is his predecessor, Crook, who remains the real Army hero of the Apache Wars.

The Ghost Dance, Wounded Knee and
The End of the Frontier

All apparent Indian resistance in the West crumbled with Geronimo's surrender. The Army's only four-star general made it official in a retirement letter of 1883. 'I now regard the Indians as substantially eliminated from the problems of the Army . . .' But Sherman was realist enough to warn of the possibility of temporary, spasmodic Indian alarms.

Just such a delayed—almost post-mortem—spasm occurred in 1890. It was touched off, ironically, by a peace-mongering Paiute mystic. Nevada's Wovoka was a half-Christianized seer, last in a long line of Indian messiahs—Popé, Pontiac, The Prophet, Smohalla, Nakaidoklini and Sword Bearer. His religion was called the Ghost Dance because he taught that praying, singing and, particularly, dancing would give the Indians a look at a joyous new world in which the dead would rise up to greet their living friends.

Many tribes adopted the Ghost Dance religion, but the Teton Sioux, Kicking Bear and Short Bull, interpreted Wovoka's prophecies to mean the destruction of the whites as a necessary preparation for the new world. They ignored his appeals to non-violence and talked instead of the medicine of ghost shirts which would turn away the white man's bullets.

General Miles was not as sanguine as Sherman about the end of Indian troubles and was ready when the Ghost Dance fervor boiled over on the Pine Ridge and Rosebud reservations in 1890. There, the Oglala and Brulé Sioux danced themselves into exhausted but euphoric stupors in which they dreamed of an American Indian holy war. Miles responded promptly by having the Army occupy both agencies and split apart the Ghost Dance's potential hostiles from Sioux friendlies.

The 600 followers of Wovoka, of both bands, then joined together in the Stronghold on the edge of the Pine Ridge Reservation. The major Sioux chiefs who were attracted by the cult were Hump, Big Foot and Sitting Bull. Hump was pacified or neutralized, but Miles ordered the arrest of the other two men. The Standing Rock Reservation's agent, James McLaughlin, urged that Sitting Bull be apprehended by his own people. The local Army Commandant agreed.

At dawn of 15 December 1890 Lieutenant Bull Head and 40-odd uniformed Indian Police surrounded Sitting Bull's cabin. Meek when he was at first detained, he called for help outside when he saw about 160 cultists watching the arrest take place. An old enemy of Bull Head, Catch the Bear, shot the Lieutenant dead. But before he fell, Bull Head put a ball in Sitting Bull's body and Officer Red

Below: The National Anthropological Archives, Smithsonian Institution, has a rich collection of photos like this view of the **Arapaho Ghost Dance**, c. 1893, by James Mooney of the Bureau of American Ethnology.

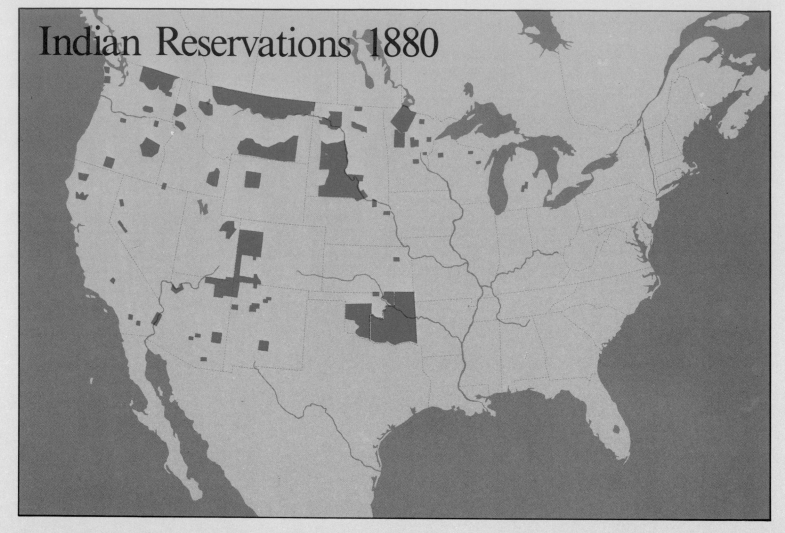

Indian Reservations 1880

Below: By 1890, most Indians had been relocated to reservations, such as the **Sioux Reservation** seen here.

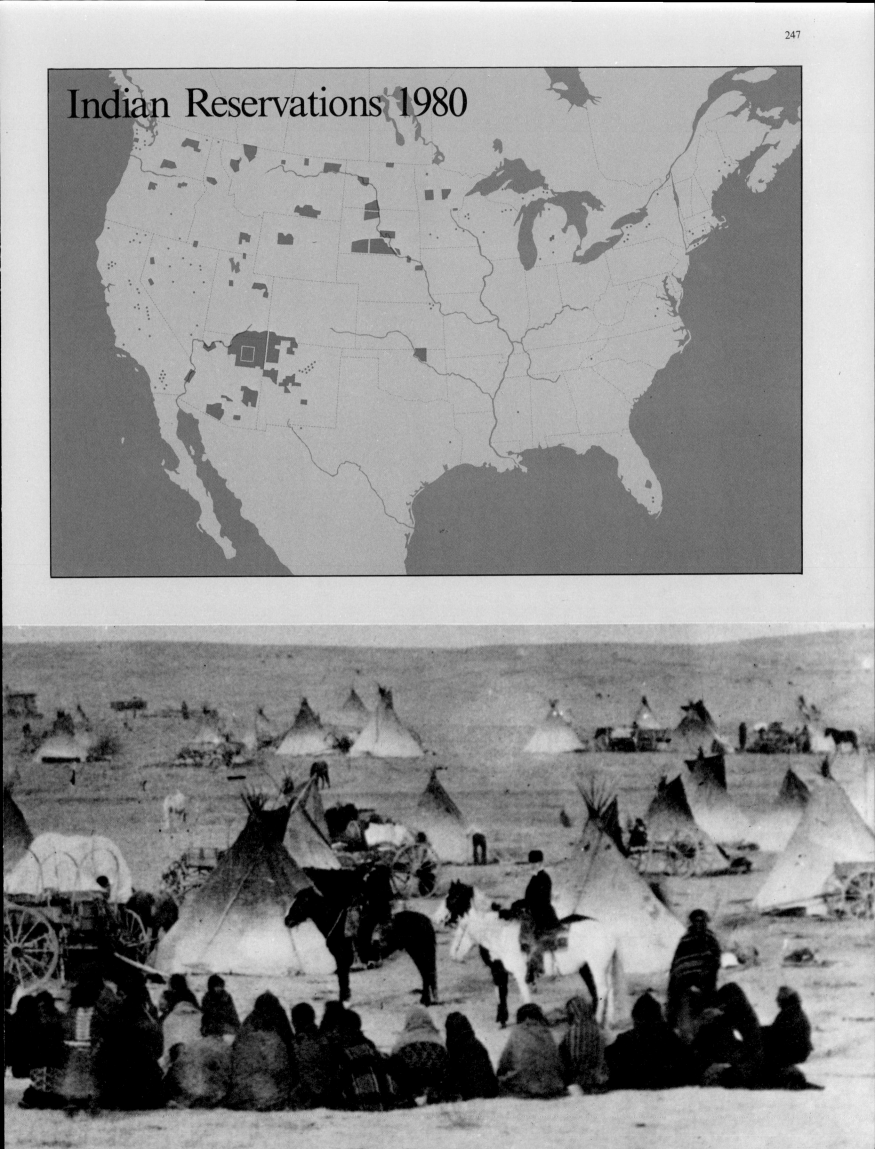

Indian Reservations 1980

Above: An unknown photographer took this picture of the frozen body of the old **Chief Big Foot of the Sioux,** one of the victims of Wounded Knee, 29 December 1890.

Below: W R Cross of Hot Springs, S D, photographed the **rifled guns, field artillery,** on the Pine Ridge Reservation in 1891.

Above: In 1891 **Army officers of the Battle of Wounded Knee** – who should have hung their heads in shame – posed proudly for the camera.

Below: After Wounded Knee wagons gathered Indian dead. *Bottom:* A mass grave was dug for the Sioux dead at Wounded Knee.

Tomahawk added a pistol bullet to his head. The police then stood their ground in a shoot-out until they were reinforced by a squadron of the 8th Cavalry. Six Indian policemen were dead or dying, and an equal number of Ghost Dancers, including Sitting Bull.

Miles moved more troops in to contain the cult. But, to his surprise, there was little or no violence after Sitting Bull's death. True, bands slipped away from the reservations to the Badlands. But Hump, for example, got most of his 400 Hunkpapas to halt their flight and surrender.

The largest band of presumed hostiles was that of old Big Foot, Miniconjous and 40 or so Hunkpapas. Miles ordered Colonel Edmund V Sumner to round up the chief, but the veteran officer stalled. He argued that an arrest was unnecessary and counter-productive, probably inciting a fight.

Big Foot, frightened by the Army's warlike preparations, fled with his people toward the Pine Ridge Agency. Miles, assuming that he was heading for the Stronghold and the irreconcilables, was angry at Sumner for letting him get away. He sent several units to intercept him and prevent him rendezvousing with the Brulés and Oglalas. One of these forces was the 7th Cavalry, Custer's old outfit.

Big Foot consented to being escorted to Pine Ridge by the military. But Colonel James W Forsyth (not to be confused with the hero of Beecher's Island, George Forsyth) had orders from Miles both to disarm Big Foot's people and to march them to the railroad for shipment to Omaha. All this was, of course, against Sumner's advice.

When the Sioux encampment awakened on the morning of 29 December 1890, its people found that Forsyth had surrounded them with 500 troops and had posted four rapid-firing Hotchkiss cannon to cover them.

As the squaws began to break camp and pack up to move, Forsyth lined up the 120 men and ordered them to turn in

Above: **Lieutenant Taylor** and **Indian scouts** at Pine Ridge, 1891.

their weapons. When only a few token guns, mostly broken, were surrendered, he searched the lodges and found arms and ammunition hidden in them. Next, he ordered a body search of the Sioux, men and women, for weapons concealed under their blankets.

The Sioux were angered by this humiliating procedure, of course, and a young shaman, Yellow Bird, began reminding the warriors of their protective ghost shirts. A few braves threw off their blankets to reveal carbines and rifles. A single soldier and a warrior got into a scuffle. Someone, probably this enlisted man, fired a shot, perhaps accidentally. (The Army blamed an anonymous enlisted scapegoat—a curious kind of Unknown Soldier for the service to single out.)

Forsyth's troops opened fire on the crowded camp at close range. The soldiers were excited, scared, perhaps vengeful, remembering Little Bighorn. Their small arms fire was deadly at such close quarters, but it paled before the bloody work of the Hotchkiss guns.

To the Indians and many sympathetic whites, the **Battle of Wounded Knee** was no battle at all, but a massacre. That it was, but only in part. It was not a massacre in the sense of the deliberate slaughter of Sand Creek in 1864. For it was also a battle or, at least, a real skirmish. Forsyth lost 25 officers and men killed, and had 39 wounded. Big Foot and his medicine man, Yellow Bird, were among the 150 Sioux dead on the frozen ground. There were another 50 Indians wounded. Probably the large number of women and children, 62, among the Sioux casualties was the result of wild firing by riflemen and Hotchkiss gunners at close quarters. In fact, some of the Army's own dead and wounded were the accidental result of gunshot and shrapnel wounds from friendly fire.

The public was horrified by Wounded Knee and compared it to Sand Creek. Miles saw it as a stupendous blunder by Forsyth. He relieved him of his command and summoned a court of inquiry. The testimony seemed to show that his soldiers tried to avoid shooting non-combatants, but that this was impossible. Miles found Forsyth to be guilty of incompetence and irresponsible disobedience of orders. The Secretary of War and General John M Schofield reversed his decision, however, and restored Forsyth to duty.

As if to prove that Miles was right, Forsyth blundered into a trap set by the Sioux at Drexel Mission. While pinned down, the victor of Wounded Knee lost one officer and

The Indian Territory 1896

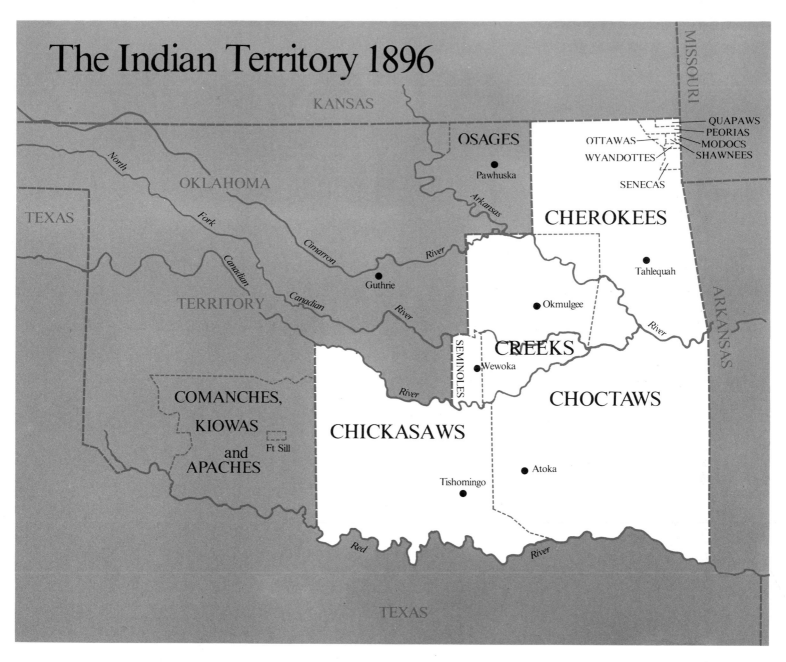

KANSAS

MISSOURI

OSAGES

QUAPAWS
PEORIAS
OTTAWAS · MODOCS
WYANDOTTES · SHAWNEES

Pawhuska

SENECAS

OKLAHOMA

North

Fork

Arkansas

CHEROKEES

TEXAS

Cimarron

River

Tahlequah

Canadian

Guthrie

Canadian

TERRITORY

River

Okmulgee

ARKANSAS

River

SEMINOLES

CREEKS

COMANCHES,

KIOWAS

and

APACHES

Ft Sill

River

Wewoka

CHOCTAWS

CHICKASAWS

Atoka

Tishomingo

Red

River

TEXAS

Above: The government established **Indian Territory** in the land west of Arkansas for the five Civilized Tribes in 1830. **Indian Territory** merged with Oklahoma and ceased to exist in 1907 when Oklahoma joined the Union.

one enlisted man, dead, and had five more wounded. He lost more face when he had to be rescued by the 9th Cavalry.

But Miles had erred, too, in ordering Forsyth to disarm the Sioux and entrain them to Omaha. As Sumner said, Big Foot could have been escorted peacefully, to Pine Ridge had the Colonel not tried to seize all Indian weapons.

Miles was more careful now. He employed a judicious mix of diplomacy and force to surround the remaining 'hostiles.' Unlike Forsyth, he left some breathing room between the two forces. And while he kept at a respectful distance, he began to tighten the circle around the Sioux at the same time that he sent Indian peace emissaries among them. They soon gave up. Kicking Bird, last to surrender, gave his Winchester to Miles on 15 January 1891.

Wounded Knee, by sheer coincidence, occurred in the year in which statisticians of the Census Bureau declared there was no longer a line of frontier settlement in the West.

The melting pot theory of assimilation had not worked in the face of the long conflict of cultures, the clashing of races, on the plains, mountains and deserts of the West

any better than in the hardwood forests and meadows of the East. So war, in place of peace, became the sorry 'solution' to what was euphemized by politicians as the nation's 'Indian problem.' After a thousand bloody actions, in which the Army had 2000 casualties and the Indians three times that number, Teddy Roosevelt's winning of the West finally came to pass. But at tremendous cost, not only for the losers, the Indians, but also for the winners.

The Army was only the cutting edge of so-called civilization. It was the power behind it, the Industrial Revolution, that conquered the Indians with its railroads, barbed wire, telegraph, six-shooters, howitzers. And the Industrial Revolution's agents were not only soldiers but farmers, ranchers, miners, townsfolk and the buffalo hunters who utterly destroyed the Plains Indians' life-support system in one short decade.

In a sense, the Army was left with the dirty work by others. It was called in at the last moment, usually, to clean up a mess made by civilians. The old Sioux spokesman was thinking of ordinary citizens, not troopers, when he sagely observed of the whites, 'They made us many promises, more than I can remember, but they never kept but one; they promised to take our land, and they took it.'

INDEX

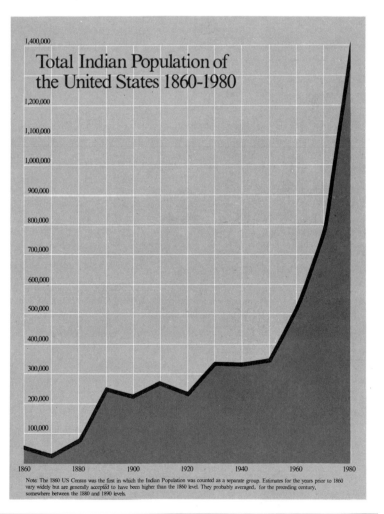

Total Indian Population of the United States 1860-1980

Note: The 1860 US Census was the first in which the Indian Population was counted as a separate group. Estimates for the years prior to 1860 vary widely but are generally accepted to have been higher than the 1860 level. They probably averaged, for the preceding century, somewhere between the 1880 and 1890 levels.

Picture Credits

Indian Population by State 1890

(Twenty most populous states.) Total = 249,273*

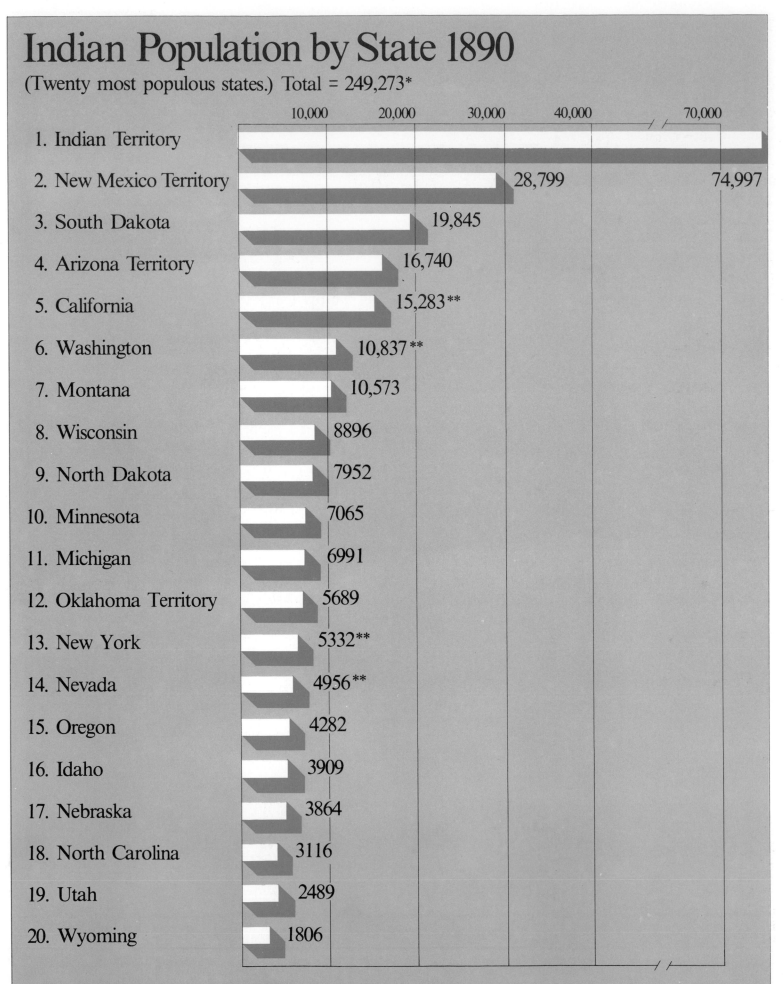

1. Indian Territory	
2. New Mexico Territory	28,799 — 74,997
3. South Dakota	19,845
4. Arizona Territory	16,740
5. California	15,283**
6. Washington	10,837**
7. Montana	10,573
8. Wisconsin	8896
9. North Dakota	7952
10. Minnesota	7065
11. Michigan	6991
12. Oklahoma Territory	5689
13. New York	5332**
14. Nevada	4956**
15. Oregon	4282
16. Idaho	3909
17. Nebraska	3864
18. North Carolina	3116
19. Utah	2489
20. Wyoming	1806

*This figure includes 568 Indians listed as War Department prisoners.

**In all of the states listed, much less than a quarter of the Indian population lived off the reservations, with the exception of Washington, where 27% lived off-reservation, California (67%), Nevada (69%) and New York (100%).